*Gender and Representation
in the Films of Ingmar Bergman*

Studies in Scandinavian Literature and Culture

Edited by
George C. Schoolfield
and
Robert E. Bjork

Marilyn Johns Blackwell

# Gender and Representation in the Films of Ingmar Bergman

CAMDEN HOUSE

First published 1997 by Camden House
Transferred to digital printing 2007

Camden House is an imprint of Boydell & Brewer Inc.
668 Mt. Hope Avenue, Rochester, NY 14620, USA
www.camden-house.com
and of Boydell & Brewer Limited
PO Box 9, Woodbridge, Suffolk IP12 3DF, UK
www.boydellandbrewer.com

ISBN: 1–57113–094–2

Library of Congress Cataloging-in-Publication Data

Blackwell, Marilyn Johns.
    Gender and representation in the films of Ingmar Bergman / Marilyn
Johns Blackwell.
        p. cm. — (Studies in Scandinavian literature and culture)
    Includes bibliographical references and index.
    ISBN 1–57113–094–2 (alk. paper)
        1. Bergman, Ingmar, 1918– — Criticism and interpretation. 2. Sex
role in motion pictures.  I. Title.  II. Series: Studies in Scandanavian
literature and culture (Unnumbered)

PN1998.3 B47B63 1997
791.43'.0223'092—dc21
                                                                96–36937
                                                                CIP

# Contents

# Acknowledgments

I WISH TO EXPRESS MY thanks to Judith Mayne; at lunch a few years ago she gave of her much-imposed-upon time and essential goodness to impart to me the courage of my critical convictions and for that I shall be ever grateful. Gratitude also goes to my colleagues Mark Roche for reading the *Smiles of a Summer Night* chapter and commenting so helpfully, Peter Ohlin for reading and offering excellent suggestions on the *Persona* chapter, and Linda Haverty Rugg for reading the entire manuscript with the sensitivity and intelligence of a veritably ideal reader. I am especially indebted to George Schoolfield whose knowledge is encyclopedic and whose heart is no less expansive; he as perhaps no other man in American Scandinavian studies has nurtured and promoted the professional development of women in our discipline. I count myself blessed that he has also bestowed on me his friendship. I should also like to thank others in the Scandinavian critical community whose friendship has eased my way toward this and other goals: Larry Scott, Jim Massengale, Ross Shideler, Steven Sondrup, Barry Jacobs, and Marna Feldt are but a few of those who make me rejoice at having chosen this profession. In Columbus I am especially appreciative of those colleagues who have supported me professionally and/or personally: Dagmar Lorenz (who has been a loyal and enduring friend throughout it all), Bernd Fischer, Helen Fehervary, and Barbara Becker-Cantarino; their generous support and understanding have sustained me on numerous occasions. Beyond my profession, Christine Altieri, Harrison Altieri Cozort, and Dan Cozort ought to appear in the dictionary as the definition of true friendship — with humanity and generosity of spirit they have saved my life more times than I can count. Their insight into the intricacies of being human continues after twenty years to amaze me. And Jens Rieckmann, Rik Sherriff, Tom and Joyce Marquart, Charlotte Patterson, Deborah Cohn, and Siv and Jerry Hood have all in his or her own way enriched my life beyond measure. Lastly, I should like to extend my thanks to my ex-husband Michael Blackwell, who supported and encouraged this project from its inception. He embodies humanity at its best — liberal of sympathy, learned of mind, conscientious of character, and generous of heart. My respect for him endures as does my gratitude.

M. J. B.
November 1996

# 1: Culture in Crisis: Feminist Critical Debate and the Films of Ingmar Bergman

THE FILMS OF INGMAR BERGMAN mirror both a crisis in and an ambivalence toward Western culture, a disruption and reinscription of cultural notions of difference. From *Torment* in 1944 (for which he only wrote the script) to *Fanny and Alexander* in 1984, virtually all his works depict a culture that fails the people who inhabit it either by being pathetically inadequate to a representation or fulfillment of their needs and desires or else by ravaging them, destroying all that might potentially bear meaning in their lives. The cultural criticism that is played out in these films is perhaps not surprising when one considers Bergman's background, a background that greatly influences his radical view of the complicity between the nuclear family and larger cultural and ideological structures. The son of a Lutheran minister who rose to become court chaplain to Sweden's royal family, Bergman learned early to equate the familial, social, and religious hierarchies of which he perceived himself a victim. He describes the environment in which he grew up:

> Most of our upbringing was based around concepts such as sin, confession, punishment, forgiveness, and grace, concrete factors in relationships between children and parents and God. There was an innate logic in all this which we accepted and thought we understood. This fact may well have contributed to our astonishing acceptance of Nazism. We had never heard of freedom and knew even less what it tasted like. In a hierarchical system, all doors are closed. . . . Many of our teachers were National Socialists, Nazi-adherents, some from foolishness or bitterness over their failure to gain academic advancement, others from idealism and veneration of the old Germany, "a nation of poets and thinkers." (*Magic Lantern* 8, 113)

Thus Bergman recognizes the connection between religion, hierarchy, and political and social intolerance, and repression. Maria Bergom-Larsson rightly sees Bergman's perception of man and woman, of the father and of society itself as connected to a bourgeois, authoritarian, and patriarchal nuclear family, even as I shall argue with her view that he does not struggle against the values inherent in this institution (168).

A significant aspect of the cultural criticism in which Bergman is engaged concentrates on the position of women in cultural contexts. As many critics have noted, women protagonists replace men in Bergman's films and become the focus of his work after 1960. Yet one seeks in vain for sociopolitical events that might explain this shift. Sweden, like most of the West, experienced social cataclysm in the later sixties, but the Sweden of 1960 was a calm, almost comatose place in which gender issues simply did not arise. However, as Leif Zern has suggested (13–29), Bergman's work seems to reflect (and, one might add, predict) social and cultural change.

Indeed, issues of gender are vital to Bergman, as attested to by his early statement that "The world of women is my universe" (*Filmnytt* 13). In effect they become a kind of nexus from which he can treat the dehumanizing effect of various cultural institutions on those marginalized by that culture. Bergman recognizes (at least implicitly) throughout his career, despite his attempts to disclaim any political agenda, that all discourse is ideologically tainted. His acknowledgment that God and the patriarchy are empty structures (a malevolent "present absence," as I shall later argue) entails drastic formal changes in his artistic practice. His production thus affords a rich opportunity for an examination of the relationship between ideology, apparatus, and discourse.

Not surprisingly, then, feminist critics have given considerable attention to Bergman, a director who furthermore has said, "Surely the slow and complex process of [women's] liberation we are watching today can only be regarded as something admirable and heartening" (Björkman *et al.*, 19). But the first wave of feminist criticism was marked by intense disagreement over Bergman's representations of female subjectivity. Molly Haskell valorizes Bergman for taking women seriously, for being "one of the five or six great directors . . . who place women at the center of their universe and honor them with a love that neither crushes nor sanctifies" and praises him for his refusal to "belie[ve] the life of the heart is somehow a less worthy subject of serious treatment than such 'large subjects' as wars, politics, religion and social causes" ("*Madame de*" 62, 65), at the same time that she sees a "mystical, fundamentalist" view of women conditioning his work. The Swedish critic Marianne Höök agrees with Haskell's positive assessment:

> The women in Bergman's films are for the most part more interesting than the men. . . . Bergman's subtle view of women has come as a liberation, and as far as women are concerned Bergman's films since *Waiting Women* (1952) have provided a glimpse of a genuine women's reality, something one has been able to identify with. His collaboration with women writers (such as Birgit Tengroth and Ulla Isaksson) obviously suited him, stimulated him and opened doors to a world in which he felt strangely at home. (84)

This opinion was, to be sure, written and published by 1962, that is to say before some of his most important works; thus Höök did not have to consider whether or not she could "identify" with the destructive impulses of Alma in *Persona* or the self-mutilation practiced by Karin in *Cries and Whispers*. Nonetheless the issues of female subjectivity raised by these two characters are all present, in however undeveloped a form, in the earlier Bergman canon; so this critic's praise for Bergman's deep sensitivity toward and incisive treatment of female experience would seem pertinent to his entire career. But a number of other feminist critics strongly oppose this view, charging Bergman with objectivizing women, with biologism and essentialism. Typical of this view are Maria Bergom-Larsson, Constance Penley, and Joan Mellen. These critics' arguments will be analyzed in detail in the discussions of the individual films they treat, but Bergom-Larsson speaks for this perception in her statement: "Woman is, for Bergman, almost without exception, 'nature.' She is enclosed within the sphere of reproduction. She is 'sex'" (59). All three critics locate in Bergman a thoroughly offensive "determinist misogyny" at odds with an enlightened feminist practice.

In an effort to mediate between these two positions, Birgitta Steene develops an argument according to which Bergman uses women characters as a "subjective metaphor" for his personal psyche — the director "project[s], through his women characters, his own personal *mythos*. . . . Women become Bergman's personae — his alter egos and his protective mask" ("Bergman's Portrait" 96, 100). But one might counterargue that using women as representations of the male self is still a refusal to grant them the autonomy of the human or, in contemporary psychological parlance, that use is abuse.

More recently, Bergman's work has received a feminist critical treatment from Mark Sandberg, who finds in the films up through *The Seventh Seal* a growing valorization of female discourse ("Rewriting"). The kinds of questions that Sandberg poses about the genderedness of certain narrative structures and framing devices in the early works are, I think, important and warrant, with other questions, the more extensive critical inquiry that I try to give them here. In the same vein, Maaret Koskinen's dissertation emphasizes issues of seeing and illusion(ism) in Bergman's work but stops short of investigating the feminist ramifications of these concerns. Given the prominence of women and feminist issues throughout Bergman's production, it is surprising that his films have received as little recent feminist critical attention as they have. While earlier feminist critics have posed interesting questions about the films, these studies warrant both expansion and reassessment. Although Penley, Mellen, and Haskell analyze individual films, they do not locate these works within the director's larger, career-long project of cultural criticism; furthermore, feminism has achieved a number of new critical and theoretical perspectives since these pieces were written, perspectives especially pertinent to Bergman's work. Bergom-Larsson, while she examines the entire oeuvre, does so by and large from a predominantly Marxist perspective in order to forward an argument that Bergman is pervasively bourgeois and reactionary; although many of her points are extremely well-taken, the specifically polemical thrust of her book prevents her, I would argue, from seeing the more progressive elements of his work. There have been, then, with the exception of Sandberg's article, almost no attempts to assess Bergman's production in light of the contributions of the feminist critical debate of the past fifteen years, a lacuna that this book tries, at least in part, to address.

But the diversity of opinion among these critics is, I think, suggestive: while feminists have certain common critical assumptions from which they operate, it bears remembering that there is no monolithic feminist critical perspective or methodology. On the contrary, feminism implies, to a greater or lesser extent, a valorization of pluralism. The variety of critical reactions to Bergman's films on the part of women/feminist critics is interesting in and of itself, for few directors have received so much attention from women. An examination of the Bergman bibliography reveals that the percentage of women critics who attend to his oeuvre is far greater than the percentage of women in film criticism at large. There appears to be, on the part of women critics, a fascination (sometimes horrified, sometimes sympathetic) with Bergman's work, and it is this fascination and its sources that serve as an impetus to this work. However one may ultimately judge them, there remains a disturbing complexity to Bergman's women characters and a plurality of spectator experience that warrant our consideration.

The ambivalence that has marked feminist responses to Bergman is, I think, not only the result of real disagreements about critical perspective, but also a product of Bergman's own ambivalence to women and to the cultural and ideological circumstances in which they find themselves. While he clearly does "take women seriously" and investigates the ways in which their lives are circumscribed and infected by the dominant cultural order in which they live, there is nonetheless a taint of biologism to them. At the same time that he claims, "I don't make any special distinction between masculine and feminine. I don't have a decided 'view of women,'" he goes on to declare, "My constant fascination for 'kvinnosläktet' is one of the great driving forces [behind my work]. It is obvious that such a dependence also entails an ambivalence; it implies a compulsion" (Björkman et al. 206). The word "kvinnosläktet" translates as either "race of women" or "family of women;" in either case, an essentialist perspective. The juxtaposition, then, of these two statements reveals the ambivalence that is the focus of this study: women, for Bergman, are both subjects and instances of ideological and cultural conflict and crisis whose behaviors and attitudes are held to norms promulgated by the criticized culture as well as to the aesthetic and psychological needs of the artist, for Bergman is ever aware that the modes of discourse the artist chooses are also ideologically implicated. For Bergman, women are autonomous subjects and yet they are also constructed by the culture in which they live and by the act of representation. It is this convergence of ideology and discourse that this book attempts to explore.

Any feminist treatment of texts produced by a male artist and of larger gender relations in those texts should expect that questions would arise as to how "authentic" a female protagonist is when she is the product of male experience — simply put, what are the feminist implications of female protagonists created by male authors? As Kaja Silverman suggests, "It is clearly not the same thing, socially or politically, for a woman to speak with a female voice as it is for a man to do so, and vice versa" (*Acoustic Mirror* 217). Relevant to this issue of voice is a study by James Carson, who finds in Richardson's "ventriloquism" "less the assertion of his authorial self than a sympathetic dissolution of the self . . . a radical example of sympathetic identification — sympathy across the bounds of gender. . . [a] making another's case one's own" (97). Furthermore, Carson finds in Richardson a recognition that "sympathy could never be complete, however much one tried to divest oneself of self" (97), and he concludes that such sympathy is extremely ethically and morally valuable. A recognition of the inevitable ventriloquism of using characters to espouse one's own views and the morally reprehensible quality of that ventriloquism compel the artist to a critique of his own authorship, as we find in Bergman's representation of vampirism in *Persona*. Hence the male artist's "use" of female protagonists is not necessarily a matter of appropriating female experience or of oppressing women, but, on the contrary, can function, as it frequently does in Bergman, to critique the masculine appropriation of women.

By way of background to this study, I should first like to look at various issues of concern to the feminist and feminist critical community and the ways in which these same issues appear in Bergman's work, both ideationally and formally. Following that, I provide a brief summary of the feminist film theoretical debate of the past two decades in order to establish the methodology by which the analyses of the individual filmic texts can move forward.

## Feminist Ideology and Bergman's Practice

Throughout his production Bergman addresses the "reality" of women's lives insofar as he focuses on certain representative aspects of female experience: "otherness," confinement/consign[ment] to the domestic or private sphere, the interruptibility of women's work, the prominence of concrete objects in women's everyday lives, certain physiological experiences such as menstruation and childbirth (both of which "contribute to a sense of being bound to physical events beyond the self, and in the case of menstruation to a consciousness of repetition and yet of the interruptibility of one's [life]"), childrearing, interdependency (here her argument is based on Chodorow's model of female child development), and contextuality (Donovan 102–105). From the valorization of female authority in *Smiles of a Summer Night*

(1955), through the assertion of female interdependence and contextuality in the 1960s films, to the exploration of the interior life and physical and psychological confinement of women in *Cries and Whispers* (1972), Bergman presents female characters who possess an interior life of their own that is not dependent upon or reflective of male realities, one "which precedes and succeeds her relationship with men and by which she, too. . . transcends her biological fate" (ctd. in Arbuthnot 44). For Bergman, as for many feminists, socially imposed roles undermine subjectivity and lead to a loss of selfhood, at the same time that human interaction seems predicated upon some roles. Thus, representations of masks, role-playing, power, and authority figure prominently in Bergman's depiction of gender issues.

Judi Roller points to another aspect of female experience that is represented in Bergman's practice when she analyzes the feminist novel from the perspective of a fundamental distrust of ideology. While she acknowledges that such distrust is also a reflection of the larger twentieth-century failure of worldviews and systems of belief, resulting from the fragmentation or discreditation of most ideologies and philosophies, she isolates this subject matter as specifically feminist when aligned with women characters (77–82), as it clearly is in Bergman's case.

Another potentially feminist dimension to Bergman's production lies in its preoccupation with issues of loss, particularly the loss of the father and/or the authority embedded in that father; at the same time the films struggle with the issues of the subject's ambivalence to that authority and how one creates meaning in the absence of authority. In this connection Jessica Benjamin's observations on Freud are pertinent:

> Freud imagined the origins of civilization in the primal struggle between father and son. The sons who overthrow the father's authority become afraid of their own aggression and lawlessness and regret the loss of his wonderful power; and so they reinstate law and authority in the father's image. Thus, in a seemingly unbreakable circle, revolt is always followed by guilt and the restoration of authority. (5f.)

But what is interesting in Bergman's case is that the revolt is aligned with an allegiance to the female, to the authority of her values and sensibilities, even as the guilt never allows the director fully to repudiate the paternal. His individual works can be seen as both narratives of loss and acts of mourning and as explorations of patriarchal authority run amok and its effects on its victims, for the patriarchy is both dead and alive, a pernicious "present absence." We can see a film such as *Wild Strawberries* as embodying the denial stage of mourning and many of the other films as suffused with the anger, bargaining, depression, and ultimate acceptance of death characteristic of mourning. Bergman's films move inward into the imaginative space where such mourning can and must take place. And at the same time that they challenge and attack the now lost authority, they also chart mourning's sense of duration and irretrievable loss. In this light, his use of still photographs takes on a special significance. As both Metz and Creekmur have shown, photographs can function as fetishized objects both forestalling and prolonging the sense of loss. *Smiles of a Summer Night*, *Persona*, and *Cries and Whispers* all address the relationship of photographs to the death of authority. In these films photographs become sites for the inscription of loss, both personal and ideological, and of fantasy both intra- and extra-diegetic.

If patriarchal authority is corrupt, illusory, or lost (as it almost always is in Bergman's work), then the relationships between men and women and between women are altered in significant ways. One of the factors that links Bergman's films *The Silence*, *Persona*, and *Cries and Whispers* is precisely the fact that all three films take as their central subject matter the relationship between two or more women. Men are either conspicuously absent or radically marginalized in these films, and, in view of the threat that male absence and female intimacy pose for androcentric culture, the relationships women establish between themselves can provisionally function as a kind of litmus test for the relationship between any given text and its feminist sensibilities.

The exposure of a thoroughgoing and deeply embedded sense of otherness in female experience is important to both Bergman's work and feminist practice, for "to internalize Otherness is almost definitionally to be unable to speak the language of the self. . . . To experience being an Other is often to feel so schizophrenically torn, that not even a clandestinely authentic 'I' dares to speak" (ctd. in Donovan, "Toward a Women's Poetics" 102). The inevitable ambivalence that arises from experiencing the self as both other and subject is a common feature for feminist texts, as is the concomitant experience of fragmentation and the mutability of subjectivity, both concerns that pervade Bergman's practice. Such films as *The Seventh Seal*, *The Silence*, *Persona*, and *Fanny and Alexander* seek a kind of dialectical integration of opposing forces both within and outside the self and yet reject a specious unity of subjectivity. While such a position is, to be sure, also prominent in postmodernist texts, it bears remembering that effect is separate from intent; that is to say, that such strategies can be feminist in their impact upon the consumer's experience of a text regardless of whether or not the artist had an avowedly feminist purpose in constructing it.

Feminist "themes" or issues, while they may serve to point us in interesting directions, ultimately are not sufficient for feminist analysis, for they do not take into account how meaning is produced within discursive systems; they neglect the relational, contextual aspect of the artistic enterprise. While it is true that "the dynamic notion of reading as a relationship between reader and text implies that no texts, 'mainstream' or otherwise, bear specific *a priori* meanings in and of themselves" (Kuhn, *Women's Pictures* 12), the fact remains that certain texts privilege certain readings or "embody preferred readings," and certain formal qualities of the text contribute to that privileging.

Although more recent feminist theory and criticism have rejected (or at least seriously questioned) the idea of a specifically feminist content, they do agree that feminist critical practice seeks to examine texts as cultural products that reinforce or oppose a patriarchal society and to investigate what kinds of texts and discursive techniques can engender a feminist experience of the text. While the discussion of recent years has rightly criticized the notion of a universal patriarchy as asocial and ahistorical, the fact remains that many particularly Western cultures have practiced gender oppression in strikingly similar ways and the commonalities of this oppression are as salient as its differences. Culture has constructed gender identities and imposed them upon women, and to ignore that insight is to engage in historical wishful thinking even as an acknowledgment of it does not preclude the assertion of women as agentive subjects.

If, as Gentile argues, feminism is less an oppositional ideology than a process that incorporates opposition into itself (6), then feminist critical practice must in some way account for the categories of androcentric culture that have oppressed or erased women. Treatment of these categories can be an important identifier of feminist potential, even as such content must be seen in the context of the whole representational field. Central to an evaluation of Bergman's work from a feminist perspective are three such concepts: binarism, the idealized male subject of culture, and the representation of the body. A major issue in feminist criticism of the last decade has, then, been the examination of the theoretical/grammatical and psychoanalytical foundations of that binarism and how those foundations contribute to the construction of subjectivity and concepts of the body.

Of course binarism of gender is, as Beauvoir points out, a social construct; masculine and feminine are cultural definitions, not biological, "natural," precultural facts. Throughout recorded history the Western tradition adduces ontological distinctions between spirit (consciousness, mind) and body that serve to reinforce various social and political hierarchies in which women are subordinated, distinctions well documented in research by Spelman and others. De Lauretis rightly asserts that "gender is . . . the representation of each individual in terms of a particular social relation which preexists the individual and is predicated upon the *conceptual* and rigid (structural) opposition of two biological sexes" (*Technologies of Gender* 5). As Butler rhetorically asks, "Does being female constitute a 'natural fact' or a cultural performance, or is 'naturalness' constituted through discursively constrained performative acts that produce the body through and within the categories of sex?" (x). This idea of gender as performance is especially prominent in Bergman's work where identity is mutable; as Livingston points out, "Bergman demonstrates that identity is never simple or immediate and that it does not reside in a static equivalence of self to self. The boundaries of self are open and fluid; its unity is not rigid, but evolves through contact with others . . . . identity is never established in isolation but is the product of a basic, inescapable reciprocity" (52, 51). Thus various of his characters not only question gender relations through their self-conscious role-playing but also periodically engage in acts of cross-dressing that extend and expand their authority both psychologically and socially/politically. Given that "the representation of gender *is* its construction — and in the simplest sense it can be said that all of Western Art and high culture is the engraving of the history of that construction. . . . [and that] *The construction of gender is both the product and the process of its representation*" (de Lauretis, *Technologies of Gender* 3, 5), a study of gender issues, as manifest in content, discursive technique, and spectator/text relations in a male filmmaker who both struggles against and longs for reabsorption into the dominant androcentric culture can provide insight into the ways in which masculine discourse can both affirm and subvert cultural institutions.

Another feminist issue that warrants exploration in Bergman's work is his treatment of how culture is embodied. Irigaray argues that the binarism of male culture is in fact a chimera, for the binary "effectively masks the univocal and hegemonic discourse of the masculine, phallogocentrism, silencing the feminine as a site of subversive multiplicity" (ctd. in Butler 19). Thus, the idealized cultural subject is male. Historically, the universal person and the male gender have been almost completely conflated; women are sex and men "the bearers of a body-transcendent universal personhood" (Butler 9), for, as Barthes has pointed out, one of the effects of ideology is to make what is cultural and therefore historically variable appear natural and immutable (*Mythologies*). If women are in dominant cinema relegated to absence, silence, and marginality, the women in many of Bergman's films would appear to be an anomaly, for *The Silence*, *Persona*, and *Cries and Whispers* all center around the issue of female subjectivity, constructed however accurately and however effectively. If "woman" is also the "subject which is not one" (Butler 10), Bergman's deploying female protagonists to speak to "universal" issues of human subjectivity is perhaps all the more remarkable. If Western cultural representations of women usually connote "otherness," then that "otherness" is a position that Bergman sees himself as occupying. While his work is characterized by an identification with female "otherness," it also presents moments in which his own feelings of otherness contribute to his "othering" of women. Accordingly we need to rethink the subject/ object dichotomy that is at the heart of so many male representations of women and to find more subtle critical methodologies for dealing with his portraits of women. If it is true, as Butler argues, that "the cultural matrix through which gender identity has become intelligible requires that certain kinds of 'identities' cannot 'exist' — that is, those in which gender does not follow from sex and those in which the practices of desire do not follow from either sex or gender" (17), Bergman's attempts to find ways to privilege, to grant authority to the other, to create "universal" human subjectivities within the bodies of women is all the more provocative. It is within the framework of this awareness of the problematical equation between gender and identity that we must also locate Bergman's recurring treatment of lesbianism.

The whole issue of the representation of women is directly, if intricately, linked with the representation of the body. This issue is an extremely complex and sensitive one for feminist analysis, precisely because of the androcentric valorization of mind, gendered as male, over body, gendered as female. Feminist criticism is then rightly suspicious of male representations (or any representation by that token) of the female body. One wonders if Jane Gallop may not be on the right track in her observation that the tendency to dismiss Irigaray as trapped in biologism bespeaks the split that makes us suspect that any sustained attention to the body must fall outside the bounds of serious thought (8). If such is the case for women attending to the issue of the female body, how much more suspect is not a male artist such as Bergman, who in films with women protagonists is interested in addressing mind-body issues and their formulation by the patriarchy. Is Bergman's preoccupation with the female body in such films as *Smiles of a Summer Night*, *The Silence*, *Persona*, and *Cries and Whispers* little more than that of a consumer with an object of purchase, simply an obsession with the otherness of femininity? I am inclined to think not, precisely because of his own identification with otherness, with marginality, and also with victimization. Bergman is, in my view, quite conflicted about the body. As his numerous interview and memoir books attest, he is repulsed and yet obsessed by all manner of bodily functions, both male and female — from digestion and sweating to breast feeding; yet films such as *Persona* (and to a lesser extent *Smiles of a Summer Night* and *The Seventh Seal*) attest equally eloquently to his recognition both of the female body as a site of the inscription of male desire and discourse and of the ideological improbity of its being so.

## Feminist Formal Strategies and Bergman's Practice

It is an axiom that the experience of an art work is as much conditioned by the discursive techniques in which it is rendered as by the content itself, and consequently feminist film criticism has explored how film strategies shape meaning. In Claire Johnston's words from her 1973 essay "Women's Cinema as Counter Cinema," "it is not enough to discuss the oppression of women within the text of the film; the language of the cinema/the depiction of reality must also be interrogated, so that a break between ideology and text is effected" (140). "Re-vision," writes Adrienne Rich, refers to the project of reclaiming vision, of "seeing difference differently," of displacing the critical emphasis from "images of" women "to the axis of vision itself— to the modes of organizing vision and hearing which result in the production of that 'image'" (35), a perception of the filmic experience that seems singularly appropriate to Bergman's enterprise with its constant preoccupation with "vision," its pervasive awareness of the complicity between cinema and ideology, and its radical challenge to that equation. Johnston proposed that only a cinematic practice that challenged mainstream dominant cinema could begin to speak for women, and some feminist critics have accordingly concentrated on what might be called strategies of disjunction, stylistic techniques that serve to undermine traditional Western male discourse. One might ask, given the extent to which the female has been connoted as other, if any disruptive practice, any challenge to the Western discursive hegemony is not feminist in effect if not in intent. Accordingly, feminists have frequently allied themselves with the avant-garde because of that movement's penchant for resisting and attacking the dominant ideology, as a result of which many of the disjunctive strategies of which feminists avail themselves are also practiced by the avant-garde. Thus, although Bergman's films may not aspire to feminism, the disjunctive devices he employs so frequently may nonetheless encourage a feminist experience in the spectator by deconstructing certain aspects of dominant male discourse.

First and foremost, the whole issue of narrative is problematic for feminism. As Gentile argues, "Narrative becomes suspect in a feminist critique due to its construction of an exclusive world view, an illusory realm complete with closure and invisible seams. The feeling of wholeness and authenticity makes it all the more difficult to detect ideological exclusions or inclusions" (81–82). Furthermore, narrative traditionally presents an image of questing men and waiting women:

> Man . . . conquers, seduces, and abandons, while Woman responds to His action of conquest, seduction, and abandonment. . . . The heroines of countless . . . fictions are locked into erotic dramas that turn primarily around the agency and power of entrepreneurs on whom their destiny depends. . . . Fundamental to the *story* that these narratives recount is a conception of *history* as manifest destiny, a history where the heroine's body figures as one among many territories traversed and claimed by heroes bent upon building larger empires. (Altman 173–73)

As de Lauretis has argued, narrative is deeply ideologically implicated. Starting from Barthes' understanding that "the pleasure of the text is . . . an

Oedipal pleasure (to denude, to know, to learn the origin and the end)" and
Scholes' analogy between the act of reading and the sexual act ("the fundamental orgiastic rhythm of tumescence and detumescence, of tension and
resolution, of intensification to the point of climax and consummation"), she
galvanizes the myth of Oedipus, Propp's *Morphology of the Folktale*, and Lévi-
Straus to conclude that there is a kind of inevitable "Oedipal logic" to narrativity, that there is an inscription of desire in the very movement of that narrative and the unfolding of the Oedipal scenario as *drama* (action); that, in
brief, narrative itself posits the possibility only of a specifically male desire
(*Alice Doesn't* 103–57).[1]

A rejection of closure, of the enigma-resolution structure, as characteristic
of avant-garde cinema in general and of Bergman's later films in particular,
also coheres with feminism since closure is "a feature of dominant
'masculine' language, to the extent that such language embodies a hierarchy
of meanings and implies a subjection to, a completion and closure of, meaning" (Kuhn, *Women's Pictures* 17). Barthes, as a case in point, makes a distinction between the pleasure of the closure of a text and the "bliss"
(*jouissance*) of texts that defy such closure. "Both are clearly relationships of
reading: the pleasure of the first is the satisfaction of completion, of having all
the ends tied up, whereas the bliss of the second is the unsettling, the movement of the subject produced by the reading" (Kuhn, *Women's Pictures* 17).

Thus both feminist films and Bergman's post-1960 works frequently incorporate new methods of narrative organization to replace a more conventional linear plot. In subverting traditional narrative, an avant-gardist such as
Bergman and feminist filmmakers come to rely on the visual instead of the
verbal for expressiveness, at least in part because of the complicity between
language and patriarchy. Thus feminism and Bergman's practice share an
impulse toward the deconstruction — the foregrounding of certain concepts
that exposes their ideological substructures — of hierarchy and a challenge of
traditional modes of discourse, tacitly responding to Virginia Woolf's call for
"less system and more sympathy."

Because it questions all forms of hierarchy, the avant-garde art or feminist
art work, like Bergman's texts, often refuses to privilege any particular viewpoint and instead employs multiple points of view that disperse and diffuse
authority in such a way that male authority is challenged and thereby engender a plurality of vision and expression. The issue of authority is vital to the
feminist critical enterprise. As Gentile puts it, "Women must find their way
to a functional identity that does not rely on the construction of an
Other; ... They must begin to see themselves as in a network of multiple
possibilities, multiple perspectives, multiple identities, where there is no clear
split between "I" and "not-I," but rather a range or continuum of existence"
(19). This issue is central to Bergman's enterprise; as early as *The Seventh Seal*

and certainly after 1960, Bergman's films refuse to grant authority to any unitary subjectivity. Rather point-of-view is dispersed across a variety of subjects, none of which has access to an indisputable "truth."

Not surprisingly, feminist texts frequently revolve around multiple diegesis. One technique for establishing this multiple diegesis is the creation of a "dialogical" text, one that "constitutes itself as an arena of conflict between two voices" (Doane, *Dialogical Text* 2), one of which may be the narrative voice of the film itself, as is the case with *Persona*. These multiple viewpoints can also, of course, engender multiple responses on the part of the spectator, an effect in keeping with feminism's attack on the impulse toward the monolithic in male culture; or, as Kuhn says, "the space for active participation in the viewing process is opened up by the different modes of address of the discourses structuring the text, as well as by the ways in which they are articulated together" (*Women's Pictures* 175). Again this is an issue that arises repeatedly in Bergman's work; films such as *The Silence*, *Persona*, and *Cries and Whispers* are all structured dialogically in order to subvert conventional spectator-text relations.

The use of the first-person or an emphasis upon the text as personal vision may also privilege a feminist reading. Whereas much countercinema, like Bergman's practice, is a personal expression of the artist's experience and concerns, dominant cinema strives for transparency and verisimilitude. While one can certainly speak of Hawks, Ford, and Hitchcock as having individual "styles," those directors erase themselves from their films far more than do, say, Bergman, Fellini, Kurosawa, or Deren. Jan Rosenberg clarifies,

> avant garde films both depict and "represent" expressive behavior. They emphasize the *emotional context* of action far more than they emphasize the social action itself. Some avant garde films dwell exclusively on the interior experience. . . . They emphasize the value of expressivity and emotion over cognition. Avant garde films are primarily valued as personal expressions of their creator's inner emotions and feelings. (68)

Or, as Deren maintains, the avant-garde film involves a "vertical investigation of a situation, in that it probes the ramifications of the moment, and is concerned with its qualities and its depth . . . not with what is occurring but with what it feels like or what it means" (ctd. in Rosenberg 71). Rosenberg further locates in such films frequent use of "themes of identity and self-consciousness" (69). In a perspective that is suggestive for Bergman's work, she conflates avant-garde and feminist film by pointing out that:

> Women's avant garde films entail and express the filmmaker's search for meaning. They include those which explore identity, childhood, and sexuality, and others . . . which probe more formal problems by experimenting with light, editing techniques, and working directly on the film emulsion. Like related forms of high art, most avant garde films by women place high

value on the careful communication of mood and feeling, on introspection
rather than action, and on subtlety. In structure and feeling, they resemble
poems. (70)

An emphasis on both the constructed nature of the text and on the text
as subjective expression, while not sufficient for, can nonetheless privilege a
feminist reading. The feminist and/or avant-garde film frequently rejects
transparency in favor of foregrounding in order to point up the constructed
nature of the fictive reality. Not the least of foregrounding strategies is that of
authorial intrusion, a prominent aspect of Bergman's post-1960 work. Roller
sees this intrusion as central to the feminist enterprise, as directly connected
with the feminist approach to authority, individualism, and ideology. She
also observes that "the fractured point of view and disjointed arrangement of
chapters often mirrors the concern the author feels about the splintered nature of modern life" (114). The closed and internally coherent narrative is
jettisoned in favor of one that opens itself up to intrusions from the real
world. Thus, self-conscious aesthetic devices that disrupt the narrative flow
can serve to interrupt the passive identification that characterizes traditional
cinematic experience and substitute for it a more critical mode of spectator
experience termed "passionate detachment" by Mulvey and "critical subjectivity" by Gentile.

Countercinema also frequently involves at least a partial renunciation of
emotional identification and a concomitant "unpleasure" for the spectator, a
deconstruction of the mergence (intense identification) between spectator
and spectacle. Thus, feminist critics and avant-garde filmmakers argue that
women's cinema should avoid a "politics of emotions and seek to problematize the female spectator's identification with the on-screen image of
woman" (de Lauretis, *Technologies* 129). By fragmenting and interrupting
the narrative, presenting "flat" characters, depicting time as nonlinear, and so
forth, one can hinder identification and engender a more critical spectator
experience. One particularly feminist strategy within this practice, then,
would be the rejection of identification with a specifically male point of view,
a strategy that pervades the later Bergman films.

Another technique that can help to foreground the constructed nature of
the fictive reality in film is a deliberate avoidance of the customary shot/ reverse shot pattern of traditional narrative film. This avoidance not only serves
to force the spectator to "maintain a distance in relation to both the narrative
and the image" (Kaplan, *Women and Film* 174), but also helps to deconstruct the androcentric "relay of looks" that is, in psychoanalytic criticism, at
the heart of cinema. Typical of Bergman's later work are the sequence in
which Märta reads her letter directly into the camera in *Winter Light* and the
repeated monologue sequence in *Persona* both of which concentrate the
spectator's attention on an individual woman's face for an inordinately long

time (filmically speaking), thereby foregrounding conventional cinema's nexus of "the look." The numerous instances in his films of direct address to the camera by a female character also highlight the constructed nature of filmic representation.

Both avant-garde and feminist cinema also frequently subvert time-space relations. Rosenberg sees women's avant-garde films as involving "the vertical penetration of an intense and privileged moment; they revolve around what an experience means or feels like. They exist outside of the dominant Western horizontal conception of time. In presenting an ahistorical, transcendent view of human experience, they implicitly deny the importance of past, present, and future. This further demonstrates their distance from the political world" (72).

One might, then, expect to find in works with a feminist import, as one does in certain Bergman films, extensive use of both linguistic and narrational repetition and interruption. And in certain texts by women, one observes that given words and images appear, reappear, and disappear, with repetition and fragmentation often replacing conventional plot as a structuring device. The substitution of "duration" for chronology can, of course, have the same effect. While it is certainly true that the ahistoricity implicit in such a perspective may seem merely to reinscribe an essentialist view of women, alternative representations of time can also subvert the linear sense of temporality that masculine culture has appropriated for its own.

By the same token, the deployment of space is ideologically implicated; as indicated above, the patriarchy has a vested interest in depicting female experience as confinement. Especially in film with its foundation in the representation of space, the deployment of that space and the relationship of female characters to it are of prime importance in expressing female subjectivity. Shot selection becomes all the more important in this connection, since it dictates whether women subjects are to be viewed (and therefore experienced as) alone or together, in sympathy with or in opposition to their environments. Thus by deliberately manipulating, as Bergman does, the "female space" of domestic interiors and the "male space" of streets and nature, one can expose and subvert the feminine stereotype of confinement.

Related to issues of feminist strategies is the concern with "feminist voice." It is apparent that in a concrete way women have been deprived of a voice in dominant cinema, that, as Silverman puts it, "sexual difference is the effect of dominant cinema's *sound* regime as well as its visual regime, that the female *voice* is as relentlessly held to normative representations and functions as is the female body" (*Acoustic Mirror* viii). One of the issues that she investigates is how dominant cinema "locates the male voice at the point of apparent textual origin, while establishing the diegetic containment of the female voice" (45). An example of this repression of the female voice occurs in dominant cinema's use of voice-over, for theoretical consensus indicates that the disembodied, heterodiegetic (that is to say belonging to an individual who is not part of the narrative) voice-over is absolutely congruent with veritably godlike authority, with achieved invisibility, omniscience, and discursive power. As Bonitzer observes: "the voice-over represents a power, that of disposing of the image and of that which it reflects from a place that is absolutely other. Absolutely other and absolutely indeterminable. In this sense, transcendent" (ctd. in Silverman, "Dis-Embodying" 134). Tellingly then, in all her research on the subject, Silverman was able to locate only one instance of a disembodied heterodiegetic female voice. But in addition to a disembodied heterogetic female voice, various other strategies appear to undercut the synchronization between the female voice and the female body: the presentation of a female voice that is not linked to a visible female body, the use of a dialectical relationship between sound and image, of counterpoint to undermine the equation, and the creation of confusion in the spectator's mind as to the "source" of a particular voice or image — these strategies serve to render "the semic code . . . inoperative by the absence of a proper name, a stable visual representation, and a predictable cluster of attributes" (Silverman "Dis-Embodying" 139), to critique the entrapment of women within masculine discourse and ideology. Voice-overs, especially those by women, can also be lent increased authority by making it clear that they are telling their own stories (i.e. a subject that they presumably know well), and, when voice-overs impart a sense of conscious, deliberate communication, they can also serve the feminist goal of distantiation. Voice-over in general and female voice-over in particular function in Bergman's films from *The Seventh Seal* to *Fanny and Alexander* in exactly this way; by problematizing the synchronization between body and voice, these films challenge the male order and lend authority to the female voice, even as the issue is complicated in *Cries and Whispers* by the film's relentless biologism.

Bergman's experimentation with (and rejection of) traditional narrative strategies and his renunciation of closure in the post-1960 films provide, then, another opening into the potential feminism of his texts. The formal techniques in his work can foreground and subvert the ideological complicity between discourse and culture; alternative narrative strategies, the subversion and/or dispersion of various kinds of authority, multiple diegesis, self-conscious aesthetics, an emphasis upon "expressiveness," a rejection of both conventional identificatory mechanisms and the appropriating mergence of spectator and spectacle, and a disruption of traditional time-space relations can all privilege a feminist experience of his texts. Thus, many of Bergman's post-1960 films can be seen as radical aesthetic experiments whose effect, if not goal, is to disrupt the cinematic structures that reinforce patriarchal ideology.

# Methodology: Psychoanalysis and
# Feminist Film Theory — A Summary

Certainly one of the most influential developments in feminist theory in the past two decades for establishing a critical methodology to analyze the feminist potential of texts is the conjunction of psychoanalysis and semiology, since the combination of the two approaches allows for the unlocking of patriarchal culture as it is expressed in individual media and art works. In its most basic form, this theory sees dominant cinema as a kind of repository for male fantasy, and one of the dubious attractions of this criticism is that it posits the male as both the perceiving and creating subject. As de Lauretis argues, "the position of woman in language and in cinema is one of non-coherence; she finds herself only in a void of meaning, the empty space between the signs — the place of women spectators in the cinema between the look of the camera and the image on the screen, a place not represented, not symbolized, and thus preempted to subject (or self) representation" (8). I designate this attraction as dubious because it disallows the presence of a female subject, but at the same time the positing of the subject as ipso facto male would seem to be a realistic assessment of our cultural situation, especially insofar as films are concerned, since even now far and away the vast majority of films are still made by men for consumption in a male-dominated society.

Laura Mulvey's influential article "Visual Pleasure and the Narrative Cinema," which set the parameters of the feminist film debate for over a decade and a half, takes as its point of departure Lacan's restatement of the "common sense" observation that women experience themselves as other in male-dominated culture, not as women, since the culture allows no real identity for women, but rather as that which is non-subject, non-self, non-male. As such, women are allotted two potential roles in the patriarchal ideology — that of mother, as symbol of lost plenitude, or as lack, symbol of all that which the male fears not having (i.e. castration). Thus, she argues, woman is identified in patriarchal culture "as signifier of the male other. . . tied to her place as bearer of meaning, not maker of meaning" (7). The *Cahiers du Cinema* critics indicate how this system operates: "in order that the man remain at the centre of the universe in a text which focuses on the image of woman, the auteur is forced to repress the idea of woman as a social and sexual being (her Otherness) and to deny the man/woman opposition altogether. The woman as sign, then, becomes the pseudo-centre of the filmic discourse. The real opposition posed by the sign is male/non-male" (Johnston 136).

As Mulvey points out, the cinema offers its spectator a number of possible pleasures, one of which is scopophilia:

[Freud] associated scopophilia with taking other people as objects, subject-
ing them to a controlling gaze. . . . The mass of mainstream film. . . portrays a hermetically sealed world. . . indifferent to the presence of the
audience, producing for them a sense of separation and playing on their voyeuristic phantasy. Moreover, the extreme contrast between the darkness in
the auditorium (which also isolates the spectators from one another) and
the brilliance of the shifting patterns of light and shade on the screen helps
promote the illusion of voyeuristic separation. (8)

Mulvey argues, then, that classical narrative film evokes a voyeuristic pleasure
connected to androcentrism and that only a countercinema that works
against spectator identification can effectively change cinema's reinforcement
of patriarchal values. Certainly a critical methodology of film that emphasizes
voyeurism seems appropriate, for, in obvious ways, film is voyeurism. Indeed,
Judith Mayne rightly argues that "voyeurism has become so institutionalized
a feature of the cinema that we tend to take it for granted" ("Woman at the
Keyhole" 54). The fascination the viewer experiences in the cinema is, in
Mulvey's view, like the fascination of the child before his mirror; scopophilia
informs both. Metz has enumerated a number of features the two activities
have in common: "the obscurity surrounding the onlooker, the aperture of
the screen with its inevitable key-hole effect . . . the spectator's solitude . . .
the segregation of spaces" ("The Imaginary Signifier" 64). The camera
functions, then, as an inscription of the scopic drive, a drive that is by definition associated with the male in the human personality.

Mulvey goes on to argue that "in a world ordered by sexual imbalance,
pleasure in looking has been split between active/male and passive/female"
(11). Since the male occupies the position of speaking and seeing subject,
woman is excluded from authoritative vision. Thus, the absence of a female
subject in film and the conflict between female presence (visible yet invisible,
heard yet not heard) and absence is central to feminist critical practice. And
given the implication of the male subject in the act of voyeurism, the status
of women vis-a-vis the same activity has to be ambiguous. The dynamics of
the cinematic apparatus seem to militate against even the possibility of a female subject and to designate women solely as objects.

There are, of course, two objections to this argument. The first would
question why the gaze is ipso facto male, to which Baudry responds. "the
spectator identifies less with what is represented, the spectacle itself, than
with what stages the spectacle, makes it seen, obliging him to see what it
sees; this is exactly the function taken over by the camera as a sort of relay"
(45), an identification clearly aligned with the (usually) male director. Kaplan
also counters that "the gaze is not necessarily male (literally), but to own and
activate the gaze, given our language and the structure of the unconscious, is
to be in the 'masculine' position" ("Is the Gaze Male?" 30). Kaplan sees this

problem as part of the sexual structures of dominance and submission that permeate our society:

> Our culture is deeply committed to myths of demarcated sex differences, called "masculine" and "feminine," which in turn revolve first on a complex gaze apparatus and second on dominance-submission patterns. This positioning of the two sex genders in representation clearly privileges the male (through the mechanisms of voyeurism and fetishism, which are male operations, and because his desire carries power/action where woman's usually does not). (29)

More recently, Steven Neale and Richard Dyer have investigated this issue from the perspective of male spectacle by looking at how the male body is represented when it is put on display. Ultimately they both conclude that even when the object of spectacle is male, dominant cinema still encodes it according to a masculinity-as-activity, femininity-as-passivity paradigm, thereby reaffirming the notion of sexual difference in the cinematic sphere.

The second argument would charge psychoanalytical criticism with assuming that female film viewers experience no pleasure in seeing films or that what pleasure they do experience is fundamentally masochistic. Bellour, for instance, claims that the only identification possible between a woman viewer and a woman character is one of masochism. Cinematic identification, then, if defined as analogous to the mirror phase, permits only two familiar polarities of identification: "with the masculine, active gaze and narrative point of view or with the feminine, specular, masochistic position" (de Lauretis, *Alice Doesn't* 78). But Judith Mayne and Ruby Rich argue that such is not the case, that, on the contrary, precisely because woman is coded for invisibility in film at the same time that the female spectator is manifestly present, the latter becomes an "ultimate dialectician," constantly juggling realities and forging new insights ("Woman at the Keyhole" 61). Their position on this issue suggests the possibility for the female spectator of a constructive engagement in the cinematic experience, a way of overcoming and even utilizing the androcentric structures of film in the development of a feminist awareness that nonetheless does not deny the ideological tainting of these structures.

Woman, then, in dominant cinema is coded for "to-be-looked-at-ness," an icon "displayed for the gaze and enjoyment of men" (Mulvey 11, 13), an observation supported in a wider cultural context by John Berger, whose research finds that the evolution of the representation of the female body from naked to nude transformed woman into an object, a commodity in relation to which the spectator is the buyer and the buyer is the spectator: "Women are depicted in quite a different way from men — not because the feminine is different from the masculine — but because the 'ideal' spectator is always as-

sumed to be male and the image of the woman is designed to flatter him"
(64). Johnston explains further:

> Lighting, camera angles, the cutting between actors and use of close shot v.
> long shot — all the techniques of filming are used to differentiate radically
> the presentation of men and women on the screen . . . techniques normally
> used . . . for women in films . . . essentially produce a specularity in relation
> to the character in a way which places her role in the film as iconic rather
> than diegetic; i.e. the classical sexual objectification of women in films. (ctd.
> in Gledhill 33)

Thus, one of the richest areas of feminist research in recent years concerns
itself with the "look," the "gaze," and the ways in which they are embedded
in the film text itself and in the viewing experience. As Williams suggests,
"the relay of looks within the film duplicates the voyeuristic pleasure of the
cinematic apparatus" ("When the Woman Looks" 83), an insight that
Bergman's films seem persistently to share; virtually all his films include moments in which the spectator is confronted with his or her own voyeurism,
frequently through a play with mirrors. From as early a film as *Sawdust and
Tinsel*, in which Anne's confrontation with the camera's gaze in a dressing-
room mirror is paralleled by characters' spying on each other, to *Fanny and
Alexander*, in which Alexander's direct address to the camera associates the
spectator with his persistent surreptitious peeping into other rooms and other
realities, Bergman foregrounds voyeurism. Even in a work such as *The Ser-
pent's Egg* from 1977, by which time he had retreated from his most radical
filmic practice, the entire plot centers on voyeurism as a metaphor for the ap-
proaching Nazi reign of terror. The "look" in essence structures our perception of the represented material, and the eye is the site of absolute authority,
just as God is often depicted iconically as an open eye. If the gaze is male, it
is to be expected that "everything conspires to condemn the desire and curiosity of the woman's look" (Williams 86). The woman's look can only destroy her subjectivity, for as Stephen Heath observes, "If the woman looks,
the spectacle provokes, castration is in the air, the Medusa's head is not far
off; thus, she must not look, is absorbed herself on the side of the seen, seeing herself seeing herself, Lacan's femininity" (ctd. in Williams 88).

As Williams has shown, powerful female looks are few and far between in
dominant cinema: the smoldering eyes of the silent screen vamp are robbed
of authority by her dubious moral status and her ultimate punishment in the
course of the narrative. When "good girls" do exercise "an active investigating gaze," it is inevitably punished and they are victimized (85). In films by
women, however, one can locate a "powerful female look" that is not punished. In Dorothy Arzner's *Dance, Girl, Dance* Johnston finds a "return of
scrutiny in what within the film is assumed as a one-way process [that] constitutes a direct assault on her audience within the film and the audience of

the film, and has the effect of challenging the entire notion of woman as spectacle" ("Women's Cinema" 141). Kaplan also suggests that certain kinds of mutual gazing can disrupt the male scopic regime. This gazing in which the viewer is also viewed and the viewed also viewer stresses the relation between the two participants in the scopic act and is not of "the subject-object kind that reduces one of the parties to the place of submission. . . . [but instead works against] the domination-submission modes [that] may be an inherent component of eroticism for both sexes in western capitalist culture" (*Women and Film* 205). Such mutual gazing "requires the viewer to address consciously the process of identification itself, the process of interacting with a particular film" (Gentile 81). Thus breaking the nexus of the look can "foreground the illusionist, naturalizing, and suturing operations of narrative cinema" (de Lauretis, *Alice Doesn't* 8).

Because of the power relations inherent in the gaze and the ways in which dominant practice encourages identification with male specularity, Mulvey and other psychoanalytical critics agree that a countercinema must subvert audience identification with on-screen characters. As de Lauretis points out, "if identification is 'not simply one psychical mechanism among others, but the operation itself whereby the human subject is constituted,' as Laplanche and Pontalis describe it, then it must be all the more important, theoretically and politically, for women who have never before represented ourselves as subjects" (*Technologies* 129).

While Mulvey suggests that countercinema must replace pleasure with "unpleasure," the question still arises as to whether or not there are some feminist filmic practices that can recoup the pleasure of identification. Several theorist/critics maintain that precisely such possibilities do exist. De Lauretis, for instance, calls for "undercutting spectator identification in terms of both vision (literally, a difficulty in seeing) and narrative (a difficulty in understanding events and their succession, their timing)," thus deconstructing the mergence of spectator and spectacle, problematizing our "'time' in film, its vision for us" ("Now and Nowhere" 154). And Kaplan, in defining what she calls the "theory film," argues that one can "replace pleasure in recognition with pleasure in learning — with cognitive processes, as against emotional ones" (*Women and Film* 138). Other critics suggest galvanizing the pleasures of puzzle-solving or of open-ended contemplation of an image (Kuhn, *Women's Pictures* 170f.) as alternatives to the voyeuristic/fetishistic pleasure embedded in most cinematic narratives. Thus, feminist criticism seems to call for a spectator attitude of disinterested intellectual play, of Mulvey's "passionate detachment" or what Kuhn describes as "an involved but critical approach" (*Women's Pictures* 172), or what Gentile calls "critical subjectivity," by which she means "the encouragement of a conscious questioning of our film experience . . . the recognition of contradictions or tension points within an individual's ideological context" (77, 68), one form of which may be what Mayne has termed the "moment of disavowal."

Gentile, however, proposes that the pleasure of identification can be turned to a feminist purpose:

> Let our filmmaker continue to utilize those film techniques that encourage identification but utilize them *multiply*. Present a film's experience from differing ... *contradictory* perspectives. This experience of contradiction will encourage a *dual consciousness* in the viewer ... thus [encouraging] a critical distance. ... Empathetic identification with adults, with children, with men and women ... [renders] gender categories ... shockingly inadequate. (79)

A further strategy for recouping the pleasure of the look lies in the possibilities of mutual gazing, an example of which would be a film in which the director pulls the spectator into and out of the identificatory process. "In this way, the viewer is personally 'engaged' or invested in the film's characters, while at the same time, she is asked to see through their behavior. ... The manifestation of conflicting viewpoints *within* the film serves to expose the choices the filmmaker makes. ... This exposure of the filmmaker's process, in effect, provides the spectator with the tools necessary to dismantle the illusion" (Gentile 81).

Mayne too, in arguing the distinction between the "woman's" film and "women's" film, holds that "women's cinema may well be characterized, not necessarily by an outright rejection of voyeuristic and fetishistic desires but by the recasting of those desires so as to open up other possible pleasures for film viewing" (*Woman at the Keyhole* 5). Furthermore, Mayne is right to raise the larger question, namely:

> the extent to which voyeurism and fetishism, as they have been defined within psychoanalytically inspired film studies (feminist and otherwise), are synonymous with the cinema. It is not always clear when voyeurism and fetishism define the cinema in an absolute sense, and when they define a specific kind of film viewing, within a specific historical and cultural context. (*Woman at the Keyhole* 4)

Keeping in mind the potential ahistoricity of psychoanalytical approaches, Mayne posits what one might call "post-psychoanalytical" insights about spectator/text relations.

But the contributions of psychoanalytic film criticism are helpful in an exploration of Bergman's work because of his consistent foregrounding of framed tableaux and acts of both voyeurism and mutual gazing. Spectator/spectacle issues are central to his entire production: his treatment of voyeurism and spectator identification in *Smiles of a Summer Night*, *The Silence*, and *Persona* suggests a consciousness of the genderedness of these activities, of the power relations inherent in them as these films explore the possibility of an authoritative female gaze and its potential for disrupting the hegemony of dominant ideology.

The importance of an accurate understanding of just how women are encoded as spectacle in films is underlined by Mayne:

> One of the most basic connections between women's experience in this culture and women's experience in film is precisely the relationship of spectator and spectacle. Since women are spectacles in their everyday lives, there's something about coming to terms with film from the perspective of what it means to be an object of spectacle and what it means to be a spectator that is really a coming to terms with how that relationship exists both up on the screen and in their everyday life. ("Women and Film" 86)

Expanding upon contemporary feminist film theory, which sees the relationship between the male viewer (voyeur) and the female object of spectacle as central to the structuring of film experience and which sees spectator identification as all but inevitably male, Mayne argues for a reading of film in terms of the film screen and its ambivalent function as simultaneous passage and obstacle and, as such, a metaphor for the female body, a surface on which is acted out the attempt of the male gaze to penetrate and appropriate the female body. Screens function, then, as figures for the spectator's contradictory and complex relationship to film by galvanizing a number of issues centering around a dichotomy between surface and depth.

As Mayne has pointed out, the metaphor of the film screen can be a pivotal one for mediating between intratextual and extratextual filmic experience, for screens "are figures . . . of the intersection of spectacle and narrative . . . the screen is both surface and passageway, mirror and obstacle," and filmgoing promises precisely the "transgression of the boundary line separating two spheres" (*Woman at the Keyhole* 31). Thus, she argues that the screen has an ambivalent status insofar as it both positions and obscures: "the screen bear[s] witness simultaneously to the necessity of the fiction of completeness and wholeness and to its impossibility" (41). Proposing a methodology whereby the gaze is investigated in its relationship to the screen, she sees the metaphor of the screen as an embodiment of enriching ambivalence, as a "nodal point in the representation of the difficulty of closure in any simplistic sense" (*Woman at the Keyhole* 43). This is, again, a theoretical approach that seems singularly suited to the films of Bergman, given the prominence of problematical screening surfaces in the post-1960 production with its questioning of the interdependence of culture, gender, and discourse and their function as both an "embodiment" of body and the interface between spectator and spectacle.

# Conclusion

By way of conclusion, of an attempt to assimilate these various aspects of the debate as to what might constitute a potentially feminist film practice, the argument adduced by Annette Kuhn in her formulation of the parameters of feminist practice is helpful. Kuhn postulates that there are two general types of oppositional practice: the use of female voices and deconstruction. By the former, she means "authentic forms of expression for women" (*Women's Pictures* 168), forms that would necessarily engender a different kind of spectator pleasure; "this is perhaps the crucial point of distinction between deconstructive texts and feminine texts. Whereas the former tend to break down and challenge the forms of pleasure privileged by dominant texts, the latter set up radically 'other' forms of pleasure" (*Women's Pictures* 168); in other words, we are talking about a cinema of "jouissance." By deconstruction, she means the "articulation of oppositional forms with oppositional contents" (*Women's Pictures* 161); in other words, a departure from the conventions of dominant cinema accompanied by a presentation of a subject matter that also stands in opposition to the traditional androcentric view of women's experience. As to how this articulation might be rendered, she considers "relations of looking, narrativity and narrative discourse, subjectivity and autobiography, fiction as against non-fiction, and openness as against closure" (*Women's Pictures* 169), pointing specifically to the possibilities for a "radical heterogeneity in spectator-text relations" through the interpenetration of the fictional and nonfictional worlds, the lack of narrative closure, and the refusal to grant the spectator a space of "unitary subjectivity" (*Women's Pictures* 171).

All these methodologies and perspectives are informative for a feminist approach to Bergman, since so much of his production is characterized by a sense of the difficulties inherent in the relationship between women and cinematic representation. One suspects that Mayne's suggestion that "the lure of film spectacle is not simply the possession of the image, but rather the simultaneity of mastery and the breakdown of the oppositions upon which mastery is based, of merging and disavowal, of passage and obstruction" (*Woman at the Keyhole* 50) is particularly appropriate for Bergman's work. For his films both legitimize and challenge the patriarchal status quo. Experiencing himself as an artist marginalized by a dominant bourgeois society and recognizing the power relations that traditional androcentric religion and culture entail and the extent to which that culture's ideology infects all forms of discourse and subjectivity, Bergman identifies with women as victims. At the same time he can only fleetingly escape his status as a male artist seeking acceptance by and integration into the dominant culture. Throughout his career, I would argue, he confronts and struggles against androcentric values at the same time that he passionately longs for reabsorption into a godhead and the comfort and solace of a perfect mother. Thus his works are individually and collectively paradoxical and ambivalent, but the paradox and ambivalence, informed as they are by a certain honesty and integrity, create a field veritably electric with energy. However, as Mayne points out, there is a great risk in arguing for a

> "both/and," since the insistence upon competing ideological and representational levels can fall into either a vague pluralism (whereby incompatibility and conflict are transformed into peaceful, boring coexistence) or a naive ambiguity (whereby the competing levels become rallying points for a quivering oscillation that effectively denies the political ramifications of patriarchal hegemony). . . . It is crucial to maintain a tension between the two functions of hegemony and contradiction. ( *Woman at the Keyhole* 25)

While it is true, as Mayne argues, that ambiguity is not an inherently radical or progressive political gesture, instances of such ambiguity can provide openings in the texts that can reveal precisely at what point and why masculine discourse fails in its attempts at hegemony.

The following film analyses will, then, examine these issues (conflating Kuhn's "radically other forms of pleasure," Mulvey's "passionate detachment," and Gentile's "critical subjectivity") with, when appropriate, specific reference to other critical parameters as outlined above. Bergman's representation of human subjectivity, the genderedness of various relationships, and the complicity between personal and familial structures with larger cultural institutions, of patriarchy, gender (including gender as performance), binarism, body, and the universal male subject of culture comes together with a radical signifying practice that centers on a subversive and disjunctive deployment of language, narrative strategies, self-conscious aesthetic devices, identificatory mechanisms, time-space relations, voyeurism, gazing, and the mergence of spectator and spectacle in an attempt to create "other cinematic pleasures" in a body of work that seriously addresses issues of concern to feminism. The films in question have been chosen precisely because they are so "canonical," that is to say "standard Bergman," and because they span the almost thirty-year period during which the director made the films on which his reputation is by and large based. The first chapter treats the issue of cross-dressing across four decades in Bergman's production in order to establish that there is a consistent questioning on the director's part of the equation between gender and subjectivity. The next chapter addresses the crisis of the patriarchal system of values and sexual economics from the perspective of the genderedness of voyeurism and its implication for female authority in *Smiles of a Summer Night* (1954). The next chapter, on "Silence as Subversion in *The Seventh Seal*," charts the continued dissolution of the patriarchy and the ways that that dissolution impacts on language, authority, and agency. The heart of the study concentrates on a group of films from the sixties and early seventies that we might loosely designate as his "women's" films, those that center on the lives and subjectivities of two or more women and their inter-actions with each other: *The Silence* (1962), *Persona* (1966), and *Cries and Whispers* (1972). It is in these films that Bergman most carefully and con-sciously examines the ramifications of the complicity between culture, gen-der, and discourse and in which he tries to find new expressive modalities less implicated by the ideology of the dominant culture and boldly articulates his abiding perception of art not as a theme but rather as "a process and a rela-tion" (Livingston 252). The conclusion then examines, as does Chapter One, a series of films from throughout his career, but now from the perspec-tive of a representation of imagination and its genderedness.

The goal of this book is not, however, to "save" or recoup Bergman as a feminist (actually, I suspect that any such argument would elicit from him hoots of derision). It is instead to argue that his work, while certainly not avowedly feminist, is nonetheless a legitimate subject of feminist inquiry, to end the "silence" of the last decade on the subject of Bergman and women, and, by engaging in what Nina Auerbach refers to as "the transmutation of men, even patriarchs, through a female prism" ("Why Communities of Women Aren't Enough" 155), to suggest that Bergman's work warrants a reconsideration by feminist critics, that it is much more multivalent on gen-der issues than we have thought and that the practice of this "elitist" film-maker frequently coincides with feminist practice. This study will, then, attempt to employ feminist theories about filmic discourse and simultane-ously to illuminate where his concerns touch upon and diverge from feminist concerns. In other words, if the purpose of much feminist criticism is to ex-amine the possibility of subverting and displacing those naturalized and rei-fied notions of gender that support masculine hegemony and heterosexist power (Butler 33f.), the goal of this study is less to provide a "correct" read-ing of Bergman's films than to engage in "ultimate dialectics" in order to suggest in what ways certain of his films are committed to this same subver-sion and displacement and to investigate how these films engender and/or subvert certain potentially feminist readings.

# Notes

[1] Susan Winnett, however, sees possibilities for a female-centered narratology based upon experiences of the body to which males do not have access. As instances of "tumescence and detumescence," "arousal and significant discharge," breast feeding and childbirth differ from the male experience of intercourse in that "both involve the potentially — but not necessarily — satisfying presence of an other" and both furthermore force us to think forward rather than backward; whatever finality birth possesses as a physical experience pales in comparison with the exciting, frightening sense of the beginning of a new life. (We should also not forget that birth is *painful*; its promise is so powerful that women often seem to forget what they have been through.) (509)

However, Winnett's proposal for an alternative narratological model revolves almost entirely around reproduction and, as such, is troubling from a feminist perspective. De Lauretis' argument is more satisfying in that it points toward ways in which narrativity is achieved and/or subverted as a masculine construct and can thus provide a potentially informative and helpful model for a feminist analysis of narrative patterns in an art work.

## 2: Subjectivity and Gender Amorphism in Bergman's Representation of Cross-Dressing

Since clothing articulates prevalent sex roles in a given society, instances of cross-dressing can serve to challenge the dominant ideology in that society. The extent to which clothing and ideology are complicit is suggested by Kaja Silverman, who points to the historical shift in men's clothing from a designator of rank and privilege to a signifier of "the solidarity between one male subject and all others. Male clothing also came increasingly to signify allegiance to a larger social order, and man's privileged position within that order" (*Acoustic Mirror* 25). Always gendered, dress usually reinforces the gender of the body beneath it, but cross-dressing undercuts this equation and has the potential of calling into question the ideology according to which gender is the ultimate truth. As Kuhn points out, cross-dressing

> highlights the centrality of gender constructs in processes of subjectivity and comments upon a culturally salient means by which a would-be fixed gender identity is marked and constructed. It subverts the construct, offering at the same time ironic comment on its status as convention. By calling attention to the artifice of gender identity, crossdressing effects a "wilful alienation" from the fixity of that identity. (*Power of the Image* 54)

To a society for whom the ultimate reality is sexual difference, the distinction between male and female, cross-dressing can appear as singularly threatening and subversive. Because "the dual body speaks dialogically" (Carson 103), cross-dressing can disrupt the monolithic in male culture. Thus art works that represent cross-dressing have the potential to engage in the feminist project of resisting dominant ideology by problematizing gender fixity, of repudiating a world-view that would define women solely in terms of their biology. Within this framework, it is significant that Bergman creates in his production three separate instances of cross-dressing. In *The Magician* (1958), *The Silence* (1963), and *Fanny and Alexander* (1984), Bergman investigates the relationship between cross-dressing and the construction of subjectivity.

For Bergman, as for many other artists who take up this motif, cross-dressing is frequently associated with performance, practiced by individuals whose life is in the theater or the allied performance arts. Such a connection can emphasize the constructed nature of gender, the idea of gender as performance. Thus Aman/Manda in *The Magician* is the assistant in a magician's show, and Johan in *The Silence* is clothed in a girl's dress by a traveling troupe of acrobats, the association between cross-dressing and performance underscores the fact that clothing itself is performance; that there is an essential distance between dress and self again calls into question gender fixity. If gendered clothing does not absolutely equate with the gendered subject, if the wearer is in some sense performing, this performance "poses the possibility of a mutable self, of a fluidity of subjectivity. . . . As a means to, even the substance of, a commutable persona, clothing as performance threatens to undercut the ideological fixity of the human subject" (Kuhn, *Power of the Image* 52–3). Dress and cross-dressing in particular constantly point to the distance between the "real" gendered self and the infinitely varied performances or personae through which the human subject expresses him/herself. It is in this sense of cross-dressing as performance and performance as an intimation of the fluidity of the subject, that Bergman's interest in the issue can be located, for his entire production is dedicated to an exploration of the constitution and construction of human subjectivity. His most radically innovative and perhaps greatest film, *Persona*, takes precisely this problem as its central focus. In his attempt to unravel the workings of human subjectivity, then, it is appropriate that he should question the gendering of that subjectivity. If a fixed subjectivity and a gendered subjectivity are, according to the dominant ideology, one and the same, then the collapse of either entails the dissolution of the other, and Bergman's production, while charting the dissolution of gendered subjectivity, consistently challenges this ideological equation.

That cross-dressing is put to different uses by male and female artists is to be expected. For instance, when Emma in *Madame Bovary* adopts male dress, "masculinity. . . becomes the mirror of her social-moral vacillations. When she dons a male costume at the end, the final disintegration of her personality is accomplished — emphasizing how inseparable are the visible and invisible manifestations of moral codes" (Todd 8). The parameters of this difference (ones that will be helpful in defining Bergman's position) have been investigated by Sandra M. Gilbert. Examining the motif of transvestism in three major male modernists (Joyce, Lawrence, and Eliot) and three major female modernists (Woolf, Barnes, and H.D.), Gilbert finds that in the male tradition false costume is portrayed as either unsexed or wrongly sexed, while true costumes are properly sexed, thus reinforcing the "rightness" of gender-appropriate clothing and of gender fixity as truth. She discovers in these authors, but especially in Eliot's formulation of the androgynous Tiresias in "The Wasteland," an implicit contention that a departure from gender fixity implies disorder and disease (405). In the feminist authors, however, she finds a tendency to treat costumes with ambiguity, a refusal to distinguish between mask and self: "on the contrary, many literary women from Woolf to Plath see what literary men call 'selves' as costumes and costumes as 'selves'" (394). For them, costumes, like selves, are fluidly interchangeable, not fixed and immutable:

> just as male modernist costume imagery is profoundly conservative, feminist modernist costume imagery is radically revisionary in a political as well as a literary sense, for it implies that no one, male or female, can or should be confined to a uni-form, a single form or self. (394)

While the male modernists seek to relocate a sense of self shattered by the cataclysmic events of the first world war[1] within a myth that reifies gender difference as the ultimate reality (thereby replacing historical "truth" with mythical "truth"), the feminists seek to define a gender-free reality beyond myth, to reveal the pure sexless (or "third-sexed") being behind gender and myth (412).

On the most elementary level, Bergman's treatment of cross-dressing differs from that of the patriarchal tradition. Since cross-dressing is perceived in that tradition as an opportunity to reassert the masculine order or to allow the male to absorb the realm of female experience so that he can better rule, it is hardly surprising that most (if not all) cross-dressers in the Western tradition are male, women largely denied this subjectivity-expanding experience since they are, after all, seen as possessing gender identity rather than human subjectivity. This male cross-dressing, furthermore, usually occurs in the genre of comedy — that is to say the genre that portrays less the development of a new order than the reestablishment and redefinition of the old order, the genre that comforts the male recipient as to the stability and perpetuation of his world. In contrast, two of these three Bergman films are distinctly noncomedic, and two of his three cross-dressers are women (either textually or extratextually) and the other a boy not yet past puberty. Thus, on the most fundamental level, Bergman's treatment of this issue distinguishes itself from the dominant male cultural tradition.

At first glance, Bergman's treatment of cross-dressing in *The Magician* would seem to participate in the conservative male tradition, since the film ends with the cross-dresser redonning her gender-"correct" clothing and with a reassertion of the potency and "rightness" of the patriarchal order, as the sun literally breaks through the clouds — thus its subsumption into the male comedic tradition. Although this early in his career Bergman still concludes his film with a "happy" deus ex machina ending in which the patriarchal order (embodied in the king's request for a performance by Vogler's troupe) is reaffirmed, he also undermines the ideological constructs behind such an ending. The verbal and visual treatment of the cross-dresser subverts a view of the film as a reassertion of the patriarchy and of sexual difference as the ultimate reality.

After an establishing long shot of Vogler and Aman silhouetted against the sky (and she is sitting in a position both higher on the hill and more central in the shot than he), the viewer next encounters Aman in the coach, where Bergman reverses back and forth between the two benches. On one side, Vogler sits on the right and Aman on the left; on the other Tubal sits on the left and Granny on the right. While these reverse shots might seem to reinforce a dualism based on gender, Aman occupies the same screen space as Granny, one of the most powerful characters in the film; unlike her grandson Vogler, she can perform real magic and has access to the potent realm behind science and the patriarchy. But Tubal tells us, "Granny's tricks are passé. They're no fun any more because they can't be explained. Granny, you ought to be dead" (309). The association of the female with the mystical powers of nature is "passé," irrelevant in the contemporary world. Thus Aman is visually affiliated with this power, at the same time that "he" is in male dress, not unlike Vogler's. Their stark black and white costumes present a coloring that always in Bergman indicates sterility and despair (see Tomas in *Winter Light* or the bishop in *Fanny and Alexander*). Aman is, then, a kind of amalgam of the character energies of Vogler and Granny, an early acknowledgment in Bergman's career of the mutability of the self. The figure of Aman/Manda with her "constantly shifting sexual identity" (*Images* 180) is, for Bergman, clearly central to the entire film: "But the real crux of the story is of course the androgyne Aman/Manda. It is around her enigmatic person that everything centers" (*Images* 167).

Significantly, too, we as viewers do not "know" that Aman is actually Manda, a woman. Many cross-dressing narratives, because of the threat that transvestism constitutes to the dominant ideology, go to great lengths to explain the motivation for the rejection of gender-appropriate clothing, thereby defusing the threat. Such is not the case in *The Magician*; although Aman does not look very "masculine," we do not learn that she is a woman until midway through the film. We know no more about the sexual identity of this figure than do the suspicious and threatening representatives of the official social order who interrogate them. Even the names of this character, Aman and Manda, may be seen as a kind of reversal of each other, a male-female mirror reflection. Thus, Aman functions, to a certain extent, like the feminist narratives Gilbert examines, to problematize the fixity of gender. And once we are given an explanation as to why Manda is disguised as Aman — because they are wanted by the police — the explanation seems flimsy indeed; given the physical profile of this troupe (one wizened old woman, one fat, jolly, and rather stupid man, one tall man with angular features, and one young woman) it seems unlikely that the police could be put off simply by Manda's disguise. And, one wonders, if they are wanted by the police, why does Vogler have his name (that it is his real name, we later learn from

Manda) emblazoned across the carriage? Thus a plausible excuse for the cross-dressing seems lacking. Rather one might speculate that Manda is dressed in gender-false clothing precisely so that Bergman can speculate on the genderedness of the artistic subject.

This problematizing effect is greatly enhanced by the verbal prominence Aman has in the film. It is s/he who articulates the dilemma of the artist both in the carriage and later when she tells the man of science and reason (evil as always in Bergman): "our activities are a fraud from beginning to end . . . . Pretense, false promises, and double bottoms. Miserable, rotten lies throughout . . . . *Nothing is true!*" (347). It is also s/he who is in discursive control when they are examined by the representatives of officialdom in the library, explaining that their magic is "a game, nothing else. We use various kinds of apparatus, mirrors and projectors. It is very simple and entirely harmless" (313). While her husband sits mute, Aman/Manda expresses the truth of their artistry, her cross-dressing providing the distance between mask and self requisite to full awareness. Significantly Vogler is also masked through much of the film, in false whiskers and eyebrows and wig, but his disguise is sexually "appropriate" and thus does not allow him to achieve the same level of awareness as his wife. The verbal prominence of the cross-dresser is reinforced through camera technique. During the interrogation, Aman is usually located closest to the camera or at the center of shot compositions as a comment on the centrality of the cross-dressing experience to the film's locus of meaning.

But once Aman is unmasked, both to Vergerus and to us, the film abandons its problematizing potential and moves forward toward an essentially conservative and conventional conclusion. Back in "correct" dress, Manda becomes a loving wife, comforting and consoling her husband in his artistic crisis, physically positioned behind him on the bed. Although she dons male dress once again to lock the attic door so that her husband can perform his art on Vergerus, when she unlocks the door out of pity for him, she is again in woman's dress. Compositionally too, she is now subordinate; while the policeman reads the decree from the king of Sweden summoning them to come and perform at the castle, Vogler is centered in the shot, while she stands behind him, an exact reverse of a shot during the earlier interrogation. The patriarchy is reaffirmed; the king saves the day and Vogler proceeds to his command performance with his loving and supportive wife by his side. The equilibrium between the sexes is restored: man is dominant, woman submissive, all within a divinely (or at least royally) sanctioned hierarchy of meaning. Thus, there is considerable closure to the text, but that closure is achieved at the expense of internal consistency. The mechanical ending depicting the sudden arrival of the king's invitation is almost completely unmotivated within the text and abandons the central issue of the film, the issue of the artist's relationship to his/her craft and the relationship between art and the human subject.

At the heart of the entire film is a conflict between the worlds of science and magic. The former sees reality in terms of empirical facts, of calculation and cold reason, and is represented by the repugnant male Vergerus. The latter is a realm of wholeness, nature, and connectedness and is represented by a woman, Granny. The artist Vogler finds himself, then, caught between these two worlds, a victim of this binarism, morally and temperamentally unable to embrace the former and without access to the latter, in part because of his gender and in part because this pole of the binary has failed, is an antiquated mode of perception. Granny's magic belongs to the pagan world, and Vogler and his culture have denied themselves access to that world first through Christianity and then through science. It is this dilemma of being subject to binarism, caught between two polarized modes of existence that so debilitates the artist. In his present level of awareness, the artist must acknowledge, as Aman/Manda does, that art is not magic; it is mere illusion and does not lead to transcendental truth — the levitation trick does not work. But the two instances of hypnosis do work, one on Mrs. Starbeck and one on Antonsson — the woman significantly is not distressed by her hypnosis (she admittedly does not know what she has said), but the man is so distraught at losing control of himself, at having his autonomy violated, that he commits suicide. In this connection, Livingston sees an analogy between Vogler's hypnotic abilities and the hypnotizing effect of a film on its audience (84). The film's anti-illusionistic impulse is so strong as to cause Koskinen to argue that it is one of Bergman's most central works (207). In *The Magician*, art, illusion and hypnosis though it may be, does offer one valuable consolation: it engenders an awareness of the mutability of subjectivity.

At the same time, Bergman associates Aman/Manda with holiness and faith: "She represents mankind's faith in the Divine. Vogler on the other hand has given up. He merely performs cheap entertainment and she knows it. Manda is very open in her conversation with Vergerus. The miracle happened once and she is herself the bearer of it. She loves Vogler despite the fact that he has lost his faith" (*Images* 167). Aman/Manda embodies, then, some mystical faith in the transcendental aspect of art that is in turn associated with a deep and essential "humanness." As such, she is a kind of "inspiration" or muse for Vogler, a symbolization of the female that reifies traditional gender categories. Although her cross-dressing is an implicit acknowledgment of the lack of gender and subject fixity, it is also an attempt to collapse binarism and to infuse masculine artistry with the generative and magical qualities associated with the female and is, as such, still a conventional and ideologically compromised representation of cross-dressing. Bergman's abandonment of the cross-dressing issue in favor of a deus ex machina affirmation of the patriarchy at the end of the film is, however regrettable both artistically and ethically, one suspects, the only possible solution for an artist still so engaged at this point in his career in a quest for God, the ultimate patriarch.

But by the time Bergman makes *The Silence* in 1963, he has acknowledged the corruption of God with all that that entails in terms of a dissolution and corruption of the patriarchy and its values. Indeed, this film marks the beginning of major changes in his work. Male protagonists engaged in quests for the supernatural are replaced by female protagonists trying to come to grips with their position in a patriarchal order that marginalizes them into nonexistence. This is also the first of two films to position a child as the central consciousness. It is this child, Johan, who is the second cross-dresser in the Bergman canon. The circumstances surrounding this incident are somewhat unorthodox. Traveling with his mother and his aunt through a strange and hostile foreign country that is relentlessly male (there are almost no women in the teeming street scenes) and whose language he does not speak, Johan finds himself in an old hotel wandering seemingly endless corridors seeking amusement, while his mother and aunt act out their own frustrations back in their separate rooms. While thus wandering, Johan espies a dwarf who tips his hat at him as he walks by. After staring for a time at a Rubenesque painting of a nymph and a satyr, Johan comes upon an open hotel-room door and peers in to discover six dwarfs sitting about the room reading the newspaper, playing cards, and repairing theatrical props amidst a great clutter of trunks and baggage. He pretends to shoot them with his toy pistol; they play along and dramatically "die." Then, laughing and smiling, they put a girl's dress on him, and all of them stand about watching one of the troupe who is wearing an ape mask do acrobatic tricks on the bed. This play is, however, interrupted when the man from the hallway enters, yells at them, orders the dress taken off Johan, and then shows him to the door. The scene is followed by a shot of the boy rebelliously urinating in one of the corridors.

The prevalent critical position on this scene is that it demonstrates the incursion into Johan's life of the same distorted and fragmented sexuality that plagues the lives of Anna his mother and Ester his aunt. Such a reading gains credence from the fact that both women meet the dwarf troupe at times when they experience their own sexuality as degraded (Anna watches them onstage while a couple next to her in the theater copulates animalistically, and Ester sees them parade down the hall just after leaving her sister, who is having a meaningless tryst with a barman). This reading is also supported by the fact that Johan's visit with the dwarfs is intercut with shots of his mother bathing her breasts, getting dressed, and putting on make-up in preparation for cruising the local bar. In the context of the rest of the film, then, such a reading seems warranted.

But a closer examination of the scene itself poses some problems for this reading, for there is no sense whatsoever in the scene that Johan experiences this cross-dressing as in any way threatening or distasteful. On the contrary, Bergman seems in his manipulation of the camera to diffuse any potential threat. The introduction of the male dwarf in the hallway seems unusual but certainly not threatening; after all, he smiles and tips his hat pleasantly at the little boy. And when Johan looks in the room, he finds these men engaged in completely "normal" everyday activities. They are furthermore photographed in long shot, placing them both in a context and at some distance from the little boy. They play along with his "shooting" of them, and their facial expressions are all friendly. Too, in the screenplay Bergman does not refer to these people as dwarfs but rather as "small people" or "small beings," as if consciously refusing to use the word "dwarf," which in the literary tradition has come to be associated with debased humanity and the truncated self (this is especially true in Swedish literature, one of whose classics is Pär Lagerkvist's *The Dwarf,* with its unspeakably malevolent title character). Further on in the filmscript, Bergman explicitly describes Johan's reaction at having this dress put on him as "a little embarrassed . . . but not at all afraid" (116).

Johan's cross-dressing occurs, then, in an atmosphere of play. Himself a "small person," he plays with gender roles among other "small people." He and the dwarfs interact in a world of pre-gender, where, because gender identities have not yet been fixed, transvestism is not threatening. The dwarfs seem perverted only to those who have accepted gender roles as fixed, the adults. Perversion, the film argues, is a culturally assigned designation, the burden of which is placed on those who accept genderedness as fixed. Thus, Johan's experience of cross-dressing diverges from most dominant cinema transvestite narratives, in which the cross-dresser is motivated either by sexual perversion (thrillers such as *Psycho*) or by a need to hide his true identity (musical comedies like *Some Like It Hot*). In either event, both genres still reinforce the idea that subjectivity is gendered and that a departure from gender fixity is a violation of the "normal" order.

But Johan's experience is also greatly dissimilar from that which Gilbert finds in Bloom's Nighttown episode (which together with Lawrence's "The Fox" and Eliot's Tiresias form a kind of paradigm of the male modernist experience of transvestism). She points to how threatening and degrading the experience is for Bloom, to the fact that it is a woman, Bella, who so emasculates him, and to the element of sadism involved in this transvestism (394). These elements are all absent in Johan's experience. On the contrary, the fact that Johan's transvestism is interrupted and terminated by a male authority figure would seem to indicate an awareness on Bergman's part as to precisely how threatening gender fluidity is for the patriarchal hierarchy.

Joyce's Bloom further undergoes a kind of "ritual sexual inversion" that Gilbert designates as a kind of "Feast of Misrule" (399), from which the male regains strength for true rule in order that the hierarchical principle of an order based upon male dominance/female submission may be recovered from transvestite disorder. By experiencing reality as a female through transvestism, the male incorporates into himself female experience the better to rule over both realms. The burden of the Nighttown episode is, then, a recovery of male potency, a reclaiming of the masterful male self, as exemplified in Bloom's emotional bonding with his "son" Stephen and his ordering his wife to bring him eggs for breakfast the next morning. But again, Johan's experience is different. The film cannot even remotely be said to portray the reemergence of the patriarchal order from transvestite disorder. On the contrary, the film ends with Johan reading and seemingly memorizing a message from his aunt, words in the foreign language, a female legacy that points to the importance of identifying with women and of transgressing boundaries. By chronicling the boy's mental and emotional development as he tries to learn from and balance within himself the emotional lives of the two older women and by incorporating into itself a scene of cross-dressing that does not designate Johan's experience as degraded or perverse or threatening, the film challenges the dominant ideology of gender and subject fixity.

Unlike *The Magician*, *The Silence* does not indulge in textual closure. At the end of the film, the boy continues on a journey with his largely uncomprehending mother while he reads a few words from his dying aunt. Kuhn finds a direct relationship between the denaturalizing potential of a cross-dressing text and its openness. She points to Barthes' contention that closure itself is "a mark of culturally dominant narrative forms, forms whose trajectory is always towards resolution, the closing over of gaps" (*Power of the Image* 56). The closed form of *The Magician*, then, is motivated by Bergman's desire to become reabsorbed into the patriarchal hierarchy, whereas the more open ending of *The Silence* reinforces the film's rejection of that hierarchy and acknowledges its bankruptcy.

But it is not until Bergman's last film, *Fanny and Alexander*, that he creates a character who embodies what Gilbert calls the "visionary multiplicity" of gender. The climactic scene that presents this vision occurs, significantly enough, in the home of Isak, whose Jewishness distinguishes him (in Bergman's view) from the oppressive patriarchy characteristic of the late nineteenth-century Lutheranism of Bergman's experience and who is connected to Alexander through the boy's grandmother. He is furthermore persistently called "morbror Isak," that is to say, uncle on the maternal side. This association between Isak and the female is all the more notable in that one would expect in Sweden that he be called "farbror" by the boy, since "farbror" not only means "paternal uncle" but also is the generic term used by all children to address almost all adult men regardless of familial relationship — and tellingly the children call the bishop "farbror Edvard." Thus, on a fundamental level, Bergman stages Alexander's epiphany in an environment that challenges both religious and gender orthodoxy.

The sequence is introduced by a repetition of a shot showing Alexander and his companion and guide Aron knocking at a door. The fact that this shot is repeated serves to reinforce the spectator's impression of simultaneity between these events and the intercut events at the bishop's house and also, like the repeated monologue in *Persona*, to imply the mergence of subjectivities. As Jacqueline Rose suggests, "The uncertain sexual identity muddles the plane of the image so that the spectator does not know where he or she stands in relationship to the picture. A confusion at the level of sexuality brings with it a disturbance of the visual field" (226).

Bergman's treatment of time is pivotal to this merging of gender. As the scene moves toward it conclusion, another repetition occurs, this time of Alexander's step-aunt bursting through a set of doors, her body engulfed in flames. The voice-over that had previously described these events in the future ("the doors will break open") repeats during the reiteration of the shot the same words, but now in the present tense ("the doors break open"). Bergman is here disrupting the inherent sequentiality of the film in favor of synchronous time, merging past and future into an immensely potent and vivid present. This time frame might be likened to Bergson's concept of *durée* but can also be linked with the time not only beyond the history from which the male modernists strived to extricate themselves but also beyond and behind gendered myth, with "the androgynous wholeness and holiness of prehistory" that Gilbert associates with "the symbolic chaos of transvestism" (415) and that can give rise to Gilbert's "wild reality beyond gender."

The being born of this time is Ishmael,[2] a character played by an actress with shaved eyebrows, but who wears "male" clothing and has a male name. Significantly the credits for the film do not indicate who plays what role; thus the viewer is even further hindered in his or her attempt to ascertain the sex of the actor. Ishmael is also referred to by Aron as "my brother," and yet s/he speaks with a higher register, female voice. As in *The Magician*, the verbal text of the film consistently refers to Ishmael as male, and yet the visual and aural evidence of the film posit this being as female. Thus, the viewer is left with an impression of uncanny dual-genderedness, of Gilbert's "third sex." (One of the first topics my students raise after viewing this film is precisely whether Ishmael is a man or a woman — gender is the ultimate truth!) Ishmael is not completely unlike the "third-sexed" Robin Vote, whom Djuna Barnes in *Nightwood* describes as "a girl who resembles a boy," and the "savage free things" and "wild things caught in women's skins" that Gilbert locates in female modernist texts. Significantly too, as spectators we are deprived of the "view behind," according to which we would know this character's "true" gender and thus be able to locate him/her in the patriarchal hierarchy.

Ishmael's androgyny points to Bergman's perception of the restrictiveness of sex roles and, specifically, to the great human potential that lies beyond genderedness, an interpretation that Bundtzen intimates when she argues that Alexander's exposure to Ishmael forces him "to acknowledge and assume responsibility for his passions and their all-too-real consequences when projected by his imaginative power" (108). If, as Paola Melchiori argues "man associates the Androgyne with nostalgia for the part of himself he projects onto the female [while] woman sees it as a dream encapsulating *rebirth* of a new Utopian individual unified under the sign of perfection" (31), Bergman's representation of Ishmael and his/her role as mentor in Alexander's artistic and psychological growth would seem to be an amalgam of these positions; Alexander, like Gilbert's male modernists' protagonists, seems to need the experience of androgyny or cross-dressing in order to achieve full subjectivity at the same time that the ending indicates that his "mastery" is aligned not with patriarchal but with female values.

But the film also suggests that non-genderedness and/or androgyny pose a serious threat to a society for which gender is all. Thus, Ishmael's room, we notice, is a kind of prison; there are locks on both the doors to the room and the iron gate just inside, and the windows are boarded up. This confined space speaks to society's fear of this person. It is no matter of happenstance that Aron's sibling is named Ishmael, for like his/her biblical predecessor, Ishmael has been exiled. The reference to the biblical Ishmael also includes the quote describing him as a "wild man," whose "hand" will be against every other man's hand, yet the only violence this character seems capable of is that of compelling others toward self-awareness, a capability quite threatening to a society dedicated to the preservation of false gender dichotomies.

But that this character is threatening also to little Alexander, who is an object of spectator identification in the film, is evident in the sexual tension in the scene. When the two males first enter, Ishmael tells Aron that he needn't be afraid, that s/he won't "eat up" little Alexander, "even though he does look very appetizing" (198). When Aron prepares to leave, he approaches his "brother" and gives him a long and passionate kiss. And later, when Ishmael is reading Alexander's mind, s/he lowers the boy's nightshirt and places his/her hand on his chest. These points all suggest that androgyny is threatening to the male subject. But this text differs from the male modernist texts in Gilbert's study by positing androgyny not as personal pathology but rather, however threatening it may be, as a vital prerequisite for a full human and artistic life as well as by implicitly rejecting the patriarchy in its ending.

Ishmael is more than a representation of the androgynous self; s/he is also a key figure in Alexander's artistic apprenticeship and therefore functions as an emissary of that world. For, in Bergman's view, society is as hostile to the artist as it is to the androgyne, since art and androgyny are linked in their implicit affirmation of the mutability of the human subject. Society, then, needs to shut away both so as to quiet the voice and obscure the visions. Thus, the "wildness" of Ishmael's character is, in the Bible, linked to his illegitimacy. So too, according to the screenplay,[3] is the boy-artist Alexander illegitimate (13), but Bergman's emphasis upon this aspect of the boy's birth is primarily intended to portray the artist as outside the mainstream of society, as a being who threatens social convention. This interpretation is supported by Ishmael's statement, "I am considered dangerous; that's why I am locked up," and when asked why s/he is dangerous, Ishmael replies that/she has "uncomfortable talents" (198).

The identification process between Alexander and Ishmael is documented visually with a variety of techniques. Reverse close-ups of each of them give way to a shot of a table in the center of the frame flanked by half of Alexander's body at the left and half of Ishmael's on the right. In tandem they move toward the center and seat themselves at the table where Ishmael asks the boy to write his own name. After he has done so, Ishmael instructs him to read it, and the boy discovers that he has written not his own name but Ishmael's. That he has done so unconsciously is evident from the fact that he stumbles over the pronunciation of the last name, thereby indicating that he did not know it before now. This identity mergence is made explicit when Ishmael says, "Perhaps we are the same person. Perhaps we have no limits; perhaps we flow into each other, stream through each other, boundlessly and magnificently" (199). This speech and the rest of the scene are filmed in a variety of camera angles and compositions taken directly from the segments of *Persona* that deal with identity mergence. The sequence in which the two characters sit across the table from each other is reminiscent of the scene in which Alma sits across from Elisabet as she intuits her feelings about her son. Ishmael further pulls a hand down over Alexander's face in a gesture suggestive of Alma's image of Elisabet stroking back her hair in the earlier film. Even the intense extreme close-ups resemble shots from the consciousness-mergence sequences of *Persona*. Again, because of its congruence with models of female child development (Chodorow 92–133), the permeability of ego boundaries privileges a feminist experience of the text.

And, as the scene continues, Ishmael begins to read Alexander's thoughts ("You bear terrible thoughts . . . . You have in mind a man's death" [199]), and, as the camera moves into a close-up on Ishmael's face next to Alexander's ear, his/her voice recounts what the boy is thinking. As Ishmael reads Alexander's mind and as the visions stored there are articulated and released, the editing accelerates with rapidly intercut images from the bishop's home, images that will culminate in the stepfather's death.

The bishop, we note, has the same last name as the scientist in *The Magician*, Vergerus, a name Bergman reserves in his canon for spiritually bankrupt, ideologically corrupt male rationalists, and he is also, of course, an officer of the church with all that that implies in terms of his complicity with the patriarchal hierarchy. Throughout his career, Bergman reuses the same names in different films, most notably Vogler and Vergerus, reinforcing his vision of the mutability of identity and undermining the fixed, phallic aspect of language, according to which the power of naming is the power of possession, of the usurpation of the identity of the other.

That it is Alexander, empowered by Ishmael, who is responsible for the bishop's and his aunt's deaths is clear from Ishmael's speech: "Have you heard you can make an image of someone you dislike and stick pins in it? It's rather a clumsy method when you think of the swift and straight ways evil thoughts can go" (199). When the policeman later tells Emilie that the bishop's death was due to "an uncanny concurrence of particularly unfortunate circumstances" (203), his statement reminds us of Ishmael's description of the aunt's cry as "uncanny." The reiteration of this word and the image of a mergence of circumstances suggest that this death is a direct result of the mergence of Ishmael and Alexander and of Ishmael's empowering androgyny. Bergman explicitly states both visually and verbally that in drawing forth a mental image and concretizing it, one makes it real. By articulating these images, Ishmael compels Alexander to a realization of his own power, his own abilities, and his own responsibilities, even as Alexander repeatedly voices his reluctance and fear of acknowledging this power. But, if the articulation of Alexander's image of the bishop's death renders that death real, then so too does Bergman's articulation of an image of androgyny make that androgyny real. Both the androgyny and the death of the patriarchy's representative are rendered as frightening, threatening, and yet absolutely necessary for growth and development.

Just before the repetition of the flaming figure, Ishmael tells Alexander, "jag följer dig . . . jag går in i dig. . . . Jag är hos dig, jag är den ängel som beskyddar dig." Because of tense structures in Swedish,[4] this statement can be translated either as "I shall follow you . . . I shall enter into you. . . . I shall be with you, I shall be your guardian angel" (200) or as "I follow you . . . I enter into you. . . . I am with you, I am your guardian angel," possibilities that again conflate two time frames, projecting Ishmael's presence in Alexander's life into the future. The lesson of androgyny and of art, the lesson of the fluidity of the human subject and of the potential power and threat of that fluidity are to follow Alexander all his life and pervade Bergman's entire production.

Again, then, but in more radical form, Bergman presents us not with images of "ritual sexual inversion" whose "sexually compensatory transvestism" is intended to allow the male to reassert the dominance of the patriarchy. On the contrary, the ending of the film depicts the death of the patriarchy and the emergence of a matriarchy. With his biological father and his stepfather both dead, Alexander's mother is to take over management of the family theater together with his grandmother (one of the few unambiguously positive characters in the film). The final image of the film, then, is of Alexander with his head in his grandmother's lap while she reads from the preface to Strindberg's *A Dreamplay*. "Anything can happen, everything is possible and probable. Time and space do not exist. On a meaningless background of reality the imagination spins and weaves new patterns" (215). But if Helena had continued on, she would have read: "The people split, double, redouble, evaporate, combine, flow out, are assembled together" (215). This vision of the mutability of human identity reflects a view of reality implicit in Aron's earlier statement to Alexander: "Uncle Isak ... he says that we are surrounded by realities, one outside the other. He says that the world is teeming with phantoms and spirits and ghosts, souls, spooks, angels, and devils" (194), and both these statements are juxtaposed in the strongest possible terms with the bishop's rigid view of an immutable human reality, grounded in the destructive patriarchy to which he has dedicated his life. Instead, Isak's mystical, cabalistic reality and Helena's Strindberg-inspired vision of the multiplicity of human subjectivity prevail.

Quite explicitly, then, Bergman leaves his narrative open, as a female voice articulates, "Anything can happen." Female authority is asserted at the conclusion of this open narrative even if the words this authority articulates come from the pen of one of Western culture's most confirmed misogynists. Bergman ultimately affirms the insight to be gained from cross-dressing and androgyny, the insight that the concept of gender and subject fixity is and remains fundamentally false. During his career, then, Bergman develops an increasingly radical vision of the implications of cross-dressing. Like the female modernists Gilbert cites, he suggests that costume and mask, not anatomy, are destiny. The consciousness mergence implicit in cross-dressing is posited as both enriching and yet an act of appropriation threatening to the male self. Reluctant though he may sometimes seem, ultimately Bergman does acknowledge that gender and subject fixity are false constructs that art in general and his art in particular can help expose.

# Notes

[1] See Paul Fussell (chapter 1), Eric J. Leed, and Sandra Gilbert (408–16) for treatments of how World War I impacted on the male sense of identity and contributed to the development of the modernist movement.

[2] Linda Haverty, citing the prominence of the Ishmael motif in Strindberg's authorship, argues for an interpretation of the Ishmael sequence in the film as, in part, a confrontation with the problems of autobiography, specifically with Strindberg's all-pervasive influence on Bergman.

[3] Although early in his career Bergman wrote quite detailed screenplays from which he deviated little in the final filming, by the 1970s his filmscripts are less filmic blueprints than loose narrative frameworks that are fleshed out later in the creative process, perhaps the clearest example of which is the "impressionistic" screenplay for *Cries and Whispers* (1972). Thus the terms "screenplay" and "filmscript" are rather misleading at this point in Bergman's career.

[4] While the forms would usually represent the present tense, sometimes the present functions as the future, as in "Vi ses klockan fem" and "Jag följer dig till Dramaten."

# 3: *Smiles of a Summer Night:*
# Voyeurism, Authority and Gender

In describing Ingmar Bergman's 1955 *Smiles of a Summer Night,* expressions such as "one of Bergman's perfect films" (Wood 72), and "a nearly perfect film" (Kael 94), pour forth from the critics. Indeed it was because of the overwhelming success of this film and because it won the Jury Prize at Cannes that Bergman was able to continue making films at all. His previous two films, *Journey into Autumn* and *Sawdust and Tinsel,* were such box-office failures that it seemed unlikely the Swedish film industry would back another of his projects. Only because of the success of *Smiles of a Summer Night* was he allowed to film *The Seventh Seal* and continue his artistic career.

From a feminist perspective, the film is especially interesting in its challenges to patriarchal values. For it investigates the complex of role-playing and subjectivity and the issues of gazing and voyeurism implicit in the cinematic experience — concerns that are central both to feminism and to Bergman's post-1960 production — and at the same time that it works within the convention-bound, and consequently pervasively androcentric, genre of the comedy of manners. In this film, Bergman attacks the patriarchy, but women are granted authority only within certain rigidly defined binary parameters. It reinscribes and subverts the patriarchy, empowering women and yet containing that empowerment within a biological definition of gender.

The genre within which Bergman is working is, like all forms of discourse, ultimately gendered. If Bergson is correct in his view that laughter is a "social gesture" with which society intervenes to correct dissension from the norm (73), comedy can be seen as fulfilling the social function of bringing back into line those who would challenge authority, including women in their questioning of the rightness of male domination. The comedy of manners that structures Bergman's film has been defined by Holman:

> [as] concerned with the manners and conventions of an artificial, highly sophisticated society. . . . Plot . . . is less important than atmosphere, dialogue, and satire. The dialogue is witty and finished, often brilliant. Satire is directed in the main against . . . [those] who fail somehow to conform to the conventional attitudes and manners of the elegant society of the time. The satire is directed against the aberrations of social behavior rather than human conduct in its larger aspects. . . . [It is further characterized by] the immoral "love game." (110–11)

In many respects, Bergman's film seems to cohere with this definition; the social stratum of his characters, their wit and sophistication, the mocking of the jealous husband and the coxcomb, and the prominence of the "love game" as a structural device are all part of the larger comedic design of the work. But within the traditional comedy of manners, the final impetus is the establishment of a new social order, the reabsorption of the socially deviant into the dominant society, and it is in this respect that Bergman departs from the convention, for there is as much of social subversion as of social reintegration in his film. To be sure, comedy can be either subversive or affirmative, but in the case of this film subversion is defined as a rebellion against traditional patriarchal values.

In defining the film's comic parameters, Marianne Höök contends that "*Smiles* does not pretend to be more than a momentary entertainment, a playing with all the clichés of the comedy of manners; the old castle, the young lovers, the duel, the elopement" (109), and points out that the film contains characters typical of the comedy of manners: the tragic couple, the comic couple, the romantic couple, and the commenting couple (110). Insofar as comedy is a reaffirmation of the dominant order, Bergman's description of the film is interesting: "The climax of my 'constructions' is *Smiles of a Summer Night*, which is based on a play by Marivaux, in the classical 18th century manner" (Björkman et al. 67). His designation of this work as a "construction" suggests a recognition of how fundamentally artificial the conventions and ideology it reinscribes are. The persistent images of "constructedness" might be seen as disrupting the androcentrism of this genre, as "denaturalizing" its patriarchal structures. If dominant cinema naturalizes its subjective vision, making that vision seem "real," absolute, and immutable, the blatant theatricality of *Smiles of a Summer Night* can subvert that naturalizing effect. The artificiality so integral to the comedy of manners is apparent in Bergman's emphasis on metaphors of theater and theatricality, even as his use of these motifs exceeds the genre within which it functions. Later in his production, most notably in *Persona* and *Fanny and Alexander*, he investigates deeply and fully the ways in which the theatrical can mirror larger concerns of human role-playing, the mutability of subjectivity and relationships, and spectator/text relations, but even in this early film theatricality serves not only as atmosphere, as comedic ambience, but also as moments of disruption that subvert the androcentric values of comedy.

Addressing the issue of theatricality, John Simon rightly points out that:

> People doing something and someone else observing them become part of the same image or are shown in rapid succession, reproducing or simulating the simultaneous interaction that is the specialty of the stage. . . . From this comparison, another one follows: that of people to actors . . . everyone in the film is acting at least one part . . . even the innocents. . . . The lovely costumes into and out of which the women are often seen changing, the elegant period decor, a certain dwelling of the camera on luxuries of various

kinds contribute to the sense of dressing up, wearing masks, playing roles. . . . The final effect of all this theatricality is to convey the unreality of reality. (112–13)

The blocking of the film is also theatrical; the actors almost never have their backs to the camera and instead stand or sit equal distances from each other in formal, often symmetrical compositions. Bergman also uses spatial planes to separate viewer from viewed, in effect re-creating the boundaries between actor and spectator in the theater and denaturalizing the narrative.

Such spatial separation is most evident in Bergman's repeated use of theatrical framing devices that remind us of our spectatorial position by turning the framed shots into objects of voyeurism. In some respects, many of the shots in the first half of *Smiles of a Summer Night* resemble photographs: flat, lacking in perspective, and rigidly framed. When we first see the Egerman household, the parlor entrance is draped with curtains that have the effect of making each character's entrance into the room that of an actor onto a stage. And, when the action moves to the "real" theater, where the prompter's box is visible in the foreground, Desirée's proscenium is paralleled by the curtained frame of the box in which Anne and Fredrik are sitting. Other instances of framed compositions abound in the film, for, by juxtaposing strictly constructed theatrical with less obviously constructed filmic viewing spaces, Bergman can suggest that space itself is an arena of subjectivity.

But the film's treatment of theatricality and "constructedness" and its impulse toward denaturalization transgress the boundaries of cinematic if not comedic convention in various other ways as well. The play-within-a-play device, for instance, enhances the overall constructedness of the film at the same time that it creates a moment of rupture precisely because it is a moment of self-conscious aesthetics. Too, the camera technique used in this scene is disruptive: the flatness of the shots of the onstage space provides a comfortable "fourth-wall removed" experience to the spectator that is then subverted by the dynamic photography used in the shots of Anne and Fredrik. The difference in camera movement encourages a comparison between these two "scenes" and a concomitant destruction of the absolute illusionism of the film with all that that implies in terms of a feminist experiencing of the narrative.

Most telling, however, are two references by the characters to the theatricality and constructedness of their lives. Desirée comments, "We're not on the stage, dear Fredrik," to which he responds, "But, dammit, it's still a farce" (69). And later in the pavilion Charlotte and Fredrik suggest how their lives are also constructed when he confirms her sense that she is "a character in a play, a ridiculous farce" (114). All these characters to a greater or lesser extent wear masks and are constrained by the roles they play, no more capable of departing the comic rounds proscribed by the social order and the comedy structured by it than the carved wooden figures prominent later in the film can leap down from the clockworks. The film posits, then, an almost tragic awareness on the part of these characters that they are all actors in a play scripted by some other authority. This sexual farce and the world order it reinscribes rob individuals of their subjectivity, the potential tragedy of which is suggested by Charlotte, who desperately rebels against her position as "a character in a play." Only Desirée's understanding of the complex play between role and subjectivity redeems the other characters.

But Charlotte's and Fredrik's exchange is, I think, important for two other reasons. For one, they provide the spectator with moments of filmic self-consciousness that disrupt his or her absorption in the fictional world of the film, thereby subverting the dominant cinematic conventions of the closed fictional world and of absolute spectator-character identification. And secondly, they point to Bergman's understanding, that to be sure does not reach full fruition until after 1960, of the fragility and mutability of human identity, an insight that challenges the androcentric notion that identity is immutable and gendered. In these dialogues he is emphasizing the fundamentally artificial and constructed nature of social reality. While these insights in *Smiles of a Summer Night* are shared by both male and female characters, in the later production they are ascribed almost exclusively to women who, because of their marginalization and experience of false roles and masks, have an essentially deeper understanding of the forces governing human subjectivity in Bergman's world.

But it is in the deployment of voyeurism that Bergman's film most extensively challenges traditional cinematic modes of viewing. As indicated in the introduction, the complicity between voyeurism and the film-viewing experience has been a central concern to feminist film criticism for over a decade, but Sandberg hints at a further connection when, in his discussion of Diderot, he says: "A spectator could only be convinced of the veracity of a scene when the actor's intense involvement in the action precluded any acknowledgement whatsoever of being observed" (*Missing Persons* 179). A disruption of spectator and/or character voyeurism, then, also thwarts the "realistic effect" that is suspect from a feminist perspective.

In keeping with its cultural connotations, voyeurism in Bergman almost always centers on sex or love. From the extraordinary Frost and Alma sequence in *Sawdust and Tinsel* to Alexander's constant peeping in *Fanny and Alexander*, voyeurism focuses on sexual activities. But voyeurism in Bergman depicts not only sex but also humiliation, the victimization of the object of the gaze. Thus Frost is dramatically humiliated when a group of soldiers jeers at him and intensifies his shame over his naked wife (the camera work notably asks the spectator to identify far more with Frost's humiliation as a dishonored husband than it does with Alma's misery). In later films the cruelty

inherent in visual dominance becomes even more intense for its subjectiviza-
tion, the characters having internalized this cruelty to the extent that they are
represented as vampires feeding on the other. Anna and Ester in *The Silence*,
for instance, constantly watch each other, as do Elisabet and Alma in *Persona*, not only out of curiosity but also out of fear and a desperate need to
absorb the other into the self.

But feminist film theory posits that voyeurism is both male-gendered and
power-centered (see Mulvey, Kaplan, Doane, Mayne *et al.*). This specularity
in relation to female characters is so dominant as to lead Silverman to argue
that the most paradigmatic of all shot/reverse shot formations is that which
aligns the female body with the male gaze (*Acoustic Mirror* 28). Because
"screen images of women are sexualized no matter what the women are doing literally, or what kind of plot may be involved" (Kaplan, "Is the Gaze
Male?" 31), any observation of the female by the male is potentially voyeuristic. The subject/object dichotomy central to voyeurism is especially apparent in the alternation between long shot and close-up, a technique that
reinforces objectification. While Bergman says that "the medium long shot is
often a most effective way of describing a farcical or comic situation, a painful
situation perhaps, by which all the participants are obliged to remain inside
the frame and sort things out for themselves" (Björkman *et al.* 109), and
most of *Smiles of a Summer Night* is filmed in the medium long shots of
which he speaks, whenever a voyeuristic activity is part of the image, the
camera usually resorts to this long shot/close-up alternation.

An analysis of the no fewer than twenty instances of voyeurism in the film
can illuminate Bergman's distinctly ambivalent position regarding male and
female authority. Precisely because it is one of Bergman's earlier and most
accessible films, *Smiles of a Summer Night* can be informative as to the basis
of the later radical filmic experiments with female authority and experience.

The first instance of voyeurism occurs at Almgren's Photo Studio, where
Fredrik contemplates a set of photographer's proofs — four of him and his
wife Anne as a couple and four of his child bride. In a series of reverse shots
from the object of the voyeurism (the photographs of Anne), to a grouping
that includes the photographer and his wife, to Fredrik alone, and back to a
zoom in on a picture of Anne, Fredrik gazes at the images with a look of
sweet melancholy on his face. His statement, "Yes, she is beautiful, Anne
Egerman," (37) and the comment in the screenplay to the effect that "He
cannot conceal a small tremor of pride in his voice" (37) suggest that he feels
a kind of pride of ownership over her, an impression strengthened by the inclusion of the patronymic that he has bestowed upon her. As Brown points
out, "The composition of the photographs also works to confirm Fredrik's
position as the dominant subject. Both he and Anne are pictured in the top
four photographs. . . . The focus of Fredrik's gaze, however, is on the four

photographs of Anne alone. Thus, Fredrik's gaze becomes an ordering principle which determines the erotic value of the object being viewed" (2f.).
Before this scene Anne has only been referred to as "that young wife of his"
(35), a representation of Anne solely in terms of her function for Fredrik that
is reinforced by the fact that she is introduced to the spectator in photographs. The photographs are crucial in introducing Anne as icon, as pure
representation and object of the spectacle. Bergman thus encourages spectator identification with Fredrik as the camera shows him in a low angle shot
that compels the spectator quite literally to look up to him, even as the melancholy expression on his face and the soft music on the soundtrack already
undercut his power as bearer of the gaze.

But there is another dimension to the photographs in this scene, objects
that achieve considerable diegetic prominence through their placement at
the beginning, middle, and end of the narrative. The similarity between
photography and fetishism that has been discussed in recent psychoanalytic
criticism is compelling: "The fetish is . . . not a symbol at all, but as it were a
*frozen, arrested, two-dimensional image, a photograph to which one returns re-
peatedly to exorcise the dangerous consequences of movement*" (ctd. in Caplan
18). In arguing that the photograph functions as fetish, Metz points to the
domain in which photographs primarily occur: "that of the presumed real, of
life, mostly private and family life, birthplace of the Freudian fetish." And,
maintaining a connection between fetishism and loss, Metz goes on to delineate three important common denominators between photography and
death: immobility, silence, and the abduction of an object out of the real
world ("Photography" 82–84). This is a connection that Susan Sontag also
makes in *On Photography*, where she suggests that all photographs, because
they emphasize the subject's death or temporality by freezing it, "are *momento mori*. . . . This link between photography and death haunts all photographs of people" (14–64). Barthes too sees the photographic referent as
retaining "that rather terrible thing which is there in every photograph: the
return of the dead" (*Camera Lucida* 9). Thus, Creekmur concludes:

> The experience of viewing photographs, as a reaction to the 'that-has-been'
> which simultaneously affirms and effaces the presence of what 'has been'
> photographed, might be described as a work of mourning, an attempt to
> negotiate between the past presence and present absence of a loved ob-
> ject. . . . [At the same time] photographs do not necessarily encourage the
> reality-testing that allows one to work through mourning, but on the con-
> trary might prolong an attachment to the lost object, . . . [forestalling] any
> painful confrontation of the reality of the object's absence. (42, 46)

In this light, the prominence of the photographs of Anne and their function
both for the male protagonist and for the larger narrative of *Smiles of a
Summer Night* are especially important. The emphasis on temporality and

death to which these critics speak is apparent, as Anne's youth and virginity are frozen in time by Fredrik, who desires to perpetuate them and forestall the losses that aging (about which he is so sensitive) entails. The photograph guarantees the real-life presence of the subject in it and is untouched by loss at the same time that it implies how much Anne's maturation as a process of time interrupted by the photograph threatens him. Thus, this is not an image of "true" identity, but of an erotic fantasy of virginity, a virginity that can only be truly possessed by being destroyed. The erotic aspect of these photographs is also evident in Fredrik's longing and lingering gaze. As he examines them in both the photo studio and later at his desk, there is on his face an expression of melancholy, of nostalgia for the lost object. These photographs thus also articulate some of the concerns that resurface throughout the Bergman production; while photographs (including the individual frames that constitute a film) do refer to a real-life presence, they nonetheless become invested by the spectator with his own fantasies about the object, and film becomes a constant chronicling of both loss and fantasy.

But Metz makes another point pertinent to Fredrik's situation when he points to photography's treatment of space. The severely delimited borders of the photograph, he argues, create an effect whereby the character who is off-frame in a photograph

> will never come into that frame, will never be heard — again a death, another form of death. . . . [That which is excluded] insist[s] on its status *as excluded* by the force of its absence *inside* the rectangle of the paper, which reminds us of the feeling of lack in the Freudian theory of the fetish. . . . The off-frame effect in photography results from a singular and definitive cutting off. . . . It marks the place of an irreversible absence. (87)

Thus, Fredrik's concentration on the four photographs of Anne alone, his averting his glance from those in which he is also included, is significant, suggesting not only that he as voyeur cannot adequately objectify her unless he is distant from her, absent from the image, but also that he is and will be forever excluded from her and the sexuality she represents to him. His exclusion also reinforces the larger narrative development that charts his displacement by his son and the displacing of the authoritative male order by a female one. I would, however, like to point out that I am not here arguing that these photographs *are* fetishes per se (although such an argument can certainly be made); instead, I would contend that they are sites of the inscription of intense psychosexual energy and are thus *similar to* the psychical mechanisms represented by fetishism.

Before returning to my main argument about voyeurism, I should like briefly to examine some of the ramifications of Metz's and Creekmur's arguments for the framing devices that are so prominent in the first half of Bergman's film, devices that create tightly framed spaces that exclude extradiegetic presences. Creekmur argues from a fetishism parallel that such "radically enclosed and 'excluded' space [can] allow . . . films to undertake the work of mourning" (45). In the same vein Metz asserts that, while film is much more difficult to characterize as a fetish because of it size and length, its multiple sensorial channels, and the speed with which its part-objects disappear, it nonetheless is an extraordinary activator of fetishism:

> It endlessly mimes the primal displacement of the look between the seen absence and the presence nearby. . . . More generally, the play of framings and the play with framings . . . work like a striptease of the space itself . . . . The moving camera caresses the space, and the whole of cinematic fetishism consists in the constant and teasing displacement of the cutting line which separates the seen from the unseen. . . . It is not simple — although still possible, of course, depending upon the character of each spectator — to stop and isolate one of these objects, to make it able to work as a fetish. ("Photography" 87f.)

Bergman's extensive use of rigidly framed compositions in *Smiles of a Summer Night* might, then, be seen as isolating people and scenes in such a way that they have a "fetish-effect," a view that is reinforced by the larger narrative chronicling of loss both personal (of Anne as erotic object) and ideological (of male dominance).

One such framed composition occurs when Fredrik returns home from work after the visit to Almgren's studio and hesitates before entering the parlor, watching Henrik reading to Anne. Another series of subject/object/ subject reverse shots frames Henrik and Anne through the open doorway. While Fredrik is momentarily separate from the parlor scene, the camera is at a high angle, adopting his point of view, and is directed at Anne and Henrik, who are seated inside. Fredrik is shown mostly in shadow, framed by heavy drapes; his hiding in shadows while Henrik and Anne — representatives of the youth and sexuality that seem lost to him — are well lit reflects the essentially surreptitious nature of voyeurism and enhances their spectator/spectacle relationship at the same time that the framing alludes to loss.

Fredrik's first statement, a condescending "Good day my children,"(38) reveals the patriarchal quality of his marriage. After Fredrik enters the parlor to join Anne and Henrik, we no longer see the scene from his perspective and instead view him from the same position as he previously viewed the young people, as a result of which his authority is undercut. Here, as elsewhere throughout the film, Fredrik is the distanced observer of youthful sexuality. This scene, then, establishes Fredrik's function as an embodiment of patriarchal forces and his position as voyeur on youthful eroticism. Thus Bergman connects voyeurism with a male need for control.

The next instance of voyeurism depicts a woman gazing at a man as Anne watches the sleeping Fredrik while he whispers Desirée's name. This scene is, however, presented with a layered shot. Again, the shot/reverse shot serves to underline the separateness of spectator and spectacle, whereas, one might argue, a layered shot obscures that distinction. Thus, Bergman here renders male and female voyeurism with different techniques, suggesting the genderedness of discourse. Whereas the film associates male voyeurism with binarism, female voyeurism is not thus implicated.

But one of the most interesting examples of voyeurism in the film occurs when Fredrik and Anne go to the theater to watch Desirée in a production of *Woman of the World*. The staging of this scene demonstrates again the gaps and distances both visual and emotional/psychological in Fredrik's marriage. He sits to the left and behind his wife in shadow, while Anne is well lit (wearing virginal white, which makes her even more visually prominent) and appears larger on screen than Fredrik. As the play begins, Fredrik is more intent on watching his wife than he is on the play, his display of voyeurism expressing his only way of relating to Anne — through a distant gaze. Koskinen makes an interesting point about the scene in which the play is about to begin: "The take is unusually long which underscores its meaning: it is as though the theater's spotlight were now also directed towards the spectators, as though the audience also found itself on the stage. Here it is not only a question of a (limited) play-*within*-a-play, but also just as much of a play *between* the stage and the auditorium" (186).

At the next critical point in this scene, the frame contains Fredrik, his back to the camera and on the left of the screen, and Anne on the right, with Desirée occupying the center of the framed theater box, but below and farther away in the viewing angle. Husband and wife clearly function here, as Koskinen points out, as cinema spectator surrogates (188). But Fredrik is positioned so that he can observe both Desirée and Anne at the same time, a position that sets up spectator identification with Fredrik's voyeuristic activity. Initially, then, the film depicts Desirée as a conventional fetishized image of female beauty, as a distanced spectacle for erotic contemplation. Fredrik's use of opera glasses intensifies the voyeuristic quality of his gazing at the same time that the framing of the shot by the edges of the theater box renders him an object of our voyeurism and thus "exposes" and undermines his authority at the same time that it positions the cinematic spectator as voyeur.

For the first time in the film, an act of voyeurism is confronted by the person being watched. Desirée interrupts both Anne's and Fredrik's watching by returning their gaze, an important action insofar as acknowledgment or permission by the object of the voyeurism diminishes both the gratification and the authority of the voyeur. The invisible wall between the viewer and the object of vision is torn down, revealing and disempowering the voyeur. Interestingly, too, in this scene where both men and women are voyeurs, Bergman uses both reverse shots and the layering shots that disrupt the rigid spectator/spectacle dichotomy and foreshadow Fredrik's eventual disempowerment. The power of the look is all the more emphasized in the important moment when Anne recognizes that there is eye contact between Fredrik and Desirée. The power of the visual connection, of this instance of mutual gazing, is so strong that Anne is overwhelmed by distress and the couple leaves the theater.

After Fredrik accompanies Anne home and sees her to bed, he stops before returning to the theater in order to watch Henrik reading to Petra in the parlor. In a layered shot that again decreases the power of the voyeur by obscuring the subject/object dichotomy, he hides in shadows, the frame including both the doorway and the scene within. His hiding in the shadows here and elsewhere increases the spectator's sense of this activity as somehow both privileged and surreptitious, somehow suspect. We see from his perspective and he is again an object of identification in his capacity as observer, even as the composition makes clear his alienation from youthful eroticism.

Fredrik and his ordering gaze are, then, the locus of spectator identification until he returns to the theater after putting Anne to bed. As Desirée exhibits herself to the audience with her curtain calls, Fredrik is shown in a layered shot watching Desirée's performance. He is again distanced from the women of the film at the same time that the layering decreases his power as voyeur. His perception of women is consistently represented as a spectator/spectacle relationship. Desirée is performing for the male gaze but is herself controlling the spectacle. She exercises a certain measure of authority over her objectification by confronting the spectatorial voyeurism.

The scene changes to show Desirée and Fredrik in her dressing room. As he discusses his marital problems, the camera work emphasizes his self-preoccupation and inability to relate meaningfully to the other. Almost all the shots in this sequence are done in medium range and present Desirée in the background looking at Fredrik in the foreground, while he stares, not at her, but rather out into space, an image that points up his essential isolation and self-absorption. But, as Desirée bathes, Fredrik approaches the screen in another act of watching that reinforces an interpretation of voyeurism as an expression of male sexual inadequacy and male fears. While physically absent from the screen, the full frame being occupied by Fredrik, she is present as a voice-over, a technique that can impart a veritably theological authority to the speaker. When asked if she is as beautiful as before, Fredrik replies: "You are as beautiful and as desirable. The years have given your body the perfection which perfection itself lacks" (59). But, because we do not see Desirée and because of the voice-over, the film suggests that Fredrik's voyeuristic power of objectification is diminishing. As Brown suggests, "By giving Fredrik permission to look at her naked body and evaluate her beauty, Desirée to a certain extent disarms his male gaze. Fredrik is still a voyeur; however, Desirée reduces the controlling power of his gaze by eliminating the element of secrecy characteristic of voyeurism. She takes charge of her own objectification and even determines the length of the exhibition" (3). Desirée continues to assert control when she imperiously dismisses Fredrik: "This is the end of the exhibition. Go sit down on the sofa" (57). In short, Desirée usurps the voyeuristic power that the film thus far has largely attributed to Fredrik.

But the scene raises another issue. The fact that Desirée uses the term "exhibition" would seem to indicate a tentative recognition on her part of gender (specifically here the feminine) as performance. This scene in which she is aware that she is displaying herself for the male gaze points both to her awareness of her body as spectacle and to a belief that she can control her own objectification. But, as an object of spectacle, the female is forever trapped in otherness, never acceding to subjecthood (Madonna notwithstanding!), and Bergman significantly jettisons this idea that the object of spectacle can control her own objectification in his later production, where in *Persona* one of the reasons for Elisabet's departure from the stage and her ensuing muteness is precisely her awareness that she is powerless over her objectification as spectacle.

But the subversive potential of this scene becomes all the more pronounced when Desirée yet again turns the tables on Fredrik. As she gazes at him appraisingly from behind a screen that hides her body and spatially insulates her, she asks her maid, "Do you think this gentleman is handsome and someone to be considered seriously?" (60). We note that she talks about Fredrik in the third person, referring to him as "den där han" ("that he"), a further gesture of objectification. The spectator does not see Fredrik here, a detail that suggests that the female gaze does not objectify (and thereby demean) its object in quite the same way as the male gaze. In turning Fredrik into the object of her erotic speculations, Desirée demands the same rights as the male protagonist, the rights of subjecthood (Brown 4), but her authority is less threatening than male authority. Her assumption of the gaze and her role reversal subvert the male gaze and eventually diminish Fredrik's ability to control both the women characters and the diegesis. Because Desirée breaks out of the confining role of object and emphasizes her independence as subject, the authoritative power associated with Fredrik's male gaze is subverted. Thus, after this pivotal scene, Fredrik's voyeurism is sharply constrained or disempowered. "In fact, after he departs from Desirée's residence, he disappears from the action of the film for quite some time. The story is now told from Desirée's point of view. The power of her gaze has enabled her to take charge of the narrative, and the other characters, including Fredrik, become pawns in her game of romance" (Brown 4). After this scene the layering of voyeuristic shots ceases; all but one instance of voyeurism are rendered through reverses, including those in which women are engaged in the voyeurism. Women, and specifically Desirée, usurp the ordering power of the gaze. The subject/object dichotomy persists but is now an expression of the (for Bergman) benevolent female forces of power. The economy of the visible is now largely controlled by women.

When Fredrik next acts as a voyeur just after Anne's visit to his study, he seems weak and confused. Even though he claims he has not consummated his marriage because Anne is so young, the sexual dynamics of voyeurism makes his non-assertion of his masculinity somehow pathetic. He seems impotent, to be using voyeurism as a substitute for sex. Once again, he looks at the photographs of Anne, but now he is even more wistful than in the photo studio. As Brown points out, "He is beginning to doubt the security of their relationship and his ability to keep Anne sexually objectified by his gaze" (4). While Fredrik disposes of the images of his virginal bride, the camera pans up to his face. The use of a pan here and layering in the previous few shots of his voyeurism along with his admission, "I don't understand. . ." (91), underscore his inability to maintain the rigid spectator/spectacle dichotomy of his earlier voyeurism.

The next instance of voyeurism reiterates Fredrik's loss of power and potency. After the arrival at Ryarp, he, Malla, Mrs. Armfeldt, and the child Fredrik are seen in a series of intercut shots sitting on the shore of a lake watching and discussing Henrik and Anne as they row past in a boat. It is obvious that Fredrik belongs onshore, associated with those who are beyond sexuality because they are either too old or too young.

The individual monolithic male gaze is further weakened by the next sequence when, through intercutting, Petra and Frid look down through the balcony window and see Desirée greeting the guests. The inclusion of multiple voyeurs further disrupts the monolithic authority of the male gaze by dispersing it across several subjects. This scene also establishes, in conventional comedy of manners fashion, that the two servants share a joyous, untroubled participation in the erotic. The association between the "lower" classes and flesh and the "upper" classes and spirit is, of course, a troubling stereotype that Bergman throughout his career never comes to question (witness the servants in *Cries and Whispers* and *Fanny and Alexander*). Instead, precisely because they are associated with nature and the "natural" order, the servants play an increasingly prominent role as the comedy draws toward climax and closure.

Men continue weakened and disempowered in the next two instances of voyeurism, which also disperse authority across several subjects. In reverse shots Fredrik, Malcolm, and Henrik watch Desirée, Charlotte, and Anne stroll to the manor house. The essential distinction between men and women in Bergman's world is elaborated here when, after introductions, the women leave the men staring awkwardly after them. And, shortly thereafter, while Desirée and Charlotte discuss their plans to reclaim their men, Bergman cuts back and forth to the men playing croquet, as the count gloatingly triumphs over the lawyer. "Seeing the latter scene first in long shot emphasizes its smallness and remoteness from immediate reality: while the women pull the strings of destiny, the men are content to play, with utmost seriousness, ludicrous little competitive games" (Simon 133–34). The window again functions as a kind of proscenium, displaying the men as objects of spectacle and investing in women the authority of vision.

The rather remarkable dinner scene at the castle presents another arguably voyeuristic situation. The massive table is arranged such that old Mrs. Armfeldt sits alone on one side, removed from the erotic concerns of her guests, all of whom sit together opposite her. Low angle shots of the mother alternate with high shots of the lovers, all of whom are somehow to be pitied. The mother is further separated from the others by a collection of ornate glassware, decanters, candelabra, bowls, and centerpieces. The sequence of shots specifically posits old Mrs. Armfeldt as the site of spectating authority on the younger people, since the position of the camera on them replicates her position and shots of her bracket the close-ups of the dinner guests. Her authority in this scene is clear from her description of the wine they are drinking: "It is also said that to every cask filled with this wine a drop of milk from the swelling breast of a woman who has just given birth to her first child and a drop of seed from a young stallion are added. This gives the wine its mysterious stimulating power, and whoever drinks it does so at his own risk" (100). At the same time that this almost mystical speech supports the sexual dynamic of the film and strengthens the binarism and relentless heterosexuality that pervade *Smiles of a Summer Night*, it also subverts that binarism by positioning a woman as the site of visual and verbal authority.

But the dinner breaks up when Henrik, disgusted by the callous cynicism of his elders, bolts from the table. After Anne consoles him, Fredrik is seen watching her, distraught by her concern for his son. As Fredrik becomes increasingly aware of Anne's love for Henrik and realizes the love she has for him is only filial and as he begins to understand that his position of power within the patriarchy is being eroded, he is increasingly victimized by his own voyeurism.

As the company disperses, then, it is appropriate that while Fredrik and Charlotte watch the others enter the pavilion in intercut shots, he stands next to a window with black pane work, a composition that reappears in *The Seventh Seal*. This gridded window contrasts with the window through which Charlotte and Desirée watch the men play croquet. In that scene, the spatial separation emphasizes the female voyeurs' authority, whereas in this scene it underscores Fredrik's isolation and victimization.

The victimization of the male voyeur continues in the next scene, as Henrik races upstairs, stopping for a moment at the same gridded window where his father stood to see Petra and Frid cavorting in sexual play outside on the lawn. Shocked by the immoral trivializing of love everywhere about him, Henrik tries to take his own life by hanging himself from a stove cord, thereby activating the trick bed, which brings the sleeping Anne gliding into his room. His gazing on her, however, although initially filmed in reverse shots, concludes with a pan from the male to the female, by which Bergman seems to be characterizing Anne's and Henrik's "authentic" relationship by an erasure of the spectator/spectacle dichotomy so illustrative of Fredrik's marriage to Anne.

The last and most emotional instance in which Fredrik appears as a voyeur occurs when Anne and Henrik elope. As they drive off from the stables, we see Fredrik in a series of reverse shots, passively watching them, withdrawing into the shadows. But male voyeurism has lost its power. Anne and Henrik are associated with sex, Fredrik with vicarious sexual pleasure. The spatial boundary between viewer and viewed is transgressed by the object of vision, who betrays the subject and, quite literally, disappears from view. Anne exerts her freedom from the possessive subject, Fredrik, as she releases her white veil in the wind, an object that clearly symbolizes Anne's loss of virginity and her taking control of her own sexual and personal identity. But we note that her assertion of self takes place within rigid sexual parameters; her liberation from the role of Fredrik's daughter/virgin bride leads only to her embracing the role of Henrik's lover/wife. To be sure, Anne is linking her life with a man who rebels against the patriarchal dominance of his father, but marriage, with all that it entails in terms of the historical subjugation of the female, prevails. The roles change but the relation to male dominance remains the same; the patriarchy is challenged and yet reinscribed.

Fredrik's realization that he has lost the object of his desire is evident through his lack of action. While he watches the young couple's flight, the camera work encourages the spectator first to rejoice for their liberation and happiness but then to identify with Fredrik's humiliation and victimization. This destruction of the power and authority that are invested in most voyeurs and the pain it causes to the viewing subject derive at least in part, one suspects, from the fact that this father-daughter relationship was taken from Bergman's own life and caused him "great confusion and sorrow" (*Images* 345). That Fredrik's victimization is directly linked to his proclivity for objectification is explained when he later tells Charlotte, "I loved them. Henrik and Anne, they were my most precious possessions . . . . But I would like to beat them, beat them for what they have stolen from me" (113). His pain is a direct consequence of his allegiance to patriarchal structures, to binarism and its consequent objectification of women.

In her room with little Fredrik (whose recurring appearances prepare us for the reconciliation of his parents), Desirée looks out her window in a series of reverse shots to observe Charlotte entering the summerhouse pavilion to join Fredrik. Her position at this window establishes a parallel between her and Fredrik, who stood in this position at a window earlier, but whereas he has been humiliated by his acts of voyeurism, she successfully manipulates the objects of her vision and is rewarded with gazing out to see Malcolm enter the pavilion to stop Charlotte's seduction of Fredrik. Her gaze has become a site of authority. And, in the last two instances of voyeurism in the film, Desirée's appropriation of the gaze establishes her autonomy and her subjecthood, just as Fredrik's loss of control over the objects of his vision entails his loss of subjecthood.

As the film approaches its conclusion, the scene in the summerhouse suggests how impotent male voyeurism has become. "The photographs are strewn across the table in complete disarray, and Fredrik is shown with his head resting face-down on crossed arms. He cannot bear to look at the pictures of Anne, because she is no longer an object of his possession. He is not a voyeur anymore, thus he cannot control the order of the photographs, the narrative, or the objectification of Anne, or the narrative" (Brown 5). When she puts the photographs in her pocket, then, the action takes on a symbolic weight connoting that she is both disposing and taking control of Fredrik's relationship with Anne, while Fredrik's prone posture, soot-covered face, and expression suggest that he is defeated.

When Desirée takes the photographs and says, "I'm putting your love in my pocket," she is not only taking control of Fredrik, but is also enacting, as Creekmur's and Metz's works suggest, an acknowledgment that the loved object is forever lost. Her action indicates that the preservation of the lost object must not be allowed, that life demands a moving on, and would seem to be the kind of compromise of which Metz speaks, a compromise that "consists in transforming the very nature of the feeling for the object, in learning progressively to love this object *as dead*, instead of continuing to desire a living presence and ignoring the verdict of reality, hence prolonging the intensity of suffering" ("Photography" 85). Significantly, however, this "compromise" is achieved by Desirée, not by Fredrik, to whom the photographs belong. There seems to be a sense here that she has taken control not only of the events of his life but also of his very psychological mechanisms, at the same time that we might see this as an act of repression motivated by the male's refusal to acknowledge loss. Thus, the compromise is incomplete and points to the ways in which Bergman's acknowledgment of loss is also incomplete.

Desirée proceeds to comfort Fredrik, who now seems merely pathetic, as though he were her child (Simon 112) — there is almost always a mother-son quality to female-male relations in Bergman. He glances at her briefly "and then quickly averts his eyes. In his powerless state, his male gaze can no longer objectify her" (Brown 5). Desirée's authority is again foregrounded when she says that Fredrik is "a good name for a little boy" and then smiles contentedly, presumably pleased with her role as mother of this adult male. Fredrik lies horizontally, accepting Desirée's solace while she is seated vertically, facing the audience; the horizontal and vertical principles at odds throughout the film are here joined. Interestingly enough, in much of the Western iconographic tradition, the vertical principle is associated with the male and the horizontal with the female. Not so for Bergman, who sees in woman a strength superior to the merely physical power of man. This image also, we note, resembles the pietá, a composition Bergman evokes again in *Cries and Whispers*, but the female aligned with the vertical principle, with dominance, is represented as mother and nurturer, and thus patriarchal structures remain intact. Nonetheless, as Simon points out, Desirée takes up a cigar on which she puffs pleasurably; early an emblem of Fredrik's masculinity and tenuous control, the cigar has now shifted mouths (132). As the film ends, Desirée strokes Fredrik's forehead gently and looks at him with an expression of both tenderness and superiority.

Bergman creates in Desirée a powerful voyeur, according women the right to subjecthood and narrative control. To a certain extent, Brown is right to suggest that "the patriarchal world order inherent in Fredrik's gaze is undermined by Desirée's female gaze. The stereotypical sexist assertion of narrative film that women must be objects of beauty and objects of male desire is overthrown" (6). But, interestingly, Fredrik is never the bearer of a completely authoritative male gaze; the spectator knows from the outset that he is posturing. Furthermore, Bergman does not consistently problematize voyeurism per se; he only hints at how voyeurism inherently humiliates the object, only tacitly questions the moral position of the subject, and does not take full account of Kaplan's insight as to the essential genderedness of the voyeuristic act itself. As the film ends, the roles are reversed but the binarism and the instrumentalization of the other are preserved.

The complicity between genderedness and voyeurism evident in *Smiles of a Summer Night* recurs consistently throughout Bergman's later films, in many of which the role of viewer and viewed constantly shifts back and forth between two female characters. In both *The Silence* and *Persona*, voyeurism is used, as in *Smiles of a Summer Night*, to establish multiple spectator identifications through multiple voyeurs, a practice that has the potential to undercut monolithic male authority, but, in the later films, Bergman also calls into question the moral and ethical dimensions of voyeurism. And, while this early film suggests the complicity of the film's spectator in voyeurism, the later films explore this relationship in much more detail. Later in his production, then, Bergman is at pains to remind us, by way of framing devices and various other self-conscious filmic techniques, that spectating is a "guilty" pleasure that is built into the film medium, that viewing space is also a potential playing space and that there is a cultural complicity between filmic conventions and the dominant social order.

Bergman's potentially radical treatment of gender issues as they are manifested in voyeurism is to a certain extent reinforced by his handling of the comedic genre within which he is working and the dominant cultural values implicit in it. As is to be expected in a comedy, *Smiles of a Summer Night* traces the destruction of an old order and the emergence of a new. Male power and authority are consistently subverted throughout the film, and it concludes, of course, with a woman having usurped control from men. Too, healthy eroticism seems possible primarily for those who are not compromised by any allegiance to the patriarchy, for those who actively rebel against it.

It is also within this restructuring of power that we can locate the film's two comic scenes of divestiture. As Törnqvist notes, such scenes are often central to Bergman's films (13). These rituals are especially interesting in light of Foucault's (and others') insight that "the body is directly involved in a political field, power relations have an immediate hold upon it; they invest it, torture it, force it to carry out tasks, to perform ceremonies, to emit signs" (*Discipline and Punish* 25). Both Fredrik and Henrik are stripped of their clothes either by or because of women and made ludicrous by their physical bodies. Anne's gradual stripping of Henrik of his robe, slippers, and pipe is, of course, a reiteration of Fredrik's emotional and physical stripping at the hands of Desirée. Both these scenes posit women in positions of control and men as somehow ridiculous, constituting a critique of male authority and dominance. Standing in front of Desirée in his preposterous nightshirt and pointed nightcap, Fredrik acknowledges the superficiality of masculine superiority when he asks her, "How can a woman ever love a man — can you answer me that?" (63). Men are, in this film, essentially ugly and sexually disgusting beings; Charlotte rages, "Men are beastly! They are silly and vain and have hair all over their bodies" (89), and Fredrik tells Desirée, "You are my only friend in the world. The only human being to whom I've dared show myself in all my terrible nakedness" (58). The literal stripping of the male body reinforces the loss of male power that the narrative charts. The reiterated motif of male exposure emphasizes, then, that male authority is superficial, that women are, in reality, more powerful. Women's "superiority" is also conspicuous in Fredrik's statement to his son after Henrik's botched attempt at sex with Petra: "The premiere is always a miserable farce, my boy, and it's very lucky that women don't take it half as seriously as we do, because then the human race would die out" (48), a tacit attack on the potency of male sexuality. Thus, the body in *Smiles of a Summer Night* is gendered as male, not female, a radical departure from dominant discursive practice.

If, in the androcentric tradition, the male body is usually disavowed and associated instead with invisibility and omniscience, Bergman is violating this tradition; to render the male visible is to relinquish the omnipotence of invisibility, to subject oneself to objectification and appropriation. Fredrik's physical exposure in Malcolm's absurd nightshirt further suggests that the male dominance both these characters embody is somehow interchangeable and based less in real authority than in posturing. Both men have an obsessive need to control and master all aspects of their own and others' lives, especially women's lives. This need grounded in sexual insecurity (one thinks of Malcolm's philandering in this connection) reflects the Western cultural equation between the penis and the phallus and the ways in which this collective belief must be constantly shored up in order for our world to perpetuate itself. But, as Richard Dyer observes, "The fact is that the penis isn't a patch on the phallus. The penis can never live up to the mystique implied by the phallus. Hence the hysterical quality of so much male imagery" (71). And, if not hysterical (for this is, of course, a comedy), then certainly overstated is the adjective for Malcolm's visual representation. Dyer finds in Hollywood pin-ups of its male stars that men are almost always engaged in some kind of "masculine" activity, a tradition that goes back to Eadweard Muybridge's 1887 series of nude photographs, in which all the male bodies are engaged in some kind of action (carrying a boulder, sawing wood, playing baseball, etc.) and all the female bodies are passive, embodying Mulvey's "to-be-looked-at-ness." Dyer concludes that "images of men must disavow [the] element of passivity if they are to be kept in line with dominant ideas of masculinity-as-activity" (66). Bergman's association of male images, particularly those of Malcolm, with actions coded as male is so self-conscious, so ironic, as to expose the false premises of the equation between masculinity and passivity. This film, then, in its representation of the male body at the very least, hints at a subversion of the male gaze by turning that gaze not upon the other in order to appropriate it but upon the self in order to foreground the dominance/submission patterns upon which patriarchal society erects its power.

At the same time, women in this film are associated with the donning and doffing of costumes, an association of women with clothing that may be a mystification of the female body, perhaps an act of fetishization on the director's part. But the negative representation of the male body and the acknowledgment (however intentional) of the female body as an object of spectacle and display for the male gaze also participate in the larger questioning of the genderedness of subjectivity that is so central to Bergman's work and to its possibilities for engendering a feminist spectating experience.

Bergman's association between the male and mirrors is, then, telling. When Fredrik first arrives home, Bergman photographs him in a foreground profile and Petra in a background frontal shot, as he primps at the mirror. This composition is one that recurs throughout Bergman's production, allowing as it does a double perspective on the characters; while we follow the actions of Fredrik the protagonist, we are also aware of Petra's ironic observation. This dual perspective on Fredrik is one that persists through the entire film; the spectator is encouraged both to identify with him as protagonist and to assess his failings as a character and a representative of dominant cultural values, a perspective with a certain feminist potential that is activated much more extensively in the post-1960 films. When he next looks in a mirror in Desirée's apartment, he wistfully acknowledges how pathetic and sexually unappealing the male is. By contrast, Desirée, despite her profession, which might provide many occasions for mirror imagery, stands before one only once, at her mother's house, an action both brief and not reinforced with dialogue. Thus, the mirror's associations as a signifier of narcissism and (for Bergman) with the inadequacy of the body and the masks one wears are linked not with the female but with the male. To be sure, Petra examines her swaying backside in a mirror, and Anne's two mirror images (one in which Petra is brushing her hair and one in which she poses thoughtfully before a full-length mirror) might undermine this interpretation, emphasizing the female as image, as spectacle of self. But the images of these girls' activities are coded positively by Bergman, whereas those associated with men are not. While the female mirror shots may reinscribe the notion of woman as spectacle, the male ones subvert masculine authority and thus provide moments of rupture in the film. While objectification is represented negatively on numerous occasions in the film, in these images the objectification of women is coded positively. Again the film at once subverts and reinscribes the patriarchy; Bergman has not yet acknowledged the full implications of his challenging of the male order.

The masculine is associated not only with narcissism, but also with rigidity and posturing. Both Fredrik and Malcolm are pretentious fools. The first shot of Fredrik, the primary representative of patriarchal values within the film, shows him seated at an intricately carved desk with many books in the background. The desk is cluttered with yet more objects — books, a decorative statue, and a vase of flowers — all imparting a certain status and ambience of cultural heritage to their owner. But the extent to which the dominant order he represents is compromised is apparent in his pompous and condescending behavior to his subordinates. This impression of him and his overbearing masculinity is reinforced by the fact that, as he leaves the office, he passes by several phallic cannons. Fredrik's failings of pomposity and superciliousness are exposed and ridiculed again when, upon his entrance into Desirée's residence, he takes a burlesque tumble into a large puddle of water. Almost always for Bergman, man is but a bumbling, self-important fool compared with the women in his films, women who, because of their greater sensitivity to the issues of the human mind and heart, will triumph over their more nearsighted male partners. Still, however, these issues are represented in binary terms; identity is still gendered at this point in Bergman's career.

The other major male character, Malcolm, is associated not only with rigidity but also with the mechanical. His affinity for guns (which makes him both ridiculous *and* dangerous) and a smoke-belching vehicle supports a view of him as embodying both the mechanical and the absurd. The trumpet fanfare that accompanies his first appearance, his uniform, the military music on the soundtrack, and his rigidity of bearing make him seem like toy soldier. His heroism and swagger are a posture, his masculinity a sham authority that is ironically undercut when a cuckoo clock erupts. That this authority (and all male authority) is false is also apparent in Desirée's stage speech when she warns that women mustn't wound men's dignity. Finally, when Fredrik is prevailed upon by the posturing Malcolm to leave, his assumed male dignity of bearing is all the more undercut when we next see him, cowering around the edge of the door in his nightshirt, compelled to wander the nocturnal streets of his city in a state of dishabille. Both these men are, then, playing false roles. Clearly Fredrik's pomposity and Malcolm's swagger are inauthentic masks that Desirée has no difficulty stripping away, a point that is emphasized when Desirée later talks of Malcolm's "perpetually functioning masculinity that bothers him a good deal" (96). Bergman hints here that genderedness is a role, not an identity, that masculine (and, we might argue, by extension, feminine although the film does not make this connection) is a gender category imposed upon the self that has little relation to the "true" self. His questioning of the equation between gender and identity in the male is a potential site of rupture in the narrative, a (however limited) subversion of the dominant cultural system.

The extent to which this film deals with issues of the patriarchy and the struggle of men to retain power is also apparent in the conflict between Fredrik and his son. The law clerks allude to Henrik's "poaching on his father's preserves," and Fredrik's announcement that he has not purchased a theater ticket for his son because the theater is too worldly for a "man of the cloth" establishes the fact that these two men are competing for Anne's affections. Fredrik's exit to join his wife in their nuptial bed takes on a tone of malicious gloating over his young son. Left alone, Henrik thrashes about the room hysterically, desperately grabbing Petra, who playfully slaps him and leaves him to throw himself onto the piano. A struggle for male sexual dominance is clearly in the air, a struggle also manifest in Fredrik's sarcastic query: "So you've taken up the guitar. I didn't know that was part of the education of the high church clergy" (46).

This competition is further manifested in the image of husband and son seated at a table with Anne between them. The men each sit in front of a large plant; the plant behind Fredrik's head is streamlined and rigid while that behind Henrik exhibits a wild, chaotic spray of foliage. While the composition indicates that the men are different temperamentally, it also posits them as rivals for possession of the woman between them. This image is also extremely formal and symmetrical, a visual icon for the homosocial struggle between father and son that lies at the heart of the patriarchal order.

Ridiculous male competition is also the basis for the symmetrical composition showing Fredrik and Malcolm flanking Desirée, engaged in a verbal duel, the winner of which is to receive Desirée as the prize. In both cases, the woman is the object whom the men struggle with each other to possess, a further reification of the homosocial quality of the heterosexual order.

Bergman's depiction of Fredrik as a representative of the patriarchy is also evident in Henrik's accusation that his father acts "like a demi-god." Fredrik further uses Henrik's reading of the Martin Luther passage about "birds nesting in the hair" to exercise domination over him and to reassert his proprietary rights over Anne. At the same time, Henrik's refusal to embrace the cynicism of his elders about love and his numerous acts of defiance clearly indicate that he is engaged in a rebellion against not only his father but also the overtly oppressive dominant order and the power it wields. After the dinner scene he directly challenges his father, who regards women and children as his material possessions: "Do you think I can tolerate anything from you? Are you some kind of emperor who decides what everyone in the house can think and do?" (101).

Although it does not play nearly so prominent a role as in later Bergman films, religion is also a facet of patriarchal domination in *Smiles of a Summer Night*. Henrik's reading from Martin Luther on virtue and resisting temptation is ridiculed, and Fredrik uses his son's religious belief to keep him in check, to deny him access to Anne. Too, we note that Henrik's liberation is depicted as a rejection of the religious strictures concerning the denial of the flesh; while previously appalled by Petra's and Frid's sexual licentiousness, once he overthrows his father in Anne's affections, the two servants are allied with him in revolt against Fredrik's authority. Religion is associated with its rejection of the body (with all that that means in terms of the repression of women), and that dogma is subverted by the development of filmic events. In this respect, the film coheres with the genre it represents, for comedy traditionally celebrates sexuality and reproduction at the expense of the rigidly self-righteous.

But for all his questioning of patriarchal authority, Bergman's depiction of character is still quite binary at this point in his career. This binarism is apparent in the various issues with which the sundry characters grapple: Henrik struggles with moral, religious, and sexual issues; Fredrik confronts his own aging, his frustrated love for his wife, and his loss of authority and subjecthood; whereas the women in the film just want to get and/or stay married. Bergman's male protagonists inhabit, then, an intellectual sphere while the female ones exist within a biological one, a distinction paralleled by the fact that men are seen in low-key lighting that allows for a nuance of light and shadow while women receive high-key lighting that robs the subject of such nuances. Although one might argue here that Bergman's lighting mirrors sexual convention in order to undermine it, such a perspective is inconsistent with the film's overarching treatment of the female body as object of beauty and male sexual desire.

Matrimony or fidelity motivate all the women in this film, and it is the men who, to a certain extent, control events by their acquiescence to or rejection of the matrimonial finaglings of their partners. "To want to get married; to belong to a man, is an axiomatic need in Bergman's films of the fifties; and, in fact, his women show no great passion or interest in anything else" (Steene "Portrait" 93). She continues:

> Bergman readily admits today that his image of female role-playing in the films of the fifties is conventional . . . . But in those days of role-playing he would have called it biological truth. He had so absorbed history's view of women in his parental Lutheran home that he believed their emotional, non-intellectual approach to life, as well as their masochistic talent for survival, to be genetic facts. ("Portrait" 94)

Thus, the film affirms the ideological tradition that women (in fiction as in real life) were permitted to attain some measure of power, of authority only through marriage, that is to say only through aligning themselves with and subjugating themselves to masculine power. As Todd points out in the case of *Pulchérie*, "the law of the father allows the heroine to accede to power only through marriage and feminine sexuality, so robbing her of the 'mastery' it seems to bestow" (*Gender and Literary Voice* 8).

The determinedly biological sphere in which Bergman's women in this film live is apparent in all the female characters. Anne, unlike her husband, is completely uni-dimensional; she is a virgin — no more, no less. The spectator is never able to see beyond this to understand the forces that lead her to make the choices she does. Rather we perceive her virginity from Fredrik's point of view. Bergman shows her at one point in a close-up with caged birds, but he connects her imprisonment with her being *denied* the wifely tasks of arranging the evening dinner menu and watering the plants rather than with the escape of such chores. Her liberation from confinement then is projected as the adoption of her proper role as wife and household manager. That Anne is sexually mature and ready to adopt the proper role that female sexual maturity entails at this stage of Bergman's thought is apparent from her curiosity in her chat with Petra, who says of sex, "It was so exciting and such much fun, I almost died!" (82). Their talk concludes with the sentiment that it would be "terrible" to be a man (83). At the same time that this view constitutes an attack on the masculine, the fact that both young women so uncritically and unthinkingly embrace their extremely restrictive roles as women indicates the limitations, at this point in his career, to Bergman's commitment to an accurate rendering of female experience.

The delineation of the character of Petra confirms this interpretation, for she is completely confined to the realm of sexuality. She joyously exhibits her chest to Henrik, thereby encouraging a spectator objectification of her sexuality as spectacle. And Fredrik even gives her a raise for her attempts to initiate his son sexually. The scene in her "mistress'" bedroom, in which she and Anne end up cavorting about and laughing on the bed serves also to delineate Petra as a sexually lusty and uninhibited character. Since she is all body, it is not surprising that she does not understand the theological tract on virtue that Henrik reads to her (51). Tellingly, her only goal in life is matrimony, and she almost has to resort to physical force to make Frid marry her. The scene in which Petra demands that Frid marry her then cuts to one of Desirée with her son, an editing choice that implies that both women have the same goal: matrimony. Thus, even Desirée, a "woman of the world," is restricted in her knowledge and action; all her control and power lie within the realm of sexuality. She is described as being void of morality, and the spectator is encouraged to see her ultimate female goal of matrimony as blinding her to the painful aspects of the dissolution of Fredrik and Anne's marriage.

Telling too is the character of old Mrs. Armfeldt, whose age places her past sexuality. She is represented as an observer of, not a participant in, any meaningful action, too old to be sexually attractive. She is a powerless matriarch whose primary joy in life is in playing solitaire and reminiscing about her former lovers. Perhaps Bergman finds her so fascinating (authoritative, compelling old women are prominent throughout his work) precisely because her body is not desirable to the male. It is she who has the voice of authority in the dinner scene, a voice imbued with a mystical wisdom that seems at least in part to derive from her position beyond gender. Speaking of May Sarton's novels, Todd finds they depict "old age for women [as] a time of wholeness and wisdom, primarily because women, always marginal and detached, have long prepared for it" (*Gender and Literary Voice* 5). Thus, old

Mrs. Armfeldt functions as both a reinscription and a subversion of traditional masculine ideology.

In contrast and as a foil to male forces, Bergman creates the formidable Desirée played by Eva Dahlbeck, of whom Haskell says, "[she] . . . is always her own person, a kind of Restoration comedienne, a woman of high style" (*From Reverence to Rape* 317). Her entrance onto the stage (and into our field of vision) is preceded by an exposition: "the personality of the countess . . . is too rich in mysterious contradictions to allow itself to be described in a few short moments . . . [her] power over men is most extraordinary . . . The Countess' lack of decency is most moral, and her influence is very ennobling to all men, whatever their class" (42–43). The role Desirée has in the theater as a "Woman of the World" is an embodiment of her reality, for the description of the countess also applies to Desirée the actress. Bergman suggests here (however problematically, from a feminist perspective) that the mask she wears is authentic, unlike those worn by Fredrik and Malcolm. The implication that the masks worn by women can be authentic, whereas those worn by men must necessarily be false, is a further indication of the extent to which Bergman's early representations of women are still compromised by objectification and binarism.

As Desirée steps onstage and begins her monologue, her speech addresses the issue of love: "Love is a perpetual juggling of three balls. Their names are heart, word, and flesh. How easily these three balls can be juggled, and how easily one of them can be dropped" (45). Love for her is fundamentally artificial, a game dependent upon societal conventions for its successful outcome, a view that implies that the true union of souls traditionally adduced as love is difficult, if not impossible, because the social constructs of human identity are so susceptible to breakdown. Love, as it is experienced in our culture, is essentially a social construction that compromises our subjectivity. Thus, Bergman suggests the complicity between human subjectivity, the relations between the sexes, and the dominant social forces that forge that subjectivity.

It is, I think, important that Desirée is an actress, a woman of the theater, for she possesses the greatest degree of understanding, knowledge, and control in the film. She is the master puppeteer, manipulating all the other characters into a course of action that leads to a comic resolution, and she possesses a certain tragicomic breadth of vision that comes from a genuine recognition of the interplay between mask and subjectivity, role and self. She is represented as possessing both the wisdom of art and the courage of life, as evidenced in her ironic verbal humor (traditionally by and large a province of the male because it is a function of the mind, of mental agility). Her wit further aligns her with Bergman himself, the creative artist, as does her authority as puppeteer over the other characters' lives. He is the artist who controls the comedy of the film while she controls the comedy of the diegesis.

There are two other interesting details about her character that are important for an assessment of the later Bergman films. For one, her mother says that she has altogether too much character, just like her father (76), a statement that might suggest that the authority she possesses is only borrowed from her father, that all authority is male gendered. This problem of the genderedness of authority recurs in virtually all Bergman's post-1960 films, where the filmmaker struggles with ascribing authority to women without defining that authority according to masculine parameters.

The second troubling detail concerns Desirée's son Fredrik. Except for two very brief appearances at the manor house, the child all but disappears from the film after he is introduced in her apartment. This decision is, I think, a ramification of Bergman's consistent difficulty in reconciling motherhood and female sexuality, a problem that plagues *The Silence, Persona, Cries and Whispers, Fanny and Alexander*, and numerous other films as well. Committed as he is in the later production to articulating women's experience, he keeps stumbling over, and never ultimately reconciles, the male binary stereotype of woman as lover and woman as mother. Of course, male discourse historically mystifies, mythologizes, and thereby manipulates women as both mothers and lovers, delineating the roles of mother and lover as mutually exclusive. Kaplan finds, for instance, in *Blonde Venus* that Josef von Sternberg's "attempts to fetishize woman" are linked to the repression of mothering in patriarchy (*Women and Film* 5). Because the patriarchy establishes an absolute distinction between these two functions, it sees women as incapable of uniting them in their own lives, projecting again a male duality onto a female unity. Interestingly, Bergman manifests a kind of awareness of this issue: "In the dream I'm working to . . . or rather: the dream is working *for* me to separate my mother and my wife. I've muddled these two up for years and years" (Sjöman 127). Bergman's representation of the maternal is clearly complicated by an ambivalent relationship with his own mother. In *The Magic Lantern* he says of her:

> I loved her . . . . My four year-old heart was consumed by a dog-like devotion. Nevertheless our relationship was not uncomplicated. My devotion disturbed and irritated her. My expressions of tenderness and my violent outbursts worried her. She often sent me away with cool ironic words and I wept with rage and disappointment. (3)

This obsessive love for the mother coheres, one suspects, with the dominant filmic representations of motherhood in the movies that Bergman attended whenever he possibly could as a young man. In part because of the influential writings of the feminist Ellen Key, there developed in Sweden in the early part of this century a kind of "renaissance of motherhood" that was played out in, among other arenas, the silent films of the era (Sandberg, "Motherhood and Modernism"), films to which Bergman was addicted as a youth.

The mother-child relationship has, of course, been iconized by androcentric culture, and the figure of the mother is especially interesting in the discussion of the role of the body in Western thought and discourse. As Nancy Chodorow points out, "Mothering perpetuates itself through social-structurally induced psychological mechanisms [and] problems in mothering emerge from contradictions in the family and the social organization of gender" (211, 213). Teresa de Lauretis is, I suspect, right in her contention that one of the problems with psychoanalytical criticism is that it posits the equation "woman = Woman = Mother" (*Technologies* 20). Motherhood throughout our culture becomes the great paradox of woman as all-body and no-body. The act of childbearing and the overwhelming presence of body in that act is disavowed so that the mother represents for the child a complete denial of body. Not surprisingly, given how ideologically implicated patriarchy is in its representations of motherhood, this is an important issue for Bergman and is a central focus in many of the films treated at some length in this study. Bergman's personal familial and larger cultural experience of the mother effects, then, not only ambivalence about her as mother, but also a lifelong inability on his part to see her as an independent being capable of healthy sexuality.

From a feminist perspective, the ending of *Smiles of a Summer Night* possesses some interesting features. Just as in the comedy of errors, various artificial devices pave the way for the comic resolution, in this case the remarkable bed constructed for the King's mistress. But the mechanical is further emphasized in the wooden clock figures and the Russian roulette scene, in which we see an overhead shot of Malcolm and Fredrik at the table, an image that resembles a roulette wheel and positions them as playing pieces, as objects. The constructedness of the ending is also apparent in the way in which Bergman deceives us as to the outcome of the duel, a structure paralleled by Malcolm's deception of Fredrik. This deception encourages multiple spectator identification with both Fredrik and Desirée, who has heard the gunshot and assumes falsely (as do we) that someone is dead. Bergman's foregrounding of tricks and deceptions at the end of the film serves, then, to underscore the constructed quality of the narrative and of the genre of comedy, with its mechanical resolutions.

At the same time, the prominence of dissolves toward the end of the film, specifically between the clock figures and the landscapes, suggests mergence and resolution. Specifically, the dissolves to increasingly prominent nature shots imply that the realignment of the couples has the blessing of the natural order, that the comic resolution has been achieved and things are now "as they should be." It is also perhaps appropriate to point out that the nature shots possess vastly different compositional principles than do the "people" shots; the characters are usually filmed in rigid verticals, verticals that speak to the false roles they play, while nature is photographed in long, leisurely horizontals, horizontals of peace and languor. The opposition of these two spatial principles, then, is one of the dominant visual rhythms of film. But, as the film comes to a conclusion, these principles are increasingly joined in shots: the aforementioned scene showing Desirée in a vertical position while Fredrik lies in her lap and the final shot of the vertical windmill with a horizontal horizon in the background both depict a joining of these two linear principles. The fusion of the nature and the human is also adduced when, on three separate occasions, Frid comments joyfully on the three smiles of the summer night: "The first — between midnight and daybreak — when young lovers open their hearts and bodies . . . [the second] for the clowns, the fools, the unredeemable . . . and the third . . . for the sad, the depressed, the sleepless, the confused, the frightened, the lonely" (109, 121, 124). The increasing dominance of outdoor scenes as well as the verbalized connection between humanity and its natural environment guide the film on its way to its comic resolution. The new sexual order is represented as somehow blessed by nature, as a result of which the film reinscribes the notion of "naturalness" of heterosexual coupling and binarism.

But, while *Smiles of a Summer Night* does indeed follow comedic tradition in ending in the marriage (or the anticipated marriage or reconciliation) of the various lovers, it deviates from conventional comedy in charting not the establishment of a new male-based order but rather the creation of a social structure in which woman is the source and site of power. At the conclusion of this reification and subversion of the genre of comedy, Desirée's control seems absolute. But at the same time we note that the conclusion of the film depicts a mere realignment of the previous female sex roles of wife and mother that continue to be subject to the laws of patriarchy. The positions change but the roles remain the same, and the binarism of the patriarchy is reaffirmed.

The fundamentally conservative nature of the comedy is also apparent in its presentation of class distinctions. Although Henrik and Petra try to have sex, their relationship remains unconsummated, and, while Petra is attracted to her employer, her attraction is unrequited and she ultimately matches up with Frid, a fellow member of the "serving" class. The hierarchy of power, both social and sexual, remains intact, even as it is, to a certain extent, subverted by the control Desirée exercises at the end of the film. The final shot of the windmill is introduced by the servants, whose joy not only serves to reaffirm the "rightness" of their social position but, even more importantly, functions as a visual image of ongoing, perpetual motion, an intimation that the "new" order posited by the ending of the film is somehow both inevitable and eternal.

The image of the perpetuation posited by the film's final shot is also interesting in light of both Metz's and Creekmur's insights. They discuss how film, because it is a succession of images through time, engages the issues of death and mourning differently than does photography, discussions that have certain ramifications for Bergman's work. Metz writes:

> The two modes of perpetuation are very different in their effects, and nearly opposed. Film gives back to the dead a semblance of life, (however) fragile a semblance . . . . Photography, on the contrary, by virtue of the objective suggestions of its signifier (stillness, again) maintains the memory of the dead *as being dead*. . . . Film is less a succession of photographs than, to a large extent, a destruction of the photography, or more exactly of the photograph's power and action. ("Photography" 84f.)

Thus, we can see Bergman's film both as an affirmation and denial of loss, as an attempt to create a new comic order and a repression of the old. As Creekmur points out, "Films, like photographs, do *preserve* action, recording and containing it even if they do not freeze it"(47). Bergman's film, then, incorporates both a willingness and a reluctance to confront, acknowledge, and accept loss both personal and ideological.

*Smiles of a Summer Night* challenges and reinforces dominant culture and cinematic values. The patriarchy is both unseated and reaffirmed; human identity is both gendered and mutable; women both rebel and submit, exercise enormous power and yet belong with certain traditional circumscribed roles; and voyeurism is gendered as both male and female, an indication of male sexual inadequacy and a vehicle for female power. Narrative and masculine discourse are denaturalized and reified. The essential ambivalence of this film is one that continues through Bergman's career for the next thirty years. He rebels against male hierarchy and power and masculine discourse, challenging and subverting the values and systems that inform dominant society, at the same time that he is never willing to accept the loss of their authority and struggles to find his place in that society and that cultural system. Female experience and his increasingly radical depictions of it are ramifications both of Bergman's revolt against the patriarchy and his longing for reconciliation with it.

# 4: Absence, Patriarchy, and Silence in *The Seventh Seal*

Whether called upon to defend or abjure Bergman's achievements, students and critics alike most frequently refer to *The Seventh Seal*. The reason for this somewhat anomalous situation is that this film is quintessentially early Bergman in both subject matter and cinematic technique, a film that prompts such exclamations as "visual splendor," "technically impeccable," "one of the most beautiful films ever made," a film that "is one of the easiest. . . to illustrate with stills: stop it at almost every frame and you will find yourself looking at a striking, distinguished and often very beautiful composition . . . . The images frequently achieve great emotional force" (Mosley 63; Taylor 135; Rohmer, "With. . ." 134; Wood 85). Mambrino evens waxes lyrical calling it "The most bounteous and most unadorned work, the most complex and the most transparent, all illuminated by an exuberance of language and yet suffused by a severe silence" (50).

But such paeans are not forthcoming from feminist critics. Typical is Bergom-Larsson, who sees in the director's work a "bourgeois ideology" manifested in a view of women as representing nature, reproduction, and sex (59). Bergom-Larsson is right, as feminist criticism has demonstrated in the past few decades, to be suspicious of male filmmakers' visions of women's experience, for as Ruby Rich pointed out long ago, "All filmmakers, male or female, superimpose their own image on top of their subject. When that subject is a woman, the male filmmaker effects a cancellation, a warping, or erasure of that subject" ("Women and Film" 100). But one might also argue that, in *The Seventh Seal*, by portraying women as controlled and ultimately erased by the patriarchy, Bergman is engaged in a project if not pervasively feminist in intention or impulse then at least sympathetic to the feminist enterprise. While it might be argued that almost all male modernists have challenged the social order, religion, and patriarchy and that that challenge has not been synonymous with a sympathy toward women and feminism, such texts can nonetheless engender a feminist experience of them. Furthermore, I would argue that this film's privileging of a feminist reading is enhanced, as other modernist texts are not, by its tacit recognition of the impact of patriarchal ideology on the lives and experiences of women. Sandberg even argues that there is in this film a convergence of metaphysical and gender-related issues of narration in which the female usurps the male narrative frame ("Rewriting" 17). *The Seventh Seal*, I think, by galvanizing issues centering on absence and silence as embodiments of a patriarchal system that distorts the lives of women, does have a certain subversive impulse, even if the film remains inconsistent and/or ambivalent in its gender perspective.

Since feminist criticism has long offered readings that expose the ways in which women characters are associated with lack and absence, such a methodology seems singularly appropriate to *The Seventh Seal*, whose epistemology revolves around issues of absence and whose foregrounding of a mysterious woman at the climax of the film has frequently befuddled critics. Indeed, *The Seventh Seal* is extraordinarily well-suited to a critical examination that takes as its starting point film theory's preoccupation with the idea that the very center of cinematic production is haunted by certain lacks and absences (Comolli, Munsterberg, Bazin, Metz, Oudart, Dayan, and Mulvey are but a few examples). Although it does not by any means address all these critics, this chapter examines *The Seventh Seal* in light of the contrast between the world of the visible and the verbal and the world of the invisible, the unnoticed, the silent.

If in male discourse women are usually portrayed as the site of absence, such is not the case in *The Seventh Seal*. Instead, Bergman locates the real absence in the male and in the religious patriarchy. For in this film, God, the head of the patriarchal hierarchy, is absent, the object of the Knight's quest. The only absence Bergman ascribes to women is an absence of interest in and association with language itself, a linguistic system that the film posits as overwrought, self-indulgent, and inadequate. Thus, instead of absence being a projection of male inadequacy onto the female, this film situates it in the male. Virtually all the female characters in the film are portrayed as having lives richer, fuller, or somehow more authentic (if still suffused with gender stereotypes) than those of their male counterparts; if the male is described in terms of absence, the female is portrayed as manifest presence, possessed of a reality more palpable (if more associated with the flesh) than the male. It is the female who is the true social being, the one who interacts authentically and effectively with others.

It is no matter of happenstance that issues of absence in this film occur in conjunction with motifs of silence and the inefficacy of language. Language as a vehicle of meaning is, of course, one of the most important manifestations of modernism. As Benstock rightly argues:

> To whatever degree other defining characteristics of Modernism operated in juxtaposition to each other, in contradiction to each other, in uneasy alignment with each other, the determined emphasis on the Word or Logos overshadowed all other divergences among these writers. The one sacred belief common to them all seemed to be the indestructibility of the bond between the word and its meanings, between symbol and substance, between signifier and signified. Multiple linguistic experiments — juxtaposition of unlike words, typographical experimentation, translations of lan-

guage into the dream world of the night or the language of the mad —
only reinforced the linguistic claim on meaning. (12–13)

In a world where God has failed the individual, writing becomes an activity
whereby the writer can meaningfully restructure reality, assuming God's role
vis à vis creation. "The artist as seer would attempt to create what the culture
could no longer produce: symbol and meaning in the dimension of art,
brought into being through the agency of language" (Friedman 98). Thus,
in a work such as *Finnegan's Wake*, Joyce realizes his dream of becoming an
Author, a "God of Creation," the absent center of a linguistic universe.

But this indestructible link between the word and its meaning has little
relevance for women's experience; deriving from its association with God's
Word, the word has a very circumscribed significance for women. Because of
its patrilineage, the Word is suspect insofar as its capacity for revealing any
ultimate truth about the lives of women is concerned. For, as Kuhn points
out, "in a sexist society, women have no language of their own and are
therefore alienated from culturally dominant forms of expression" (*Women's
Pictures* 167). Thus, if we can even call authors such as Gertrude Stein modernists, they are distinctly failed modernists, reveling not in the power of language but rather in its waywardness and protean shiftings. Not surprisingly,
one frequently finds in the writings of women that female characters fall silent or collapse into verbal incoherence, unable to express themselves in a
linguistic system that insists upon their nonexistence. Carolyn Allen's analysis
of Djuna Barnes's *Nightwood* is instructive in this connection: she points out
that women characters express themselves verbally in terms of negation:
"un-," "no," and "never" reinforcing the inability of the dominant linguistic
and social system meaningfully to express the experience of women's lives.
Also prominent are formulations with a negative force: words such as
"debase," "turn away," "whore," "stop," "foreign," and "fear." And admo-
nitions to be silent also participate in the novel's acknowledgment of the inefficacy of male language. Allen goes on to point to the frequency of first-
person and action-verb usage in the speech of female characters while the
male speech in the novel is characterized by abstract nouns such as "soul,"
"mind," "compulsion," and "manner," stative verbs, Latinate word choice,
and mixed metaphors (106–18). Thus, in important ways, language and the
artist's perception of it are issues of gender. Interestingly, language in *The
Seventh Seal* is contaminated precisely along these lines. Male and female
characters express themselves differently, and that difference coincides with
gender distinctions. Bergman foregrounds the fact that male patriarchal
authority is corrupt, as a result of which its language becomes abstract, self-
serving verbiage, while women struggle for a less compromised mode of expressiveness.

Dominant cinema tends to treat men and women differently when it comes to the mastering of language. In classical film, it is the male who is identified as mastering speech, vision, and hearing while the female is associated with silence or thwarted or unreliable speech, rendered by her biology incapable of seeing, speaking, or hearing accurately. The male is, furthermore, allowed access to what Foucault calls "discursive fellowships, whose function is to preserve or reproduce discourse, but in order that it should circulate within a closed community, according to strict regulation, without those in possession being dispossessed by this very distribution" (225). In contrast women do not have a voice, either figuratively or literally, in dominant cinema. As Silverman points out, woman "is excluded from authoritative vision not only at the level of enunciation, but at that of the fiction. At the same time she functions as an organizing spectacle, as the lack which structures the symbolic order and sustains the relay of male glances" ("Dis-Embodying..." 130). Thus, as Johnston and Cook assert, Marlene Dietrich "is depicted as only having an existence within the discourse of men . . . . She is 'spoken,' she does not 'speak'" (95). Female characters are consistently identified with discursive inadequacy. Hollywood seems absolutely fascinated by the idea of verbally stunted women; in films such as *Shock*, *Dispossessed*, and *The Spiral Staircase*, female characters lose their voices, and in *Johnny Belinda* the main character is born incapable of speech. Doane sees this situation as "paradigmatic for the genre. For it is ultimately the symptoms of the female body which 'speak' while the woman as subject of discourse is inevitably absent" ("Woman's Film" 76). Silverman, whose work in this area is path-breaking, argues:

> Her linguistic status is analogous to that of a recorded tape, which endlessly plays back what was spoken in some anterior moment, and from a radically external vantage. The participation of the male subject in the production of discourse may be limited, and contingent upon his "willingness" to identify with the existing cultural order, but the participation of the female subject in the production of discourse is nonexistent. ("Dis-Embodying..." 132)

One manifestation of this sound regime is a contrast between the disembodied male voice and the synchronized embodied female voice. Voice-overs, for instance, are almost always in classical cinema associated with the male, possessing an authority the female voice lacks. Silverman goes on to summarize:

> These differences [are projected] at the formal as well as the thematic level. Not only does the male subject occupy positions of authority within the diegesis, but occasionally he also speaks extra-diegetically, from the privileged place of the Other. The female subject, on the contrary, is excluded from positions of discursive authority both inside and outside the diegesis; she is confined not only to safe places *within* the story (to positions, that is, which come within the eventual range of male vision or audition), but to the safe

place *of* the story. Synchronization provides the means of that confinement. ("Dis-Embodying. . ." 132)

The reasons for this positioning of the female voice are obvious. A purely silent woman character becomes the "dark continent" inaccessible to interpretation, impossible to master and contain (thus, film's recurrent need to extract speech from silent female characters), whereas a woman who speaks but is not seen is even more dangerous since she has the authority of the invisible, which places her beyond the control of the male. "To dis-embody the female subject in this way would be to challenge every conception by means of which we have previously known her, since it is precisely *as body* that she is constructed" (Silverman, "Dis-Embodying. . ." 135). Thus, feminist criticism has frequently focused on the silences that surround women in film texts.

But the silence of Bergman's women in *The Seventh Seal* is not, I would argue, the silence of erasure or disembodiment; rather, it is the silence of subversion, of resistance to and ultimate rejection of the patriarchy, for silence becomes an authentic, positive response to the crisis in communication engendered by the patriarchy, even as that subversion is thwarted by the conclusion of the film. That there are gaps and inconsistencies in his treatment of this issue is only to be expected given Bergman's continuing reluctance at this point completely to reject God. Since God is the mainstay of the patriarchal linguistic system, Bergman's ambivalence about his absence and the concomitant loss of authority appears as an ambivalence about women and language. Thus, while inconsistent, *The Seventh Seal* is an exemplary film for an investigation of the God/woman/language complex that pervades his entire production.

The issue of silence arises the moment *The Seventh Seal* begins. As the film opens, a cymbal crash precedes the credits, following which the screen goes black, the music crescendos, and a shot of an ominous sky erupts into the frame as a choir sings "Dies irae, dies illa," which is again followed by an ominous silence. This opening shot serves to set the tone for the rest of the film: the curiously flat and blank sky and the immobility of the bird complement the crashing noises that are juxtaposed with deep silence to establish absence as one of the key issues of the film. A disembodied male voice-over then recites from Revelations VIII, 5: "When the lamb had opened the seventh seal, there arose in heaven a silence which lasted about half an hour." The voice that recites this passage is that of the character of Death, who enters the diegesis shortly hereafter and who is posited by the rest of the film as a representative of God and of the inaccessibility of "meaning." Thus, the male voice and its assumption of authority define the entire film, at the same time that language and authority are associated with God and the Holy Scripture. Silverman's argument, then, that the disembodied male voice-over achieves a veritably theological status (49) would seem born out here. Sandberg too argues that the level of enunciation and production are equated with the voice of God: "The total synchronization of cinematic image and soundtrack . . . creates the narrative expectation that we are dealing with a secure text in which voice and image are inseparable. The whole of this film, the opening sequence tells us, is being narrated from on high" ("Rewriting" 17); but, since the rest of the film charts the corruption of language through its association with the patriarchy, this corruption has to extend, I would argue, to include the scripture readings at the beginning and end of the film. The disembodied male voice-over at the beginning of the film can be seen as privileging a male perspective, as ascribing authority to the specifically male, but we might also see the nonsynchronization of voice and body as an intimation of absence, as a tacit articulation of how powerful and palpable absence can be. In this argument, we might look at this treatment of voice and authority as suggesting that dominant cinema's analogy between voice and authority is predicated upon false distinctions, a product of an erroneous equation between authority and language.

It is this half hour of silence in heaven that is at the center of Bergman's film. Ayfre's interpretation that the seventh seal is "the last, the one whose rupture leads to the supreme revelation of the secrets contained in the Book of God" (112) is, ironically enough, correct in that the film demonstrates that there are no such secrets, that God is silent, lost, and/or absent and the religious and social institutions based on his authority void of any real value. The screenplay also emphasizes the silence that pervades this landscape: "The restless movement of the sea has ceased, the water is silent" (139). That this silence is directly connected to the absence of God, to the bankruptcy of the patriarchy that derives its authority from God, is evident in the text's statement that this silence occurs in heaven. But it is interesting that while it is defined as male in heaven, it is represented as female on earth, for it is the film's female characters who embody and enjoin silence, while the males chatter on in a desperate attempt to reinscribe the word with spiritual authority.

This absence and loss of male authority is evident not only in the Knight's futile, anguished searching, but also in the figure of Death. God and his emissary Death are a palpably present absence. The presence of Death is equated with the presence of absence as we know from his statement to Block late in the film that he knows nothing. He embodies God's absence at the same time that he is manifestly material and present. Even Death's drastic binary coloration — the white of his face incorporating no color and the black of his robe the fusion of all colors — articulates both presence and absence. Or, as Törnqvist puts it, Death is "definable only as a negation: an absence of life" (39).

We see how destructive this absence is in the fact that every reference in the film to organized religion, to religious institutions, is negative. Jöns' description of the crusades is telling: "For ten years we sat in the Holy Land and let snakes bite us, flies sting us, wild animals eat us, heathens butcher us, the wine poison us, the women give us lice, the lice devour us, the fevers rot us, all for the Glory of God" (152). This "holy" enterprise, then, is a travesty, but Jöns intimates here that women are a scourge of God, a view that is contradicted by much of the rest of the film and that goes more to delineate Jöns and his misogyny than to explicate Bergman's attitudes.

But this patriarchal religion fosters even greater madness in the grotesquely howling procession of flagellants. Jof and Mia's song is drowned out by the chant of these wandering fanatics who whip and scourge each other, their eyes raised heavenward, their mouths agape in anguish, their bodies streaked with blood. As the procession enters the square, the camera views them in low angle, suggesting the townspeople's fear and fascination. Close-ups of Block, Jöns, and the Serving Girl alternate with close-ups of the townspeople falling to their knees in terror. A high-angle shot of the flagellants shows them collapsing to the ground in disarray, the angular lines of their bodies and the crosses they bear intersecting chaotically, for, in Bergman's view, they represent the kind of discord that results from both the Knight's personal fanaticism and that of organized religion. They are representatives of a patriarchal order run amok, chaos personified.

As a priest, played by the ever-grotesque Anders Ek, harangues the townspeople, Bergman locates him in the foreground of the frame, his crucifix behind him on a diagonal, with Jof and Mia watching fearfully from the background, a separation that suggests a sharp distinction between the religion of fear represented by the Monk and the values embodied by Jof and Mia. As the brutal tirade continues, the camera cuts to reaction shots of the Knight and his companions and the townspeople, manipulated into fear by this fanatical religious terrorism. As the Monk concludes his doomsday harangue, Bergman cuts to an extreme high-angle shot of him under the outstretched horizontal beam of the crucifix, a shot that suggests how oppressed he is by his vision of a cruel and ruthless God. For him, as for the "witch" and the townspeople, God is "a scourge, the cause of plagues and death . . . . Religion becomes for them suppression, cruelty, persecution, the burning of innocent girls as witches" (Holland 267). In a high-angle long shot the flagellants rise and move on in awkward, lurching movements partially obscured by smoke from the censers. A cut of them leaving the frame dissolves into a shot of barren, parched ground, a device that makes these fanatics seem like a kind of nightmare at the same time that it associates their faith with loss and meaninglessness.

But, while all the representatives of organized religion (the depraved monk Raval, Death, and the monks who guard Tyan at the church, preside over her burning, and lead the flagellants) are portrayed as callously indifferent at best or morally bankrupt at worst, it is primarily through the character of the Knight that Bergman articulates the annihilation of human values that the patriarchy and its religious institutions embody. In terms of visual composition, dialogue, and narrative development, the Knight's search for the absent patriarch is represented as both futile and destructive.

The first physical background Bergman allots to his main character is a desolate, barren bed of rocks. The slightly high angle with which this shot is taken assures that no sky or water is visible; rocks fill the frame, a visual metaphor for the Knight's spiritual state. It is also significant that in this first shot of the protagonist, his eyes are widely, vacantly open; he seems incapable of repose, troubled, sleepless, and empty. The Knight's pale face, white against the cold grey rocks, is so impassive as to appear almost dead. While one might not wish to put too fine a point on it, the deadly pallor of the Knight's face throughout the film is rendered in white, that color which in the optical spectrum is no color, but rather is an absence of color. This coloration (or absence thereof) also, of course, embraces Death with his clown-white face set off against black garments, a high tonal contrast that participates visually in the film's thematics of abstraction, which are most clearly expressed in the recurring image of the chessboard. The Knight and Death and the patriarchal religious hierarchy that defines them both are manifestations of an untenable binarism that infects and victimizes human existence.

The compositions in which the Knight appears visually reinforce his isolation and the extent to which he is implicated in male absence. Block has incorporated the absence associated with the patriarchy into his own life and his quest for a silent and absent God, an act that has destroyed him as an effectual human being both socially and spiritually. His entire life is an embodiment of absence and loss. In the introductory sequence, for instance, the Knight is consistently photographed off to one side, the rest of the frame vacant, occupied only by flat grey and white surfaces or shadows. Throughout the later church scene, too, large areas of the screen are in total darkness, a darkness and absence suggestive both of Block's state of mind and of the patriarchal religion that has created that state of mind. Thus, in the introductory sequences, we see no two-shots of the Knight and his squire; rather, the only character with whom he shares a frame is Death. And when Block and Jöns ride off from the beach, Bergman cuts between them; they do not share the same space for there is no significant human contact here. This isolation is further reinforced in subsequent scenes both in the church and at the witch burning, where the Knight is isolated from his conversational companion by the bars both of the confessional and the cart in which Tyan is transported.

And, in the latter scene, the Knight's alienation is underscored by Bergman's choice to cut back and forth in fully thirteen reverse shots between Block and Tyan rather than to show them in a two-shot. Isolation and alienation are again consistently depicted in visual metaphors of binary opposites, opposites that are generated by an ideology that posits the ultimate distinction as that between God and the Devil, spirit and flesh, male and female.

The reverses in the introductory sequence between the Knight and the pounding surf also reveal this absence, for here nature is devoid of growing, living things. Another cut shows the Knight entering in long shot to wash his face in the water; a blank, bleak sky occupies fully two-thirds of the frame, and the cold opaque sea another one-third. Nature reflects ideology here and throughout *The Seventh Seal*. The next shots of water, sky, and rocks reinforce this connection as the Knight kneels to pray but seems unable to do so. These shots conclude with a pan down to a chessboard set up on the rocks in the foreground, a visual statement that the problems that disturb the Knight and interfere with his prayer are binary in nature, like the chessboard and the figures upon it.

We note too that the Knight is portrayed as an absent husband, that from his wife's vantage point he embodies absence. He becomes that which anguishes him. His preoccupation with the absence of God ultimately erases him into absence, and his attempts to get God to speak doom him to the literal silence of the grave. The problem that is being played out in the metaphysical realm is also being reenacted on a familial level, a parallel that recurs throughout Bergman's work; sickness and death in the realm of the divine are reflected in the debilitation of the family and its members.

That this abstract problem is religious and patriarchal in nature and that religion itself is, in Bergman's view, essentially binary and inhuman is apparent in the scene in which the Knight and his squire stop to visit a church in the area. The parched, dry earth, the stark, high contrast lighting, and the rigid, angular lines of the white stucco building characterize religion with images of harshness, oppressive heat, and barrenness.

A long shot of the Knight with his back to the spectator shows him in the apse in front of an altar above which hangs a particularly grotesque crucifix. On either side is a small window and over it all rises a vaulting arch, which in medieval iconography would indicate a protective presence. Here it is used ironically to stress the fact that Block has come seeking some kind of solace and protection, only to find emptiness. God's solace is an illusion. The Knight's essential solitude is all the more emphasized by the fact that his confession is framed before and after by shots of Jöns in moments of fellowship. Block's search for meaning and God alienate him from human values and community.

Throughout this scene, Bergman photographs the Knight in close-up or medium close-up shots, often in profile or semi-profile, a composition that renders his facial features flat and two-dimensional. Harsh, high-contrast lighting and the black-and-white shadows of the confessional that appear behind the Knight reinforce the binary aspects of the Knight's quest, while dominant high-angle shots suggest Block's diminishment in the eyes of both the spectator and the director.

It is in this scene that the viewer finds out why Block receives the visual treatment he does. He tells the confessor:

> Now I live in a world of phantoms. I am imprisoned in my dreams and fantasies . . . . Is it so cruelly inconceivable to grasp God with the senses? Why should he hide himself in a mist of half-spoken promises and unseen miracles? . . . What is going to happen to those of us who want to believe but aren't able to? . . . Why can't I kill God within me? Why does he live on in this painful and humiliating way even though I curse Him and want to tear Him out of my heart . . . . I want knowledge, not faith, not supposi-tions, but knowledge. I want God to stretch out His hand toward me, re-veal Himself, and speak to me . . . . I call out to Him in the dark but no one seems to be there . . . . My life has been a futile pursuit, a wandering, a great deal of talk without meaning. (149–51)

The crux, then, of the Knight's problem, of his isolation, despair, and self-doubt, lies less in the silence and absence of God than in integrating this ab-sence into his own life and allowing it to corrupt and destroy him.

Interesting too is Bergman's use of church sacrament here and elsewhere in his production. Sacramental acts embody for the church the mechanisms of remembering; through them its members are instructed to engage collec-tively in an "imitation of Christ." But for Bergman this imitation of Christ only reinforces God's betrayal of his son, and the rites contain more of a for-getting than a remembering, a forgetting and loss of the authentic self en-gendered by patriarchal, hierarchical structures.

Telling too, then, is the later milk and strawberry scene, a kind of com-munion conducted not by the rigid male hierarchy of the church but by Mia who, with Jof and their child, comes to represent a more "authentic" relig-ious alternative. Although the knight can recognize the values Mia repre-sents, he does not allow this recognition to alter his own life as is evident in his use of language. He continues to reflect in ostentatious literary metaphors on the "meaning" of this meeting: "I'll carry this memory between my hands as carefully as if it were a bowl filled to the brim with fresh milk. And it will be an adequate sign" (176). In this sacrament the Knight seems to find the remembering that is missing from the church's sacrament of confession. But, as Barthes and others have demonstrated, precisely this search for a sin-gle, unambiguous meaning is itself a bankrupt enterprise, ideologically suspect. Significantly, as he utters these words, we see him in close-up; by insisting upon living his life under the lodestar of the patriarchy and its semiotic system, he isolates himself from the very forces he prizes. It is immediately after this isolation in close-up and the Knight's ironically depicted verbalization of fellowship that he goes back to his binarily-colored chessboard to resume his game with Death, the embodiment of God's present absence. He leaves the group, still in long shot, to return to his private hell of isolation and close-ups.

The fact that Block is engaged in a traditional "quest" through stations where he is presented with problems to be solved or conquered can also be seen as an indication of his complicity in the patriarchy. As de Lauretis has argued, narrative in general and the quest in particular are often (if not always) deeply compromised by patriarchal values because they posit a male quester who must conquer and subdue female-gendered obstacles (*Alice Doesn't* 105–57). Because the Knight's life has become an embodiment of absence, his quest is perverted and self-destructive, resulting not in his conquering the female obstacles of de Lauretis' argument but rather in his being consumed by the very male absence that so torments him. Thus, it is significant that by 1960 Bergman abandons traditional narrative in favor of other structuring devices, a development that coincides with his intensified challenging of traditional ideologies, both aesthetic and social/cultural, and his heightened efforts to depict and understand female experience.

Telling too is the contrast between the vision that the Knight has of the figure of Death and that visited upon Jof, who is consistently associated with female values. Jof sees not a palpable absence but rather an impalpable presence in his vision of the immaterial Virgin Mary, a vision that, because she is teaching the baby Jesus to walk, stresses the female aspect of divinity, as reflected in Jof's and Mia's names. For Jof and Mia, the issue of God simply does not arise. He has a vision of the Virgin Mary that indicates his need for some transcendental truth, but that truth is simply imparted; it is not sought, as is the Knight's. It even becomes a point of (however slight) contention in Jof's relationship with Mia, since she thinks he is lying about it. Jof's vision of Mary is, then, unnecessary. Evidence, proof of God's existence, for which Block is searching is somehow superfluous to their lives. Block has a lack that he feels must be fulfilled while Jof and Mia do not experience any such lack. To a full and rich life, God is superfluous, the absence of a structuring patriarchy unimportant (or at least this is the case until the last scene of the film). But, significantly, Death, in his capacity as a male-gendered present absence, has the power and authority to make people act, to compel them to certain deeds, while Mary, as female absent presence, has virtually no agency.

The issue of God's absence, however, pervades the entire film. Bergman designates the evil that suffuses the world of his film as a product of this spe-

cifically male absence, as a manifestation of male inadequacy, as we see in
Jöns' bawdy song, in which he intones: "Up above is God Almighty / So
very far away / But your brother the Devil / You meet on every level"
(140). That evil and the Devil are but mirrorings of an absent God is apparent too in the fact that the whole world of the film is infected, as we see in
the plague that is ravaging the human landscape. Jöns speaks of the terrible
things that have been happening: "Two horses had eaten each other in the
night, and, in the churchyard, graves had been opened and the remains of
corpses scattered all over the place. Yesterday afternoon there were as many
as four suns in the heavens" (140). And in the tavern, we hear that "people
are dying like flies . . . . Worms, chopped-off hands and other monstrosities
began pouring out of an old woman, and down in the village another
woman gave birth to a calf's head . . . . Judgment day. And the Riders of the
Apocalypse stand at the bend in the village road" (164–65). Again we see
that in Jöns' very male view, this "God" expresses his malevolence through
women. This pernicious absence contaminates female sexuality. It is the
bodies of women that give birth to deformed creatures, and it is women who
infected the crusaders with lice. For Bergman, the female body is the ultimate presence, especially in its ability to bear children; his entire production
is preoccupied with the maternal and child-parent relations. In *The Seventh
Seal* absence affects those who are most present, most abundantly alive, and
thus women are co-opted by death, their bodies infected with it.

But the absence of God is central also to Jöns' experience when he stops
and asks the way of a man sitting beside the road. After he finds out that this
hooded figure is dead, the Squire informs his master that the man was
"extremely eloquent" (141), a statement that, while ironic, nonetheless indicates that silence is a profoundly eloquent statement of its own, that silence
has its own power and authority that surpass language.

Language itself, with its patrilineage through God, is culpable, deeply
suspect. The mutual dependence of language and culture was apparent to
Bergman as a child, as we know from his accounts of his family's punishment
strategies: "The immediate consequence of confessing was to be frozen out.
No one spoke or replied to you" (*The Magic Lantern* 8). The complicity
between God, the father, the family, and language was impressed upon
Bergman, then, at an early age and is one that pervades his production.
While the Knight is given to syntactically complex, imagistic, and abstract
speech (like the men in Barnes's *Nightwood*), Jof and Mia express themselves
in the simplest, most direct possible terms. The Knight's obsessive rational-
ism finds its linguistic correlative in his mastery of language. The extent to
which logic and rationality, those qualities Bergman finds so culpable in
Block's character, dominate masculine culture and its language is apparent in
language's tendency to define other modes of being in terms of what they

are not: *ir*rational, *in*consistent, *un*conscious, *il*logical, and *un*reasonable. Language embroils even the sympathetic Jof in difficulties, as we discover when we hear that his bragging has repeatedly landed him in awkward situations. And, in the milk and strawberries sequence, he announces that, with Skat gone, he will have to assume the duties of "the director of the company," for which pretentiousness Mia gently upbraids him. Thus, even he is implicated in the negativity of language. The loss of God and his authority also entails the loss of authoritative language.

But such is not the case for the film's women. They participate in a different linguistic regime; their language use falls into two categories: they express themselves either in straightforward, syntactically direct language or else through silence. Three of the film's positive women characters — Mia, the Serving Girl, and the Knight's wife Karin — specifically initiate silence at some important point(s) in the narrative, and the other positive female figure, the "witch" Tyan, embodies the concept of silence in her very character. Indeed, some feminist theory aligns women with silence, with the view that there is no authentic women's speech, and therefore the only authentic posture is one of silence, a posture that serves as both statement of and resistance to dominant male discourse. It may be true, as Christine Makward argues, that such an alignment "is dangerously close to repeating in 'deconstructive' language the traditional assumptions" according to which woman is "incapable of speaking as a woman; therefore, the most female course of action is to observe an hour of silence, or to scream . . . . Women resign themselves to silence and to nonspeech. The speech of the other will then swallow them up, will speak *for* them" (Baym 49). But the silence of Bergman's films is not the silence of Silverman's and Makward's arguments, the silence to which women are relegated in a linguistically aggressive male regime; instead, it is the positive, appropriate, and only response to a patriarchy whose authority and language are thoroughly corrupt. Thus, ironically, it is the women characters who reflect on earth the silence in heaven to which the "seventh seal" of the film's title alludes, an allusion based less, I would argue, on a projection of male inadequacy onto the female than on Bergman's valorization of women's more accurate perceptions, more authentic responses.

Not only silence, but also shot composition, differentiate the female from the male in the film. As a case in point, Bergman's establishing shot for Mia shows her in a covered wagon lying beside both her husband and their fellow actor Skat. She is associated with forces of fellowship and community, almost always shown in two-shots, while the Knight and his God are connected with forces of isolation, as reflected in the one-shots in which he appears. Wood points to several other salient distinctions:

> The background for the Knight . . . was rocks, waves and barren moorland; for the players it is lush grass, peace, fertility. The sunlight with the play of

shadows seems kinder; birds trill where previously we heard only the rau-
cous, unsettling cry of gulls. The disposition of trees and branches makes an
exceptionally graceful composition, into which drapes and shawls slung
over the tree fit harmoniously, as if the human here were a continuation of
the natural instead of a discordant anomaly. (84)

The Knight's high-contrast lighting gives way to a soft, even light in the Jof
and Mia scenes. The binarism in the Knight's lighting has been resolved. We
notice too that the actors sleep inside a wagon, protected, while the Knight
and his squire sleep outside, exposed to the elements. Their wagon forms an
arch that functions unambiguously as a protective line, while the arching
vault of the church rises ironically over the Knight. There is warmth and security here, not the cold and exposure of the beach. When the Knight and
Jöns awaken, each isolated on a separate part of the beach, their faces show
their fatigue; we see their tired and drawn horses drinking saltwater from the
sea. Mia and Jof awaken differently, smiling, happy. As the camera moves inside their wagon, Bergman shoots from a high angle to create an impression
of intimacy that is reinforced by the low-contrast lighting and the long duration of the shot.

   We notice too that the Knight's anguished close-ups are replaced with
contextual medium and long shots when Mia is the subject, and that
throughout this segment foliage is much more prominent than in the shots
of Block and his squire; the Knight's landscape is a barren wasteland suggestive of desolation, while Jof's and Mia's is lush and verdant. As Holland suggests: "Bergman gives us the certainty . . . of life represented by Jof's family
in light, airy frames; quick cuts tend to replace the slow dissolves used for the
religion of death [represented by the knight]" (268).

   As the sequence continues, Mia and Jof recline on the ground and play
with their child, occupying the same spatial field high on the screen that
during the knight's sequence was given over to a bleak and forbidding sky;
Bergman seems to be indicating that they and the forces they represent can
displace the metaphysical absence that surrounds Block. Mia, Jof, and Mikael
are here and elsewhere positioned close to one another, a detail that suggests
their emotional and spiritual intimacy. The parents' love for their child and
for each other is everywhere apparent, and the horizontal lines of both their
environment and their postures reinforce the peace of their lives.

   When Bergman later cuts from the tavern to a shot of Mia on a hillside,
this contrast is even more apparent. Significantly, the relational perfection
that Jof and Mia embody is possible only because Skat dies — the absence of
his pretentious authority as "director of the company" allows for the emergence and assertion of the female values the couple represents. The tavern
scene, with its recounting of atrocities that God has visited on the world, directly indicates the malice and/or indifference of the patriarchy, whereas the

hillside scene (which leads into the milk and strawberry sequence) reveals the strength Mia in particular and women in general possess, in Bergman's view. The gurglings of a baby replace the gruntings of pigs from the previous scene. The inn was a dark, oppressive, enclosed space where the patrons seemed almost to be hiding, while the campsite is open and free. Mia and her family are outside, part of nature. As Steene argues, "Thematically, we see first mankind at strife, then mankind at peace; mankind surrounded by hysteria and frantic noise, mankind resting to quiet music; mankind in fear of death, man at peace with himself" ("Milk. . ." 17). In almost every respect, then, the milk and strawberry sequence functions as a counterpoint to the tavern scene. The lines of the framing reinforce this distinction. The smooth, undulating curves of the grassy slope are given volume by a leafy, round tree, and the heavy, circular wagon wheels, coupled with strong horizontals, evoke a mood of ease and tranquility.

As the scene progresses, Bergman continues to point up the central position Mia occupies in the film: when she is talking alone with the Knight, she is situated higher in the frame, looking down on him, and in numerous shots she is located at the center of the frame between other characters. Too, when Jof lies in Mia's lap and she ministers to him, she, like Desirée in *Smiles of a Summer Night*, is a stereotype of the comforting and nurturing wife/ mother. It is not surprising then that it is Mia with whom Block talks about his disillusionment, that she rather than Jof is the spokesperson for the alternative values of the film, for she is a kind of redemptive maternal figure for Bergman.

The meal that Mia and Jof share with the Knight, the Squire, and the Serving Girl is also shot in a style that contrasts markedly with that used in the Knight's scenes. Long shots replace Block's anguished close-ups with a camera range that emphasizes fellowship and community, a sense of the integration of the individual into nature. The long shots stress the group as a whole, a unified social unit, with the nurturing mother at its head. When Jöns and the girl arrive, they drop into reclining postures on the ground like the others, postures that suggest that they are spiritually as well as spatially in harmony with the dominant horizontal lines of nature.

The only time the camera frames Mia in close-up is when she is lying on the ground, her head in a diagonal that replicates a shot of the Knight in the opening sequence. While the Knight stared vacantly upward in his shot, Mia comments quietly: "One day is like another. There is nothing strange about that. The summer, of course, is better than the winter, because in summer you don't have to be cold. But spring is best of all" (174). Her language, unlike the Knight's, is simple and unpretentious, taking as its subject her direct relationship with nature. Mia is posited as embodying traditional "feminine" maternal values that give her speech strength and authenticity.

But her association with the natural order is, of course, double-edged, for, while it implies that women are less corrupted by patriarchal ideology and that their experience represents a positive alternative to the Knight's destructive binarism, it also represents them as part of the biological continuum "flesh" that stands in opposition to male "spirit" and "mind."

But Mia not only challenges male discourse through her direct and authentic speech; she also does so by enjoining silence. Aware of the inadequacy of language, Mia turns to her husband, when they are standing together outside their wagon in their first scene, and admonishes him ,"Jof!. . Sit still. Don't move . . . . Be completely silent . . . . Shh! I love you" (146–47), a choir of women's voices faintly heard singing chords on the soundtrack. Although she does not overtly claim that language is corrupt, her admonition to silence indicates that, at the very least, it diverts us from real meaning and is inadequate to an expression of what constitutes the value of human reality.

Significantly, too, the soundtrack that accompanies this admonition is the same one we hear during Jof's first vision. In describing that vision, he says, "It was completely silent everywhere — in heaven and on earth" (143). The silence motif, the same soundtrack, and the fact that the Virgin Mary is not dissimilar in coloring and appearance from Mia not only associates Mia with Mary but also establishes silence as a positive response to the language of the patriarchy. She, like Christ's mother, becomes, by virtue of Bergman's stereotyping, yet another instance of absent presence. She is palpably, tangibly present and yet very much an idealized, "non-real" woman.

It would obviously be misguided to claim Mia as a sensitive depiction of women's reality. For one thing, we note that Bergman assigns the capacity for divine vision not to her but to her husband, the (albeit arguably) ineffectual Jof. More importantly, however, the values she embodies are closely aligned with those that the patriarchy historically portions out to women — a closeness to nature and a capacity for "maternal plenitude." In this respect, Bergom-Larsson is right in contending that:

> [Woman] . . . is permitted to represent values lacking in the man's world, such as emotionality, growth, strength, warmth, wholeness, intuition, maturity, enclosing maternalness. Man, on the other hand, represents the opposite pole, intellect, questing, sterility, coldness, exploitation, fragmentation, violence, immaturity. Bergman's films provide a distillation of the patriarchal ideology's conception of women, at the same time that they contemptuously dismiss the same ideology's masculine ideal. (59)

While this argument does not sufficiently take into account Bergman's post-1960 representation of female subjectivity and the genderedness of filmic practice, or the ways in which his criticism of the "masculine ideal" privileges a feminist reading of his texts, it does acknowledge the limits at this point in his career of Bergman's understanding of certain gender issues. While *The Seventh Seal* demonstrates insight into the destructive power of binarism, as far as men are concerned, it retreats from equivalent insights into the ramifications of binarism for the lives of women. Both Bergom-Larsson and Donner rightly argue that this representation of women finds its roots in bourgeois Swedish social structures, that "his entire vision of people and society in different ways is formed in relation to the patriarchal structure, often in desperate attempts to liberate himself from its iron grip" (Bergom-Larsson 168), and Donner's conclusion that Bergman both despises and longs for reabsorption into that society (72) is even more to the point as this film and his subsequent production attest.

But if Bergman's camera work, shot compositions, and use of silence with respect to the character of Mia present a tacit criticism of God and the patriarchy, that criticism becomes overt in the figure of the young "witch" Tyan. Outside the church early in the film, the Knight sees a girl sitting in stocks: "Her face is pale and child-like, her head has been shaved, and her knuckles are bloody and broken. Her eyes are wide open and yet she doesn't appear to be fully conscious" (152). This pitiable girl (she is consistently called "the child") has been abused and tortured because the church thinks she has had intercourse with the devil, that she is the cause of the plague ravaging the countryside. Such a claim is, of course, ludicrous, but it is significant that the church should place the blame for all this evil on a woman, projecting its own failings onto the female, that a male power structure should displace its own sexual desires onto the object of those desires, claiming that woman is evil rather than locating that evil in itself.

But in the church scene the Knight seems all but indifferent to the extent to which this pathetic child has been brutalized by the church; he is interested only in what she can tell him about the devil. And, as he and Jöns leave the churchyard, her whimpering is aurally overshadowed by the Squire's beginning anew his bawdy song, an action of extraordinary callousness. It is true that Block upbraids a monk for having broken her hands (for which the church's representative refuses to or cannot offer an explanation) and he gives her a sedative, but when he questions her more extensively, the two are separated by the bars of the cart, a composition like the iron grid in the confessional; this half-dead girl is to Block and Jöns little more than a source of information about God and the devil or, as Sandberg puts it, "[They] are struggling for the narrative rights both to her silent terror and to the opacity of existence in general" ("Rewriting" 20).

What is pathetic about this girl is the fact that she herself has been deluded by the church into believing that she has had intercourse with the devil. Jöns asks Block "Who watches over that child? Is it the angels, or God, or the Devil, or only the emptiness? Emptiness, my lord!. . . Look at her

eyes, my lord. Her poor brain has just made a discovery. Emptiness under
the moon" (186). That her emptiness and Block's are one and the same is
underscored by the fact that the music for Block's first sequence is the same
as that which introduces this scene. The extent to which women reflect male
absence and inadequacy is further evident when Tyan tells Block that if he
wants to see the devil all he has to do is look into her eyes: "He is with me
everywhere. I have only to stretch out my hand and I can feel his hand. He is
with me now too" (184); women mirror male inadequacy and evil. We note
too that as she dies, her face reveals horror and despair, and she attests to the
presence of the devil falsely and under duress, even as she has come to believe
that she is guilty of the charge a masculine society has leveled at her. She is a
reflection of that which has been violently imposed upon her. Having as-
similated the belief system of a religion that brutalizes her, Tyan dies reflect-
ing the emptiness of that belief system, the absence at the center that co-opts
the lives of women and absorbs them into its vacuum.

   Tyan's victimization is rendered all the more grotesque through Bergman's camera work: diagonals predominate and she in one frame is filmed in
an expressive and drastic foreshortening. The low angles from which the
spectator sees her all through the burning scene present her in radically composed frames and foster a sense of unease, her silence and her terror a privileged insight into the ontological distortions of patriarchal ideology.

   But it is the silent Serving Girl who most eloquently and extensively
demonstrates what role women play for Bergman in the patriarchal structures
of absence and silence. Historically, Bergman scholarship has had difficulty
with this figure, puzzling over her prominence at the end of the film. Only
Sandberg has addressed her role in the film in any kind of critically satisfac-
tory way. Not only is she more prominent throughout the film than has been
assumed, but her position in the narrative is neither surprising nor inconsistent if examined in the light of recent feminist theoretical/critical insights.

   Her "muteness" is part of a larger concern throughout the film with issues of silence and language. After the telling use of silence in the opening
sequence, a sequence that equates verbal expression and language with God
and the Word, the scene between Jöns and the corpse, as mentioned earlier,
intensifies the equation between silence and eloquence. Sandberg asserts that
"The significance of the girl's muteness for the narrative issues . . . is that one
finds in her the extreme depiction of diegetic and discursive interiority — she
is completely 'spoken' by others" ("Rewriting" 20), at the same time that I
would argue that silence and interiority achieve a kind of narrative authority
precisely because language and the patriarchy are so corrupt.

   When Bergman introduces her, she is about to be raped by Raval, the
malevolent former monk who convinced Block to go on the crusades; his
intended violation of her, then, is seen as a direct extension of his complicity

with the church. But, he tells her first, "There's no point in screaming. There's no one to hear you — neither people nor God" (155), a statement that aligns her silence with an acknowledgment of God's malevolent absence. The girl, like Tyan, is a victim of the patriarchy. When she then joins up with Jöns and Block, she never utters a word, but does appear consistently in our field of vision. Indeed, during the harangue by the flagellant monk and in the encounter between Skat and Plog in the forest, she is featured as prominently as Block himself. She also appears in a number of other scenes, often at the center of the visual composition, as at the witch-burning, where her silence is contrasted with the wordy metaphysical debate between Block and Jöns. Too, she is the focus of the spectator's attention during Raval's death scene, when she tries to give him the help for which he is begging while Jöns tells her, "It's no use. It's no use. I know that it's no use. It's meaningless. It's totally meaningless. I tell you that it's meaningless. Can't you hear that I'm consoling you?" (194). But the mute girl seems unchanged; language has no power to console. Silence is an essentially positive stance in light of the corruption of patriarchal language (a position also manifest in Elisabet's adoption of muteness as resistance in *Persona*). The loss of male authority entails a loss of the productive relationship between language and meaning, language and action.

The question arises, then, as to why, when Bergman directs the spectator's visual attention to this character time and again, critics and audiences are so befuddled by her prominence at the close of the film. One might speculate that Bergman is pointing out how compromised the audience also is by its dependence on purely linguistic meaning, demonstrating on an extratextual level that ironically that which is merely visually evident is not sufficient for spectators even in so essentially a visual medium as film, an insight that Bergman repeatedly invokes in his post-1960 production.

The silent girl's authority increases as the troupe enters the castle and the camera lingers on her face, a visual treatment allotted to none of the others. In this final representation of Block and his companions, women achieve far greater prominence than the men, both visually and aurally, as the girl and Block's wife Karin join character energies to carry the sequence. A cut reveals Karin in long shot next to a fire, a shot that establishes a sense of the possibilities for warmth and nurturing that she bears within her, possibilities the Knight has turned his back upon in his quest for knowledge of the divine, even as it again points up Bergman's inconsistency in and ambivalence to issues of binary definitions of women. When she and her husband meet, close-ups show the disillusionment in both their faces as she smiles softly and compassionately at her long-absent, much-tormented husband. While she does not manifest her disillusionment and insight in silence, as does the mute girl, she nonetheless is differentiated linguistically from the men in the film by her simple, quiet, direct utterances.

A dissolve to a close-up of the girl is accompanied by Karin's voice reading, "And when the Lamb broke the seventh seal, there was silence in heaven for about the space of half an hour" (199), an instance, however brief, of disembodied female voice-over. The same text that at the beginning of the film was read by a male voice-over is now appropriated by a female voice that is only subsequently synchronized. Sandberg argues that "this brief flirtation with non-synchronization [of voice and body] ruptures the emphatic synchronization of heavenly voice and image in the film's establishing shot in which the same scripture is read" ("Rewriting" 21), but we note that there is no equivalent synchronization between the female voice and image. Women do not have the requisite authority (as they will in later films) to produce images. Only Jof and the Knight have that power, an especially important gender distinction for an artist whose life is devoted precisely to the production and creation of images.

But we note too that, except for the initial male voice-over, there is constant synchronization between the male voice and the male body, and the same is true for women, except when Karin reads from the Bible. Both male and female bodies are, then, held to synchronization, except when reading scripture. Thus, while the male voice-over has more authority than the female voice-over because it is not subsequently synchronized, the telling distinction seems to lie less in who is doing the speaking than in what is being said. One might argue that by foregrounding synchronization only when scripture is being articulated, the film centers more on an investigation of the authority of God and his word than on the attempt, so common in dominant cinema, to reinscribe the authority of the male voice over the female voice and body.

While Bergman's synchronization of the female voice with the female body may indicate a reluctance to abandon certain patriarchal constructions, Sandberg sees Karin's reading of scripture as lending increased aural authority to a female voice, an authority underscored by camera technique:

> Both image and voice . . . finally tip the scales against the male discourse represented in Jöns and Block. The mute girl's power to attract the camera's interest at every turn, to displace the initially firm alliance between the protagonist Block and the visual attention of the narrative, creates a neat parallel with the larger discursive movement from the dominant male narrative voice to its feminine counterpart. ("Rewriting" 21)

A tracking back reveals the troupe seated at a table eating silently as Karin reads; she is now in charge of both the meal she is serving, the text she is reading, and the narrative of the film. This and subsequent camera work compel the spectator to see and perceive these events through the Mute

Girl's eyes; she becomes the consciousness through whom this reality is mediated. The scene continues with yet more dissolves while the camera increasingly isolates her face. When the camera pans to an isolated close-up of her, she turns to look at a torch next to a window, and the camera follows her look. Thus, her vision, both literal and figurative, is granted authority. A series of zooms and pans creates a kind of vertiginous reality, during which Karin's voice continues reading on the soundtrack. Significantly, too, a two-shot of Karin and Block tracks back to reveal the girl at left in close-up. As her face indicates that she sees something, the spectator increasingly identifies with her vision, with her look, a technique that Mulvey indicates is quite rare in dominant male cinema precisely because it does lend authority to female experience. Nonetheless we note that, while we shared Jof's vision, we do not see what she is looking at, a strategy that deprives her vision of the authority of male spectating.

With the arrival of Death at the castle, the camera cuts to an extreme close-up of the Mute Girl and then tracks back as she walks forward, tears on her face. In the background Jöns and Block come stand behind her, and Karin enters in close-up on the left, so that the two women share the foreground of the shot and the two men stand in the background. A pan left shows even Lisa standing in front of her husband Plog. The reverse pan right isolates half of Karin's face at the left of the frame and the girl's face in the center, while the Knight is visible in the background, praying in profile between the two women and apart from his squire, refusing again to accept the solace of community. Again women are foregrounded visually as well as aurally.

Block is located next to a small window through which light is streaming, a light that certainly seems ironic in this context. As the Knight prays and Jöns babbles on cynically, Karin admonishes them to silence, "Quiet, quiet," to which Jöns responds that he will be quiet, but only "under protest." Again Sandberg rightly reads this scene, seeing here "the last gasp of the male discourse of metaphysical debate, which falls silent only under coercion. That the silencing voice is that of Karin confirms the impression of discursive control suggested by her appropriation of the scripture reading" ("Rewriting" 21). During all this dialogue, the camera still isolates the girl in close-up as her lips begin to move as if she were struggling to speak, and the scene concludes with a zoom in on her radiant face as she quietly and dramatically declares, "Det är fullbordat." The Mute Girl literally acquires voice and visually displaces the men in the film.

In the King James Bible (John 19:30), this last statement is usually rendered as "It is finished," but the Swedish version of the original would be better translated as "It is accomplished" or "It is completed." These are, of course, Christ's last words on the cross and embody a terrible irony, that

God's plan entails the sacrifice of his own son. The association of the Mute Girl with Christ, both through her words and through her sufferings and victimization by a representative of the repressive social and religious order, is interesting, for here and in the later films Bergman persistently attempts to chart women's victimization by the dominant order. His positioning the Mute Girl in the place of God's son undermines the legacy of power that is passed down from male to male and also grants the female drastically increased authority. But what is it precisely that has been finished, accomplished, or completed, and why is this final statement made by a woman who has not previously said a single word in the film?

Mosley designates this statement as "words of affirmation" (63), while Sarris argues that the girl "embrace[s] the prospect of death" (88). But Silverman might counter that in dominant cinema "woman's words are shown to be even less her own than are her 'looks.' They are scripted for her, extracted from her by an external agency, or uttered by her in a trance-like state" (*Acoustic Mirror* 31), and such is the case here. The girl's words are uttered in a "trance-like state," and Karin's reading has been "scripted for her." The close-up of the girl's face shows an almost sexual rapture. This woman's first and final utterance almost seems like an embracing of absence, a sexual submission to a God who has seduced her, for her face in close-up is suffused with radiance, illuminated by a beam of light that reminds one of the fact that the immaculate conception is described as the penetration of Mary by a shaft of God's light, for sexual difference and male sexual need are always the foundation of the patriarchy.

"Det är fullbordat" implies the fulfillment of God's will and the finishing, the death of the human. Both silence and absence are implied in this moment of fulfillment, which is itself a prelude to the final silence and absence. These words are, after all, words of prophecy, penned by the apostle St. John. Karin also reiterates the words of the prophet; she too is a mouthpiece for a literally canonized male voice whose vision is effected. The male prophecy is, then, fulfilled. The (self-)destruction ironically implicit in the patriarchy is accomplished. Thus it is difficult to agree with Sandberg that the narrative chronicles an emergence of a genuine female voice. Both the Mute Girl and Karin begin to speak by reciting scripture that is of course divinely sanctioned. This form of speech is secondhand discourse, not an expression of authentic subjective experience. Scripture is, of course, ritualistic language. The voice of God, not of the individual human subject, its goal is to some extent the erasure of the individual in favor of the communal. While ritualistic language is what Foucault calls a "discursive fellowship," the language of community, of social bonding, those forces Bergman so prizes in his later work, it is also an expression of a closed system that by its very nature unites its members by excluding others. As the later film *The Rite* demonstrates, ritual is frequently corrupted by the community it serves, a bloodthirsty misuse of communal values. Thus, the speech that Karin and the Mute Girl achieve is not the language of self-articulation. Instead these women seem to have been co-opted into the vacuum of the male semiotic system. It is also well to remember that the mute girl's statement, as a repetition of the opening line of the film, provides textual closure, an order artificially imposed by a dominant cultural value system, so as to legitimize itself.

The girl's statement is further complicated by Bergman's visual technique. She clearly sees something that we do not, experiencing a kind of epiphany, but we are given no interpretive signposts for this event. Whereas Mia was present to comment on Jof's vision and the Knight and Jöns attempted to speak Tyan's vision, nothing and no(body) is interposed here either to interfere with or to dilute the authority of her vision. Is she experiencing a divine revelation or a subjective delusion? Her speech seems almost imposed upon her. Is this voice somehow the voice of God or that of delusion or both? Bergman provides us with few interpretive indicators to guide us, even as the foregoing argument would suggest that in this moment God and delusion coincide, a further reiteration of the bankruptcy of the patriarchal system. While this utterance can be seen as a legitimate, clearsighted vision of the inevitable consequences of the malevolent patriarchy that has consistently wrought death and destruction throughout the film, these two women are speaking the masculine truth of the film, not the truth of who they are. One might instead see the Mute Girl's statement as an attempt by the film to extract speech from the female in order to master the "dark continent" that a silent woman represents to the male imagination.

The biblical source of this utterance underscores both the finality of these events and the malevolent, inscrutable patriarch behind them, at the same time that the irony of the original statement includes an acknowledgment that only through artistic articulation can the bankruptcy of articulation, of language, be rendered; only through presence can absence be represented. Having chosen silence as the only appropriate reaction to a corrupt world and its compromised language, this authoritative voice affirms that death is the only release from and the logical conclusion of this ideological system. Her previous silence only lends added authority to this utterance. A female voice, then, rises out of silence to become the privileged voice of the narrative, at the same time that that voice speaks a "male" truth rather than a female one. At best we can see the emergence of Karin and the Mute Girl as speakers of scripture as imbuing them with an insight into the corruption of the patriarchy, as new "seers" whose vision is clearer and who may point the way to some new religious alternative centered on female values, analogous to Jof's Virgin Mary-based religion. This interpretation is reinforced by the parallels between the Mute Girl and Christ; she might, then, be seen as a new kind of divine progeny who can initiate a more positive religion to re-place the vengeance-based tradition of arbitrary divine power as represented by the Old Testament Yahweh.

But the Mute Girl and her acquisition of voice remain troubling:

> The Mute Girl's lack of a name . . . reflects the contradictory role that un-articulated female experience plays in Bergman's narrative strategy. In one sense, the mute girl's anonymity is her strength, because it epitomizes her existence outside articulation in male discourse. In another, her nameless-ness reveals the problems inherent in such marginal status, since any discur-sive 'victories' must necessarily go unmentioned. (Sandberg, "Rewriting" 24)

In summation, Bergman's penultimate scene imparts to the female more visual authority than to the male, creates spectator identification with the fe-male gaze, undermines the tradition of patrilineage through the Mute Girl's association with Christ, and hints at the emergence of a new, more authentic and responsive religion based on female values. At the same time, however, he portrays women as lacking the authority necessary for the creation of im-ages and delineates what authority they have as at least in part derived from their biology. But perhaps most importantly, the female voice in the film is not an authentic articulation of female reality; instead, it speaks a truth that is specifically gendered as male. In many respects, I think, this scene is para-digmatic for Bergman's problematic relationship with female experience; while he recognizes the ways in which female reality is subverted by the pa-triarchy, sympathizes with it, and sees in it values not compromised by the male hierarchy, he cannot reject a biological definition of woman or grant her the power to speak with her own voice, precisely, one suspects, because of the threat that such articulation poses to the male artist.

But the film does not end here. Rather it continues on to present Jof's vi-sion of Block and his companions doing a dance of death on a distant hill-side. There are, however, significantly two people missing from this scene — Karin and the Mute Girl. Bergman's explanation that the scene was shot hastily after the main actors had left for the day seems somehow inadequate to explain this omission. In light of the emergence of female authority (however negotiated), these two glaring absences in the last scene seem meaningful even if not calculated. One could effectively argue, I think, that this omission/absence coheres with the film's presentation of God, Death, and the male as an absence at the center that co-opts the lives of women into its vacuum. The juxtaposition of the scene in the castle and the subsequent dance-of-death shot indicates that the mute girl and Karin are literally pulled along into this meaningless quest and then erased from it. Sandberg again provocatively points out that the absence of these two women from the Dance-of-Death shot is both a victory, in that they completely escape the closure of the narrative, and a defeat, in that their escape is virtually unnoticed by the vast majority of viewers. Their fate is completely overshadowed by Jof's concluding vision, which points metafilmically to Bergman's imagination as the ultimate organizing principle of the film. (24)

While Sandberg is certainly right here, the problem of Jof's final vision is complicated by two instances of identity mergence. The transition dissolve from the mute girl to Mia suggests a kind of synthesis, an early variant of the sort of identity mergence that so many of Bergman's later films chart, a strategy of disjunction that can serve the feminist enterprise by calling attention to dominant narrative's attempt to "naturalize" its view of subjectivity as fixed and immutable. Interestingly, Bergman acknowledges a connection between identity mergence and the loss of patriarchal authority: "That which had formerly been so enigmatic and frightening, namely the supernatural, does not exist. Everything is of this world. Everything exists and happens inside us, and we flow into and out of one another. It's perfectly fine like that" (*Images* 241). The collapse of the patriarchy for Bergman entails an acknowledgment of the mutability of subjectivity.

Bergman would seem with this dissolve to be suggesting that Mia tacitly embodies the same insights and authority that the girl does. If that is the case, Bergman is not successful here, for while Mia and her husband Jof seem in many respects a kind of last-ditch effort to demonstrate the possibility of overcoming the patriarchal binarism represented by Block, Mia herself is a "binarized" figure, and the female pole of binary thought collapses once the male pole is destroyed, since it is generated by the patriarchy and its existence depends upon the continued vitality of that male pole. Without the male half of the binary equation, the female half cannot stand. Thus, while the film centers on a questioning of the validity of male patriarchal authority and the binarism that that authority creates in order to perpetuate itself, it stops short of questioning the ramifications of that binarism for the lives of women.

The second instance, equally troubling, is embodied in the vision itself, for Jof is, significantly, the only other character in the film besides Block who is not dying and yet is able to see Death. Significantly, this final vision, in coloration, in composition, in subject matter, and in ideology, is parallel to the Knight's vision of Death. Jof's final vision, then, serves to recoup him for the male forces of the film. Jof must, for Bergman at this stage of his career, learn the lessons of manhood. A male life that does not include an alignment with the Father, however problematic that alignment may be, is not a truly male life. One suspects that it is precisely because of Bergman's need to merge the forces and values represented by Jof and the Knight that he uses so many dissolves throughout the film. In other words, Jof inherits from

Block the legacy of the destructive father, even as Bergman reiterates his idealization of the family unit, both mortal and divine, in Jof, Mia, and Mikael.
We note that in the final shot Jof puts his arm around Mia and the camera
pans with them while we hear the strumming of a lyre and the heavenly choir
of female voices from Jof's earlier vision. This soundtrack would seem, then,
to suggest that the two visions, one of birth and life, one of death and finality, complement each other and finally form a unified perception of life.

Thus, the film seems to argue for the emergence of a new definition of
the male. Bergman has consistently associated Jof with Mia and the traditional female values of community, fellowship, family, and closeness to nature. He is one of the first instances in Bergman of what we might call the
feminized male, a man whose life is enriched and enhanced through his association with women and female values. At the same time, however, Bergman's feminized male (Oscar in *Fanny and Alexander* is another example),
while well-meaning and authentic in a way that more "manly" men are not,
is rather bumbling and ineffectual, his association with these values serving
somehow to undercut his potency and agency. Indeed, Jof's capacity for vision seems very much predicated upon these "feminine" values. We notice
that his vision early in the film is not one of God the father or even of Christ
the son, but rather of Mary the mother. Bergman even confesses that it is no
matter of accident that his actors are named Jof and Mia for "naturally
they're Joseph and Mary, it's as simple as that" (Björkman *et al.* 116). He
continues on, "I infused the characters of Jof and Mia with something that
was very important to me: the concept of the holiness of the human being. If
you peel off the layers of various theologies, the holy always remains . . . . I
believe a human being carries his or her own holiness and it is 'intra-natural,'
it has no supernatural explanations" (*Images* 236, 238).

*The Seventh Seal* seems, then, to be trying to posit an alternative religion
of affirmation, represented by Woman as Mother, against the religion of destruction embodied in a cruel and indifferent paternal God. But such a con-
stellation is extremely problematic, for the Virgin Mary (and Mia with her)
are nothing more than naive, quasi-idealistic, and simplistic projections of
male needs; after all, the primary, if not only, importance Mary has within the
Christian ideology is as mother to the male. Furthermore, the association
with the Holy Family still keeps Jof and Mia firmly within the tradition of
Christianity, a fact that undercuts their subversive potential.

Bergman's film, then, is Janus-faced: it posits a vision vitalized by an idealized, creative (and feminine) force and yet the terms of existence are set by
the ultimate patriarchy, God's ordering of the world. Jof's final act of imagination is presented as a synthesis of male and female values but cannot hold,
however many dissolves the director may use; for the imagination, as con-
ceived by Bergman, seems to demand that dualism and masculine preroga-

tive be overthrown. At the same time, by concluding the film with a (very visual) vision, Bergman is again the modernist reasserting his control over reality and valorizing the structuring influence of the male artist.

In *The Seventh Seal*, Bergman presents a patriarchy whose silence and absence indicate its inability to impart values to human life. The silence associated with the female in this film is both quantitatively and qualitatively different from that associated with the male; women's silence is, in an albeit limited sense, positive, an appropriate response to corrupted male language. But *The Seventh Seal* works both with and against itself — to depict the victimization of women by the patriarchy and its institutions and to reinscribe them within the order, to posit the emergence of female authority and to undercut it by reasserting woman's "proper" place as a function of male needs, as mother and wife, beings in touch with larger "natural" forces, and to suggest that female experience is somehow truer and more authentic than male experience at the same time that only male experience can overcome binarism and that the structuring creative imagination is gendered as exclusively male. For all its ambivalence on these issues, however, the film serves to demonstrate that, as far as God and the patriarchal philosophical, social, and linguistic structures that locate their power in him are concerned, "things fall apart; the centre cannot hold."

# 5: *The Silence:* Disruption and Disavowal in the Movement Beyond Gender

*The Silence* (1963) is the third of Bergman's trilogy of "chamber films," so named after Strindberg's musically-structured chamber plays. The films that comprise the trilogy — *Through a Glass Darkly* (1961), *Winter Light* (1962), and *The Silence* represent a major shift in Bergman's filmic enterprise, a transformation that was to determine the nature of his entire subsequent production.

Male critics have by and large granted rather begrudging approbation to this pivotal film, of which Bergman himself has said, "at [its] bottommost layer lay the collapse of an ideology and a way of life" (Björkman *et al.* 181). Even Vernon Young, who usually disdains Bergman's work, acknowledges that "*The Silence* rewards effort; at its core there is a kind of rancid integrity which compels one's recognition, if not one's affection" (213). And Donner approvingly describes its context:

> Whereas Bergman, *ancienne manière*, observed nothingness in the eyes of the young witch in *The Seventh Seal*, in this film he provokes direct experience of it. In *The Seventh Seal* we are told that God does not exist; in *The Silence* the death of God has become palpable, a matter of deep pain formulated not verbally but in the actions, expressions, and gestures of the characters . . . . And whereas in *The Seventh Seal* the dialectic is conducted in the head, through language, here it is expressed physically, and operates directly upon our emotions. (120)

The questioning of the patriarchy implicit in the earlier films now becomes an overt acknowledgment of the bankruptcy of male hegemony and entails a rejection of male discursive and cinematic convention. The film's title alludes, of course, to the silence of God, the silence in which humanity must try to construct new meaning for itself.

Feminist critics have, however, found the film troubling. Mellen argues that Ester, one of the film's protagonists, "lives an empty futile life because she has not accepted the demands of the female body, because she refuses the female sexual role" and that she is a manifestation of Bergman's view that "men move in an ethical realm,. . . women in a biological one" (298). And Bergom-Larsson sees in the film a completely dichotomized vision of the world that derives from patriarchal values, arguing, "Without God, Bergman seems to think, the world is split, dichotomized into inner and outer, into intellect and body, into masculine and feminine — the synthesis, the totality remains unattainable" (137). While she is certainly right to see the film as dichotomized, I would argue that all Bergman's films embody an awareness of binarism but that this film is an attempt (however successful and however negotiated from a feminist perspective) to move beyond binarism by both denaturalizing its categories and disavowing gender.

*The Silence* implicitly recognizes the connection between "the collapse of an ideology" and the bankruptcy of traditional narrative. It has little narrative and no real plot development. Rather *The Silence*, like Strindberg's chamber plays, subordinates thematic content to the evocation of mood, plot continuity and diegesis to the portrayal of psychic states; the film makes sense "not according to what happens, but to *how* it happens" (Brightman 242), its narrative propelled forward less by action than by mood, emotion, and character. Of his technique, Bergman says: "The film is chamber music — music in which, with an extremely limited number of voices and figures, one explores the essence of a number of motifs. The backgrounds are extrapolated, put into a sort of fog. The rest is a distillation" (Björkman *et al.* 168). Immediately after completing this work, Bergman called film "a language . . . beyond words," ("Den fria") and continued on to maintain, "I find it easier to compare film, not to theater or the novel, but to music. In fact, I think of film and music as equals of a sort. In pure film and pure music there is a feeling that goes directly to some deeper level of the listener or viewer" (Alpert 41). He also says: "By working directly on the audience, music is by nature closely related to film, also rhythmically" (Billquist 265). This musical structure, one notes, functions for many women artists such as Duras and Dulac, as an expressive mode not corrupted or depleted by masculine language. The development of a musically structured filmic practice represents an attempt to move beyond conventional (male) discourse. *The Silence* galvanizes a set of diachronous images of objects, lights, and people, evoking a visual and aural sense of a patriarchal destructive present absence that infects all human life.

The germinal image for the film came to Bergman in a daydream: "Four strong young women are pushing a wheelchair. In it sits the skeleton of an ancient old man, a ghost. The old man has had a stroke, is deaf and almost blind" (*Images* 104). This image clearly suggests the impotence and death of male authority and the energizing alterity of female experience that underlie virtually all Bergman's post-1960 films. Critical of the male dominant order, the film embodies, I think, an impulse to move beyond gender at the same time that this movement entails a rejection of all sexuality, male and female, a complete disavowal of the body. The film posits the corruption of the male sexual order and tacitly argues that both male and female sexuality are perverse. For Bergman, as for most male artists, there is only one sex, only one sexuality. In essence, in "taking down" the male order, he disallows the possibility of the healthy female subject, investing the liberating possibilities of subjectivity instead in the sexually immature male protagonist. The only viable subjectivity for Bergman now is one that is non- or pregendered, at the same time that it is, of course, biologically male. *The Silence*, then, charts both the collapse of the patriarchy and its systems and reinscribes them. It is this simultaneous disavowal of gender and movement beyond gender, as informed by recent feminist criticism, that this chapter will investigate, by examining Bergman's use of disjunctive strategies and gender categories (both diegetic and extradiegetic) in his treatment of the public and private spheres, the representation of subjectivity, female sexuality, voyeurism, screening surfaces, and space. Like Ester, Bergman is engaged in the transgression of boundaries, a project that entails both connection and appropriation. I would like to suggest that this film both deconstructs and reinscribes binarism, that it addresses gendered subjectivity in terms of both character and apparatus and constitutes the continuation of an increasingly radical, if problematic, exploration of issues of feminist concern in Bergman's work.

The very structure of the film suggests a criticism of male ideology and discourse. While *The Silence* is structured around a journey, this particular journey-quest differs from those in earlier Bergman films. Here the journey is not liberating, but stifling, not goal-directed, but seemingly aimless, the obstacles to effective progress defined as masculine rather than feminine. Furthermore, the journey is undertaken not by a lone male, but by two women and a child. The landscape to be conquered is, unlike the one in de Lauretis' argument, overwhelmingly male in nature, the masculine constituting a series of obstacles to the female questers and the boy protagonist. Bergman has, to a certain extent, inverted the paradigm of the male quest, and, while inversion can simply be a perpetuation of the paradigm in new terms, here the director is clearly engaged in a challenge to the ideological tainting of narrative. This notion of narrative as ideologically compromised also surfaces at the end of the film, for its closure, while informed by a sense of ritual passage and initiation, is nonetheless deeply problematized.

The patriarchal order in which the filmic events occur is described in Anna's extended monologue to her sister:

> (When Father was alive, he decided things. And we obeyed him. Because we had to. When Father died you thought you could carry on the same way.) It's just that you always carried on about your principles, how meaningful everything was, how important! But that was just talk. Do you know why? Everything existed for your self-importance . . . . And that's the truth of it. You can't *bear* it if everything isn't "significant" and "meaningful." . . . When Father died you said: "Now I don't want to live any longer." Well, why are you living, then? (136)

The lines in parentheses occur in the screenplay but not in the final film and emphasize the less obvious connection in the rest of Anna's speech between the bankruptcy of the patriarchy and the plight of the two sisters. Anna demonstrates here an insight into the destructive effect of the patriarchy, into its false values and self-validation, even as she fails to see that Ester is as much its victim as she. Throughout the film, Bergman represents the loss of God the Father as entailing a loss of meaning in human life; the patriarchy is an empty shell, a vacuum that female values must fill. The equation between male order and meaning, then, is undercut by the ending of the film, which posits the emergence of new meaning derived largely from female experience.

The world surrounding the three protagonists is defined as unremittingly male and profoundly hostile, its every manifestation tinged by war; tanks flash past the train window, another rumbles past the hotel, and the train is carrying soldiers to or from some unspecified military site. Houston argues that "the mysterious war carries great significance for the film as a whole, suggesting that the private hatreds and antagonisms of individuals and the great, impersonal conflicts between nations somehow mutually reflect and reinforce each other with silent inevitability" (143). While she may be right that the film establishes a parallel between the macrocosm of the war and the microcosm of the sisters' relationship, the matter is, I suspect, not quite so simple. For there are fundamental differences between the hostility of the (male) war and that between the two (obviously female!) sisters; beneath the conflict between Ester and Anna is a personal bond of shared experience and commitment, expressed in their attempts to reach out to help the other. By contrast, the mysterious war is impersonal and abstract, a metaphor for a destructive absent patriarch who even in his death ravages humanity. Bergman has said of this background, "It's a country preparing for war, where war can break out any day. Whether it's a civil war or what, I couldn't say; but all the time one feels it is something perverse and terrifying" (Björkman et al. 184). That he associates this male environment with both perversion and terror is a further indication of the extent to which this film charts a crisis of faith in male culture.

That the world in which this film takes place is explicitly masculine is also apparent in the town where the hotel is located. The streets, the cafe, and the theater are filled with men. Except for the two female protagonists, women are virtually absent from the film. Men bustle about shouting noisily in a language neither the protagonists nor we understand, underscoring the alienation of this masculine reality. This city, we learn later, is named Timoka, an Estonian word for "pertaining to the executioner" (Björkman et al. 183) that intimates again the hostility of this male world. The searing white light Bergman uses both in the introductory train sequence and in the shots of the town is also descriptive of this male reality and is "terrifying" for Bergman (Sjöman 77), a metaphor for the oppression associated with an inimical male reality.

This city is further characterized by shots of an emaciated horse pulling a heavy cart, images that are bracketed by shots of Ester. Thus Cowie argues that this animal "like her own spirit,. . . is shrivelled by circumstances" (*Sweden 2*, 180). But rather than seeing this camera work as establishing an equation between Ester and the horse — an instance of the projection of male failings (for the horse is a part of the relentlessly male outside world) onto the female — one could argue that the camera suggests the ways in which corrupt male culture (for the horse is almost always associated with the masculine) impinges upon and infects female reality. Too, every time Anna wanders into the public sphere, she is humiliated and degraded, and the only other woman in that space (who has sex in the theater balcony) is similarly degraded. Although the film posits public space as male and threatening to women, private interior space is susceptible to invasion from without. As Cowie suggests (*Sweden 2*, 180), the insulation of the interior is not complete; the noises of the street (the tank, the airplanes that awaken Johan from his nap, the ominously booming bells, the foghorn, and the shouting of the men below) penetrate into the family's rooms as does the movement of the tank, which sets the glass on Ester's table trembling. Such incursions disrupt the differentiation between private/interior and public/exterior and suggest that these individuals can never escape the threat of male aggression.

Since one of the male stereotypes of women is confinement ("range is masculine and confinement is feminine" [Ellmann 87]), a rigid distinction between the public sphere (defined as masculine) and the private sphere (defined as feminine) characterizes dominant cultural expressions. But, as Kaplan points out, this stereotype can be problematized through the filmic deployment of space and the kinds of activities that take place within different spaces (*Women and Film* 96–99). Thus *The Silence* demonstrates the ineluctable interconnectedness of the public and the private and treats the psychological manifestations of this untenable distinction.

The very absence of a male adult protagonist in this film indicates a major change in Bergman's work. That this change should coincide with his acknowledgment of the death of God (and his pernicious cultural legacy) suggests an awareness of the complicity between ideology and aesthetic structures. Steene sees this shift as one in which "women then change from objects to subjects" ("Portrait" 97), but the degree of subjectivity and the nature of that subjecthood are, as we shall see, problematic. Nonetheless, the focus on female protagonists does indicate a recognition of the insufficiency of patriarchal discourse and ideology. The entire film might be considered an exploration of the boundaries between the self and the other characteristic of the feminist enterprise.

With the exception of the dwarfs, the adult males in *The Silence* are depicted as marginal at best and repugnant at worst, their impotence and/or lack of integrity an extension of God's impotence and moral bankruptcy. The old waiter, the most positive adult male in the film, is usually seen as a God substitute or a harbinger of death (Kustow 141, Young 215, Penlington 31). He is stooped and bowed by age, pathetically eager to please, his doddering actions confined to the traditionally female role of server. While Cowie may be right to see him as "a retainer of simple goodness in the tradition of fröken Agda, Isak's housekeeper [in *Wild Strawberries*]" (*Sweden 2* 180), his nurturing role combines with his extreme age to render him feminized and impotent, an implicit acknowledgment of the bankruptcy of the patriarchy. His association with death and castration and Johan's fear of him reinforce this interpretation.

When Johan espies him in a little cubicle eating his dinner, the waiter catches sight of the boy and performs a pantomime in which he wraps a sausage in a piece of lettuce, bows this strange figure in Johan's direction, and then bites off its head, a rather obvious gesture of both aggression and castration. After Johan approaches, the old waiter shows him a series of photographs placed diagonally within the film frame: the first depicts a couple, the second a funeral bier with children in the background, and the third a bier with adults around it and a single child off to the left. The waiter, in pointing to this figure and then to himself, implies that he is that child. He would, then, draw Johan into his own funereal reality, into the world of death with which he is associated. These photographs are, quite literally, the momento mori of which Sontag speaks; in the dominance of the absence effect over the presence effect of photography, they narrate loss and suggest an at least partial acknowledgment of that loss.

For Johan the waiter is frightening, and yet he is also feeble and rather silly. The fact that Johan takes the photographs and shoves them under a carpet might indicate that he rejects the funereal reality of this demoted and trivialized patriarch, but the metaphor — as the *Scenes from a Marriage* episode entitled "The Art of Sweeping under the Carpet" suggests — also hints that this action is escapist and that Johan does not fully come to terms with the threat of castration embodied in the old waiter.

If the waiter in the hotel is compromised and marginalized by his associations with the patriarchy, the waiter in the cafe is repugnant and brutal. The occupation of these two men is, I suspect, not a coincidence, for the waiting profession is severely marginalized by our culture; very low in the social hierarchy and lacking financial stability, this profession is dissimilar to those practiced by, for instance, Doctor Isak Borg in *Wild Strawberries*, and even Pastor Tomas in *Winter Light*. The fact, however, that Bergman uses a hierarchy of professional status to indict his male characters indicates that he still carries a good deal of patriarchal "baggage," that he has yet to examine the ramifications of some of his insights. But the waiter in the cafe is far more repugnant than the hotel waiter and is associated with violent male sexuality. Brusque, hairy, and coarse-looking, he has hurried, brutal sex with Anna, his face impassive, even when he cruelly sodomizes her while she weeps uncontrollably. He enters the private space occupied by the three protagonists, bringing with him the violence, hostility, and hatred of the male public sphere.

Attempting to navigate his way in a world dichotomized between male and female is young Johan, from whose perspective we see and experience much of the film. Metaphors of vision are so prominent that Koskinen argues that "*The Silence* is the first Bergman film in which observation, the very act of seeing constitutes the center of both the narrative and the narrating" (104). The film begins as Johan comes to the train window, looks out at us, and rubs his eyes, as if to see more clearly. As a voyeur, he peeks into realities both male (the soldiers on the train and the dwarfs) and female (he spies on his mother when she enters the hotel room with her lover). Johan's voyeurism, while clearly a method for sorting out sexual roles and identities, is very different from that in dominant cinema. If adult male voyeurism entails the appropriation and objectification of women, Johan, like Bergman, is engaged in an exploration of sexuality less to appropriate and objectify (although they do that too) than to arrive at some new and less rigid and restrictive sense of sexual desire and subjectivity beyond gender. Thus Bergman suggests that voyeurism is essentially androgynous but becomes sexually implicated by dominant ideology, even as such a suggestion flies in the face of recent critical insight as to the essential genderedness of the voyeuristic act.

The book Johan is reading, *The Hero of Our Times*, is, as Steene indicates, "a name tag rather than an indication of his reading habits" (*Ingmar Bergman* 106), for the film invests in him the complete authority of subjectivity. The mobile camera of the opening sequence follows him around the train compartment and out into the corridor, voyeuristically probing, consistently following his eyeline, establishing a point-of-view structure through which the spectator is locked into the fantasmatic world projected on the screen. As Koskinen suggests, "Through him the spectator comes to participate in the process of meaning, through our own growing awareness (of the film) we engage . . . in precisely the act of communication of which the film's adult characters are incapable" (112). In his movement, for instance, from one bench of the compartment to the other, the camera follows him, but, when his mother does likewise, it does not. When cuts appear in the film, they consistently do so after shots of one of the two women, while shots of the boy usually pan over to one of the women or to an object before cutting away. Such camera work would seem to represent Johan's identity and experience as somehow more fluid than that of the two women. Furthermore, on several occasions the boy turns from profile to a full-face close-up that sug-

gests agency and direct address to the audience. Johan's vision is further cor-
related with the spectator's point of view by the film's many low-angle shots
that are appropriate to a child's perspective.

Thus, although this is one of Bergman's first films to foreground women
and their experience (as the filmmaker perceives it), the central positioning of
Johan might call into question just how committed Bergman is to an exploration of "women's reality" and to a challenging of male hegemony and discourse. A view of the film as reinscribing male authority is supported by the
identification between Johan and Bergman himself; both are engaged in attempts to define themselves in terms of, and come to some truth about,
male-female binarism. Notably, however, this is the first Bergman film in
which the protagonist is a prepubescent child. Unlike the Knight in *The Seventh Seal* or Isak Borg in *Wild Strawberries*, both of whom are indicted for
their rigidity and allegiance to androcentric values, this male child is defined
as living an experience in which gender roles are not yet fixed because sexuality is still amorphous.

But the prominent position of two sisters within the diegesis is also interesting, since self-sustaining female communities are so threatening to a male
culture that sees itself as the only source of authority and of life itself. As Auerbach has noted, "Initiation into a band of brothers is a traditional privilege
symbolized by uniforms, rituals, and fiercely shared loyalties; but sisterhood . . . looks often like a blank exclusion. A community of women may
suggest less the honor of fellowship than an antisociety, an austere banish-
ment from both social power and biological rewards" (*Communities of
Women* 3). She goes on to point to the significance of all-male communities,
citing King Arthur's Round Table and the fellowships of *Moby Dick, Heart of
Darkness, Treasure Island, The Treasure of the Sierra Madre, Billy Budd*, and
*The Caine Mutiny* as cases in which, whether the community is destroyed or
reasserted, it retains its magnitude as a "vessel of significance."

In contrast to these all-male fellowships, female communities such as the
Graie, the Amazons, and the Muses share the fate of existing in exile, beyond
the frontiers of civilization, of being desexed (the Amazons are said to have
cut off their right breasts in order to shoot arrows better and the Graie are
beyond childbearing years), and yet of embodying some transcendent ideal
that assists the hero in his quest. As Auerbach again points out: "As a recurrent literary image, a community of women is a rebuke to the conventional
ideal of a solitary woman living for and through men, attaining citizenship in
the community of adulthood through masculine approval alone" (5). Since
they exist seemingly independent of the patriarchy and occur most frequently
when male authority is absent, these communities threaten the male cultural
tradition. The bond between sisters (literal or figurative) is in the male tradi-

tion associated with obstacle, with that which must be conquered and destroyed in order to allow for the reemergence of the male order.

Thus male discourse develops a series of strategies for undercutting the potential threat of a group of women gathered together beyond reach of male authority, one of which strategies is to emphasize the "unnaturalness" of such fellowships and to characterize them with the mental and emotional "diseases" of narcissism, lesbianism, and physical illness, external manifestations of the "disorder" of these women's lives. Other strategies exist to underscore women's confinement — by restricting their physical mobility, for instance, the artist can also restrict attempts at moving beyond male authority; by emphasizing that these women are forever waiting, desperately praying for the return of "normal" male authority, the artist can assert that, for woman, waiting for the male is life itself. Not surprisingly, then, many depictions of female friendships occur against a background of a far-off war where the men are engaged in defending the very community and values they have temporarily deserted. Thus, *Lysistrata, Little Women,* and several Jane Austen novels, like *The Silence,* all take place during wartime. Furthermore, as a film such as *Mädchen in Uniform* attests, the mere physical absence of the male can still be accompanied by an overwhelming presence of male authority: the introductory montage of that film establishes a mood of "military preparedness, steeples and archways, bugle calls and the marching rhythm of soldiery" (Rich 102). All these strategies, of course, reinforce the patriarchy's insistence upon seeing women as fundamentally insufficient unto themselves, as dependent for the meaning of their lives upon external male authority.

But Bergman departs from male discourse in this respect; while Anna and Ester do exist in a pervasively male world, the military authority outside is corrupt and senseless; there will be no reemergence of a "right" male order (except as embodied in young Johan), and the confinement of these women is an aspect of the hostile male present absence that infects their lives. Thus, the sisterhood in *The Silence* has a feministly subversive potential. The absence of a dominant male protagonist and the positioning of the sisters' relationship within a hostile male environment subvert the dominant tradition. But the representation of that relationship as hostile and "perverse" and the reification of gender binarism in it undercut that subversive potential.

This reification occurs primarily in the representation of two adult protagonists differentiated along lines of masculine/feminine, male/female. The two sisters are represented as deeply gendered in a film that strives to disavow gender, at the same time that their experience of gender and binarization as repressive coheres to depict them both as victims of male sexual and ideological dominance. Male ideology projects its hierarchical sexual system onto the female.

Binaristic oppositions between the two sisters appear in both lighting and framing. Anna is consistently photographed in dark spaces — in the theater and in rooms where she turns out lights and lowers window blinds. By contrast, Ester's room is brightly lit, although not so brightly as the outdoor scenes. The association between darkness and femininity and light and masculinity is, of course, a gender stereotype, but because of Ester's sexual ambiguity, the binarization is disrupted. Significantly, too, the only character allotted "natural" lighting is Johan; almost all the shots in which he appears as well as the corridors associated with him are lit in a soft grey light. The fact that only a sexually immature child receives this lighting speaks to the film's impulse beyond gender at the same time that Johan's biological sex, of course, reinscribes the subject as male.

The binarism of the two sisters is also apparent in Bergman's compositions. Anna tends to move horizontally within the frame while Ester moves forward or backward and the camera records her in alternately high and low angles. Ester is shot in rigid verticals and Anna in horizontals or languorous diagonals. Yet Ester's horizontal positionings on the bed align her with her sister; the illness that places her there extends to Anna, as both are "infected" by the patriarchy's ordering. These lines and angles are also resolved at the end of the film when Johan, after receiving Ester's letter, throws himself on her in an embrace. The coming together of the sexually ambiguous Ester and Johan in a line that the film has associated with Anna marks Johan as the subject and suggests a mergence of these character energies, a mergence of sexual ambiguity and nongenderedness that signals a culmination of both narrative and spectacle.

Binarism also emerges in Bergman's treatment of dress. Anna consistently appears in low-cut, body-hugging dresses that emphasize her as sex object, while Ester dresses in severely tailored clothes. Throughout much of the film, she is dressed in "masculine" pajamas, not unlike those Johan wears, a detail that reinforces both the connection between nephew and aunt and Ester's association with the male. Too, Anna is constantly ministering to her body with baths, creams, and make-up, while Ester's body seems both to fail and repulse her. As Kustow points out:

> Anna's incessant washing set against Ester's heart-rending chokes, gulps and spasms defines a relationship and a difference between the two women . . . a cut from the rounded curve of Anna's breast settling into cool white pillows to Ester's burning cigarette makes us feel the abyss between two kinds of existence; the whole delicate poised rhythm and pattern . . . gives occurrences resonance and enables them to echo with a range of almost imperceptible harmonics. (142)

But the distinction between the two sisters is illusory, for the male sexual regime of the film compels one sister to engage in self-objectification and the other in disavowal, both reactions to dominant culture's view of the female body as other. Bergman represents the female body as that which must be overcome or disavowed in order for the young protagonist to move beyond gender, at the same time that he intimates that woman's body is not hers but exists only as a projection of a corrupt male sexuality.

This ambivalence to the female body and its role in male culture is underscored by Bergman's camera work, which follows the male tradition in showing more of the woman's body than the man's during the sex scenes. Too, recent psychoanalytic theory points to the isolation of female body parts as an aspect of the sexual hierarchy that informs cinema. By fragmenting individual body parts, the male viewing subject (who coheres in this instance with the male director) defuses the threat of castration; by dismembering the female body through strategies of objectification and fetishization, the subject eliminates the threat that female sexuality poses. In this light, the isolation of body parts in *The Silence* is informative. Twice early in the film, Anna's feet and legs are isolated in the frame. The male child through whose subjectivity the spectator experiences much of the film remarks that her feet are walking about "completely by themselves," a statement that suggests fetishism by implying that they are disconnected from the rest of the body. It is appropriate, given her consistent objectification, that it should be Anna's rather than Ester's or Johan's feet that are fetishized. Too, Teghrarian makes the interesting observation that Johan's comment about his mother's feet approaches self-reflexivity, that it is only film itself which has the ability to fragment Anna's body in this way (112f.); thus, the film may be seen as foregrounding and therefore denaturalizing cinema's fetishistic strategies.

Shots of isolated hands are even more prominent in the film. We repeatedly see close-ups of Ester's, Anna's, and a dwarf's hands. The first word that Ester learns in the foreign language is "kasi," which, we are told, means "hand." This prominence of isolated hands is, however, somewhat complicated by Bergman's statement that:

> The aim is to make people, write people. To what extent I succeed, I don't know. But it's a striving I have had and have; instead of drawing construction designs to try more and more to draw a human hand. I mean: it stands out more and more to me, in this strange age of non-art, as being very important that we don't lose the human being out of the center, but keep searching for an expression by which to portray people — a personal form of portrayal. (Sjöman 80)

Thus, at the same time that hands symbolize a human connectedness that critiques and transcends a corrupt divine patriarchy, an affirmation of the human and the female as opposed to the male and patriarchal, one might see in his obsession with these images a kind of visual fetishism that derives from his desire to contain the female body and his ongoing reluctance fully to acknowledge the loss of male cultural and sexual potency, an interpretation supported by the fact that Johan's hands are never photographed in isolation from his body.

Given the potential fetishism of these hand shots, it is not surprising that there are virtually no close-ups of Johan's body parts except for his face, a shot that connotes agency and subjecthood rather than fetishism. That Bergman should fetishize his female characters is, I think, understandable, given his acknowledgment of the silence and destructive present absence of God. The recognition of the death of the father cannot help but result in fragmentation; the projection of that fragmentation by the male onto women is, sadly, almost inevitable. That he should try to recoup that fragmentation through the use of a male child narrator, to re-create and thereby perhaps change personal and psychological history, is absolutely if regrettably consistent.

But, if the camera's treatment of Anna and Ester is fetishistic, it also supports a spectator experience of them as subjects. They appear throughout the film in facial close-ups that emphasize authority. Indeed, close-ups dominate to an extent almost unprecedented in Bergman's career and disrupt the cinematic convention of woman as spectacle, and female-female exchanges far exceed the male-male ones, indicating again a questioning of the patriarchal hierarchy according to which the male is the enunciating presence. These close-ups are of paramount importance for Bergman:

> Our work in films must begin with the human face. We can certainly become completely absorbed in the aesthetics of montage; we can bring objects and still life into wonderful rhythm; we can make nature studies of astonishing beauty, but the approach to the human face is without a doubt the hallmark and distinguishing feature of the film medium. (Alpert 41)

Bergman increasingly depends upon close-ups and extreme close-ups to carry his films: "[They] are a passion: to be right up close to people. To look them straight in the eyes and to try to get their mental movements to reflect in their faces. And to convey this to the audience in as direct and naked a way as possible" (Sjöman 203). Thus, while close-ups of body parts fetishize women, close-ups of their faces position them as conscious and active agents who are alternatives to adult male subjects. It is Johan's experiencing of these women both as body and as subjects that must be rejected that allows a movement beyond gender for the young protagonist who is both male and not male.

The binarization of the body that is both reinscribed and subverted by the camera appears also in Anna's association with the "typically feminine" (as both sex object and mother) and Ester's with the "typically masculine" in both her identification with her father and her profession. As far as the mother is concerned, *The Silence* coheres very much with patriarchal ideol-

ogy, and its art works in establishing a series of strategies to discount, displace, or erase the mother. Kaplan argues that the mother's role

> demands that she have no voice, that she be at the service of the nuclear
> family, abnegating herself. Thus, paradoxically, while literally present and
> fulfilling enormous demands physically and emotionally, the mother is psy-
> chologically *repressed*; qua herself, she is absent to the family and society.
> The father on the other hand represents the dominant Law and is thus psy-
> choanalytically present, while literally absent. He is subject, in control, and
> given the voice, in contrast to the silence forced on the mother. (188)

Thus, the male artist develops strategies to dispose of the mother: he can
render her repulsive, foolish, or inadequate, he can kill her off during the
course of the narrative, or he can simply eliminate her from it. Tellingly, the
sisters' mother is never mentioned in *The Silence*; she is effectively erased.
One might, however, point out that male authors are not alone in their erasure of the mother; many women authors, including Jane Austen, consistently portray mothers as foolish, stupid, negligent, or absent, their dominion
over their families classic instances of "mis-rule." As Todd points out, "Good
mothers are hard to find in any novels and inadequacy is the main maternal
characteristic in male and female fiction alike" (*Women's Friendship* 411).

Since dominant ideology needs to believe that motherhood represents
subservience to the male, nonmaternal women such as Anna are revealed to
be essentially inadequate, incomplete, for male ideology's linkage of woman
to her "biological destiny" serves to control and contain her. As in almost all
his films, the mother in Bergman's *The Silence* is a "bad" mother, one who
selfishly neglects her child, and it is the sexually ambivalent Ester who cares
for and nurtures the boy. It is interesting too that several Bergman films position the mother as sexually degraded — Alma's orgy in *Persona* is linked
with pregnancy and abortion, Maria in *Cries and Whispers* is both promiscuous and a bad mother. Not only is there no healthy sexuality for mothers in
Bergman's world, but the maturation of the male child specifically requires
disavowal of the sexually active mother. The mother as an "embodiment" of
body must be overcome and erased. Bergman's own extremely difficult relationship with both his parents contributes to his hostility both to the figure
of the mother and to patriarchal culture.

Ester's association with the father is apparent both in her identification
with him and in the fact that she has a profession that involves intellect and
language. Hans Nystedt even goes so far as to claim that Ester symbolizes
"the church" (40). It is she who, through her search for meaning, is "clearly
in direct line of descent from the Bergman-projection figures of earlier
films — the Knight, Vogler, Pastor Tomas" (Wood 130). This issue of the
parent-child relationship is a volatile one for feminists. Traditionally, female
characters have been confronted with the choice between identifying with a

weak, stupid, absent, or, at best, idealized-into-impotence mother or with aligning themselves with an active, vital father. It is hardly to be wondered at, then, that most female protagonists in the Western tradition opt to identify with their fathers; from Elizabeth Bennett's closeness to her father in *Pride and Prejudice* to the Hollywood figure of Daddy's little girl, the only opportunity open to strong women for human development lies in identification with the father and rejection of the passivity and victimization of the mother. And yet such identification also entails a certain denial of the self, a rejection of one's "femaleness." Bergman's female protagonists are also confronted with this dilemma, but (especially in *The Silence*) this issue of parental identification is problematized and foregrounded such that patriarchal culture and its attendant binarism are challenged. Ester's father identification and obsession with a search for meaning rooted in the familial and metaphysical father are represented as destructive, even as Anna's apparent embracing of meaninglessness, as rooted in the body, is also destructive. Only the pregendered male child can move beyond gendered meaning.

But Ester of course is not male, an especially interesting point in view of the fact that in the original script Ester and Anna were a man and a woman (Björkman *et al.* 19). Bergman needs, I would argue, a woman to show how gender categories infect relationships and to denaturalize them and yet also to dichotomize women into "all-body" or "no-body" in order that both alternatives might be rejected. In short, Ester must be female in order for Bergman both to disavow and to move beyond gender.

While Bergman has said that, roughly put, "Anna is the body; Ester is the soul" (Sjöman 130), this statement is, of course, a vast oversimplification. As Wood points out: "If Ester were merely 'soul' she wouldn't have to masturbate . . . and if Anna were merely [body] she wouldn't feel guilt. Each sister, in fact, possesses in a suppressed and perverted form the more obvious attributes of the other" (123). We see this essentialist doubling at the beginning of the film when the two women sit on opposite benches of the train compartment; the opposition between them is superficial, for they are linked by a single camera pan and also occupy the same positions on their respective benches. Binarism dissolves into essentialist doubling in the two sisters' experience of sexuality. For Anna, sex is compulsive but empty and degrading, ultimately isolating, as is apparent in her reaction to the couple copulating in the theater; repulsed, she flees the scene. When crying and moaning after her confrontation with Ester, she is sodomized by the waiter, she does not resist. But female sexuality is both demeaned by its interaction with and dependence upon a corrupt male sexuality, as represented by the repugnant waiter, and is degraded in and of itself. The film demonstrates the ways in which women have been appropriated by male culture and yet inscribes a degraded sexuality onto women. It is Anna's biological body as much as her willingness to make herself an object to this corrupt male sexuality that degrades her.

For Ester, female sexuality has also been debased. As she suffers another attack of her illness, she shouts her revulsion:

> It's a question of erectile tissue and mucous. A confession before supreme unction. I think semen smells nasty . . . . I found I stank like a rotten fish after being impregnated . . . . It's a silly part, and I don't want to play it. I didn't want to accept my poor role. But now it's so lonely . . . . We try out attitudes and find them all meaningless. The powers are too strong for us, I mean the *monstrous* powers. You have to take care, moving among ghosts and memories (140).

The female body is infected by the male. This conflation of degraded male and female sexuality, death, role-playing, memory, and religion suggests that the patriarchy has poisoned human life and sexuality, rendering them meaningless and monstrous.

But the indignity inherent in indulging the body is not limited to its interaction with male sexuality. Ester's masturbation is also humiliating and isolating; photographed from a high angle, Ester's body is severely foreshortened in the frame, the pillows and featherbed and the dominance of her hands in this shot reminiscent of Johan a few minutes earlier when he, surrounded by a fluffy featherbed, used his hands to enact an airplane battle. Ester's masturbation takes on associations of violence and death from Johan's play. As she reaches orgasm, the camera zooms in on her head, upside down in the frame, her eyes wide open and her teeth clenched until finally she thrashes her head about violently on the pillow (a shot that prefigures Alma's nocturnal thrashings in *Persona*). This extreme foreshortening renders Ester and her sexual activity grotesque, as does the concluding diagonal. This scene is, then, paradigmatic for Bergman's treatment of female sexuality at this point in his career; while acknowledging how corrupted it is by male sexuality, he nonetheless so thoroughly grafts it onto women that debased sexuality becomes linked with their biology. While it has been objected that masturbation "has been taken away from women" ("Women and Film" 101), this representation is presumably not how feminism would like to have it returned.

Bergman's depiction of sexuality as illness has very much troubled feminist critics. Ester's recurring attacks and her masturbation not only occur in the same place but also are photographed and edited similarly. The recurring bed imagery, then, designates the site of sexuality as a site of illness. Zern suggests, rightly, I think, that beds in Bergman's films "mark out . . . the boundary at which all life-and-death events are played out and where oppositions are generated and resolved" (143). The aligning of women with pain, illness, and blood allows the patriarchy to dismiss women as physically and therefore universally inferior. Thus, Hollywood gives us Bette Davis' brain tumor in *Dark Victory*, Loretta Young's deafness in *And Now Tomorrow*, and Dorothy McGuire's and Jane Wyman's muteness in *The Spiral Staircase* and *Johnny Belinda* respectively. As Todd again points out, "Sickness is a mark of female debility" (*Women's Friendship* 407). Significantly, however, the disease from which Ester is suffering is never given a name. This refusal to name the illness universalizes the disease into a transtemporal malaise designated as both male (by association with the film's representation of threat as male) and female (because Ester has it), projecting onto a woman a male disorder. The connection between sexuality and illness, while located in the female, is also clearly a product of the hostile male universe that pervades this film. Actually, Bergman to a certain extent inverts the connection between the female and illness when he makes it clear that Ester's sickness is an inheritance from her father: she says, "Do you know what they call my condition? Euphoria. It was the same with Father. He laughed and told funny stories. Then he looked at me: 'Now it's eternity, Ester,' he said. He was so kind, though terribly big and heavy, weighed nearly 400 pounds. . ." (140). Ester's disease is a legacy of the patriarchy, of the grotesque, oppressive Father both divine and familial. Thus, the notion of woman as the site of illness is both reinscribed and subverted.

The position of the dwarfs in this sexual regime is illuminating. While they are associated with a snakelike dance in the theater, the copulating couple, and, later, Anna's being sodomized, that association is undercut by their behavior. They are in no way dark and menacing; instead, they chat amiably back and forth with each other and behave perfectly "normally." This seeming inconsistency can be resolved by looking at their first appearance in the film, one which, precisely because it is the first time the spectator encounters them, is privileged. As indicated in chapter two, Johan's experience of the dwarfs and his cross-dressing in their midst is distinctly nonthreatening; only when a representative of male hierarchy and power enters and exerts his authority does the boy experience the dwarfs as hostile. I would suggest that the dwarfs do not partake of male corruption precisely because they are marginalized by dominant male culture; they connote otherness and sexual ambiguity and yet are male. The dwarfs are for Bergman an embodiment of the nonthreatening other that is biologically but not culturally male.

Johan's position in this sexual landscape is pivotal, precisely because he is pre-pubescent and his sexuality still not fixed. That his quest, however, is a sexual one is apparent from the kinds of activities in which he engages and the objects with which he is associated. His prolonged concentration on the painting of the nymph and the satyr, his cross-dressing with the dwarfs, the toy six-shooter that he takes on his adventures, and his urinating in the hotel corridor as an act of rebellion against male authority all cohere to depict his development in the film as a sexual one.

Thus, the film emerges as a kind of initiation in which he examines gender alternatives and finds them wanting. While he clearly loves his mother, the physicality she evinces toward him suggests excess and suffocation: she wraps him in a curtain, rubs cream all over his body, and kisses him repeatedly and almost obsessively, at which point the boy pulls back from her. His development as a protagonist is linked to the rejection of the mother and the female body and to an increasing identification with Ester. The shot of the boy outside the room in which his mother and her lover are having a tryst associates him with Ester, who finds herself in the same position shortly thereafter. It further extends Ester's subsequent confrontation with her sister and her disapproval of Anna to Johan. Gradually, then, there is a convergence between Johan's consciousness of events and Ester's, a mergence of subjectivities that crosses the boundary between the self and the other and is further defined in terms of a rejection of both the male objectification of women and the female body itself represented in Anna. This association is furthered by the foreshortenings of both Johan and Ester; Anna is never foreshortened. This drastic angle appears to be a kind of visual metaphor for these characters' potential for insight into the ontological distortions of Bergman's world, a potential that devolves back upon their shared sexual ambiguity and frustrated subjectivity.

The film's impulse both to move beyond and to disavow gender is also evident in its representation of nonheterosexual desire. As Bordwell, Thompson, and Staiger have noted, the classical Hollywood cinema "almost invariably involves heterosexual Romantic love." In a sample of 100 films, Bordwell finds that ninety-five involve romance in at least one line of action, while eighty-five make it the principal line of action. The very depiction of potential lesbianism in film is subversive; thus, physical contact between women is an extraordinarily explosive issue in male-authored renderings of female relationships. And, while the prospect that emotional bonding with another woman could undermine her dependence upon the male is disturbing, the prospect of his being displaced sexually is an object of virtual horror to the male imagination.

Despite the subversive possibility of lesbian love relationships, however, depictions of them occur relatively frequently in female fellowships depicted by male authors, such depictions serving as a kind of male turn-on: lesbianism is degrading, an abomination in the sight of God the Father, and therefore pleasurably reinforces the male view of women as inferior. The only variant of lesbian love that seems morally acceptable to the male artist is that which serves to initiate a woman into sexuality, after which she discovers in the arms of a man "true" sexuality. As Brantome asserts, lesbianism is "merely the apprenticeship of the great business with men" (Todd, *Women's Friendship* 322) (such is the case with Anne's and Petra's frolicking on the bed in *Smiles of a Summer Night*). Or, as Mayne observes ("Women and Film" 91), the male imagination can dismiss the threat of lesbianism by associating it with childhood, by attributing it to a pre-adult level of development (as seems to be the case, again, in *Smiles of a Summer Night*). Too, the threat that female homosexuality constitutes to masculine culture can be minimized, as Irigaray argues, "if female homosexuality is regarded as merely an imitation of male behavior" (194). Thus, the alignment of lesbian desire with masculine/feminine, active/passive dichotomies undercuts its subversive potential. But, if not "recouped" in these various ways, it can function as a desire for another kind of representation not bounded by the kind of sexual hierarchy described in psychoanalytic theory. Nonheterosexual desire, as Wittig puts it, "is also the desire for something else that is not connoted. This desire is resistance to the norm" (114).

As noted, heterosexual desire as a function of both male hegemony and female biology is depicted as dark (such encounters occur in literally dark places and the male partner is dark in complexion and hair coloring) and degraded, an activity no longer capable of containing "meaning" or value. Against this empty heterosexual desire, Bergman posits Ester's "desire" for her sister Anna. While the relationship between the two sisters can certainly be subsumed into the categories masculine/feminine and, in some respects, Ester seems like a "butch" reinscription of male binaristic categories onto female sexuality, the designation of Ester as sexually ambiguous privileges an interpretation of this relationship as part of both the film's disruption and denaturalization of binaristic categories and its impulse to move beyond and to disavow gender. At the same time that Bergman's questioning of patriarchal structures leads him also to challenge the heterosexism that is the cornerstone of those structures, all sexuality is rendered culpable because of its complicity with the threatening body.

That there is a sexual tension between them is clear, and yet Ester's desire for her sister is not merely an inversion of male sexual desire. After telling Ester about where she slept with the waiter, Anna confesses that it was a lie, to which Ester responds, "It doesn't matter," an attitude that seems singularly unjealous in a potential lover. When Anna then tells her about having sex on the church floor, Ester responds with, "I understand." She concludes, "It torments me . . . because I feel so humiliated. You mustn't believe I'm jealous" (130), following which she kisses her sister slowly on the cheek and places her hand on her shoulder. In a woman otherwise so self-aware, there is no reason to disbelieve her on this point. And later after Anna rails at her sister, Ester rises and strokes her sister's hair, "her face. . . completely calm. Its petrified expression of pain has dissolved and been succeeded by an almost imperceptible smile. She looks at her sister, without superiority, sympathetically, with tenderness" (137). Her obvious love for Anna, her tenderness even in the face of Anna's vicious tirade, and her lack of jealousy all render her "desire" for her sister a very ambiguous proposition.

Too, Bergman never designates the desire between these women as specifically lesbian. While one might interpret this as evasion, a reluctance to name the unnameable, it might rather be seen, I think, as a representation of desire that disrupts gender categories in its attempt to disavow and transcend them, a view supported by the fact that Ester does not have a stable gendered identity. Ester articulates her desire as distinct from heterosexual desire, but also from homosexual desire, a desire for "something else not connoted," for a connection that transcends sexuality. This desire is similar to that between Aron and Ishmael in *Fanny and Alexander*. Both incestuous pairs seek a connection so intense that it is characterized as a blood relationship; the individuals suggest different aspects of a single "cosmic" self that seeks reintegration. In this sense they are reminiscent of Frey and Freya of the Scandinavian mythological tradition; originally one nongendered being, they have been split, and the incest that occurs between them is an expression not of perversity but of a longing for reunification and reintegration. Thus, through the incest motif, Bergman challenges the idea of fixed identity and foregrounds the social constructedness of the notion of the perverse. The most "perverse" sexuality in the film is that of the heterosexual couple in the theater. We can, then, read Ester's desire for her sister as a deconstruction of the whole concept of the perverse.

Bergom-Larsson's argument that "it seems as if the progression beyond the world of silence that the film seeks will occur through so-called spiritual humanistic values, a fellowship that seems to exclude sexuality as belonging to 'the powers'" (138) is in part correct; sexuality in this film has been demeaned by both male culture and the female body, but the movement beyond it occurs not through "humanistic values" but through radically alternative values and forms of discourse. Sexuality is here hopelessly compromised by its grounding in both patriarchal values and the body. Thus, Ester's desire functions both as that which is culturally other and as that which refuses that designation, a hope for the possibility of a deep, intense connection beyond social construction and beyond gender.

In this connection, Johan's relationship to his mother is also interesting. When Ester says softly to Johan, "We love mamma, you and I," he looks away and nods resignedly, suggesting that this love is a source of pain to him. The film seems to equate Ester's love for her sister with Johan's love for his mother, thereby removing both from the category of "normal" heterosexual desire and at the same time stressing the connection between "love" and the disavowal and erasure of the female body. If Ester's desire for Anna repre sents a longing for the reintegration of the self, then Johan's is an impulse that must be disavowed. Again Bergman's work charts a deep and thoroughgoing ambivalence to the mother and the female body.

Pertinent here is an argument advanced by Koskinen, who sees Ester's and Johan's desire for Anna as "analogous to the relationship of desire in which the spectator stands to the film fiction itself. . . . Anna becomes the sign itself of . . . 'fullness,' the fictive world the spectator tries to put together — a metaphor for the spectator's desire for meaning and wholeness. Anna is, so to speak, *the body of the fiction*" (115). While one might adduce this view to designate Ester's (homosexual) desire as spurious, as an attempt at appropriation like that of the cinema spectator, it could also be part of a larger argument in which *The Silence* is an attempt to represent a new kind of desire analogous to the new kind of filmic experience Bergman is attempting to create for his spectator, an experience that embodies a feminist disjunctive potential in its acknowledgment that the appropriation of the body is as morally reprehensible as it is ultimately impossible.

The impulse to move beyond gender in *The Silence* also surfaces linguistically. The very title of the film indicates the central role language issues play, and one of the most striking features of the introductory sequence is its almost complete lack of dialogue. The silence on the train contrasts with the linguistically uninterpretable shouting of the men in the city. Language, because it is a hierarchical system linked with patriarchal values and God's Word, is deeply suspect here (and throughout Bergman's work); when the patriarchy loses its authority, male language becomes senseless babble. Like certain feminist practices, Bergman's work rejects traditional modes of discourse and seeks to discover new expressive modalities less implicated in patriarchal ideologies. Again one can observe a similar ambivalence toward language on the part of male postmodernist culture of recent years, but the difference in these positions lies in the fact that, if language is highly negotiated for men, it seems all but impossible for women, as it does for Bergman after 1960.

Like such women writers as Barnes, Woolf, Duras, Wittig, Cixous, and Le Dantec, Bergman explores the "consequences of the loss of linguistic innocence in texts which inventively question the necessarily mediating status of language" (Gillman 22). Irigaray militates for a feminine language that operates outside the parameters of "an Aristotelian type of logic," for, as Audre Lorde put it, "the master's tools will never dismantle the master's house" (ctd. in Donovan, "Towards a Women's Poetics" 99). As Caroline Allen has shown in her study of Djuna Barnes, some feminist authors consistently express themselves in terms of negation as a way of saying "no" to patriarchal language (11). Other women artists tend toward a language of synonymy rather than antonymy, toward a language that is fundamentally nonoppositional, a style that is metaphoric and oblique like that so prominent in Bergman's practice. Thus, Kate Millett proposes that "the flowing verbal monologue or dialogue [is] a suitable form for feminist art" (Register 17), a proposal that receives support from Chodorow's theories of child psychology, wherein she contends that girls "fail to separate from their mothers because the mothers fail to separate from them with a resulting fluidity of boundary between the self and others" (Baym 52). The inclusion of a fluid, formless style within a feminist aesthetic has, however, been criticized by Elaine Showalter and Nina Baym on the basis that such a formulation tacitly affirms the masculine stereotypes of women as formless and incoherent. But Baym argues for another way in which fluid language is grounded in female experience: "There is one source for the idea of the *adult* woman's language as unbounded, polysemous, and the like — a residual memory of our mother in the days before we understood her language, that is, in the days before we had a language of our own" (55). Although such an argument is, of course, open to charges of biologism, the fact is that part of the experience of women's lives is their experience of their bodies and to ignore that truth is to effect an erasure and displacement of the female body every bit as effective as that which patriarchal ideology has historically practiced. Thus, while not unproblematic, Bergman's increasing use in films such as *The Silence, Persona, Hour of the Wolf,* and *Cries and Whispers* of a fluid, subjective style that incorporates interior monologue sequences can be seen as privileging a feminist experience of his texts.

Although by no means purely positive, language in *Winter Light* still retains some power — Tomas's final prayer serves to commit him to a stronger relationship with Märta — but in *The Silence* language initially seems completely nonfunctional. Bergman himself says, "[In *The Silence*] language has ceased to be a means of communication: they can't talk to each other" (Björkman *et al.* 183). In earlier Bergman, we heard about the silence of God; now we experience it. As Persson puts it:

> As a means of contact, as a tool for transmitting a feeling, [words] are most often helpless,. . . dark, foreign things, pragmatically useless . . . . As far as dialogue is concerned, *The Silence* entails something completely new in Bergman's production. Words are used very sparingly, often more for the sake of voice or intonation than of content . . . . Words are dangerous things. In simple circumstances they are unnecessary, in more complicated ones they easily become lies; therefore silence is preferable. (228–30)

Language is corrupt and women, while insightful of that corruption, are nonetheless victimized by it; they are silenced and silent. They and the film seek a language beyond gender. But the mastery of that language is finally denied women; it is achieved only by Bergman the artist and the boy protagonist who is identified as both male and nonmale.

Anna, we note, is associated with the hostility of language. In both of her extended monologues, she expresses hostility and even hatred toward her sister, shouting out her rage at the Father. Furthermore, she seldom speaks, making contact with the waiter in the bar without a word and telling him after sex how nice it is that they do not understand each other. She shouts at her linguistically preoccupied sister, "Can't you be quiet!" Anna's comparative silence is a strategy of resistance to male language, to its efforts to describe and circumscribe. By not speaking, by not communicating, she (like Elisabet in *Persona*) imagines that she can isolate herself from pain. But, because Anna is represented as almost pure corporeality, silence is also aligned with a repression of female subjectivity; the female body is silenced. While silence can be a strategy for women to resist the oppression of language, and much of the film charts precisely a resistance whereby meaning is transmitted through image rather than words, the film ultimately asserts that, even though language is contaminated and highly negotiated, the complete rejection of it, of communication itself, is not resistance but acquiescence.

Instead of resisting language, the sexually ambiguous Ester is complicit with it. A translator by profession, she is "someone whose life is dedicated to ensuring the diffusion of works of the creative mind across the silencing barriers of language" (Mosley 118). At the same time that it connects people and cultures, translating is a cerebral occupation gendered as male by dominant culture and, for Bergman, suspect. What speech occurs in the film is almost always ascribed to Ester; it is she who tries to communicate through language to Johan, to Anna, to the waiter, and to herself. Bergman's first shot of her in the opening sequence shows her with a sign written in the foreign language behind her, and it is to her that Johan turns to find out what the sign means. Like the window to which this sign is affixed, language is a kind of screen that separates and connects people, permeable and yet impermeable. The fact that the language spoken in this country is "foreign" and that the waiter and Ester still manage to communicate points to precisely this combination of permeability and impermeability. The "male" language she uses in her profession and her quest for meaning are designated as corrupt, while her efforts to use language to connect, to transgress boundaries are coded positively. Ester is sexually ambiguous and as such represents the possibility of a subjectivity that transcends gender. But, because she is biologically female and therefore, for Bergman, implicated in degraded sexuality, she can never attain the enunciating status that Johan, as a pregendered male (so to speak) can.

Music functions throughout *The Silence* as a kind of alternative language not compromised by hierarchical systems. The word "music" is the first word that Ester's and the waiter's languages share as cognates, and music presides over the one moment of fellowship all three family members share. While

Ester sits in her room, Anna in hers, and Johan in the doorway connecting
the two, Ester generously suggests that they try to leave the city as soon as
possible, and Anna indicates that she is concerned for her sister's health.
Anna, although she does not know what the music on the radio is (an igno-
rance that in the context of the film indicts her,) nonetheless admits that it is
"pretty," a statement that leads to a tentative peace and connection between
the two women; even the lighting is soft and gentle in this scene. But the
peaceful mood created by this language beyond gender is broken when Anna
stubs out her cigarette to leave for her assignation with the waiter. Female
sexuality, victimized though it may be by patriarchal value systems, destroys
the peace beyond gender. Bergman's binaristic representation of the two
women, then, dissolves into yet another essentialist doubling, for both Anna
and Ester, victimized by language and struggling to cope with it, represent
the failures of the patriarchal linguistic system and of their own bodies' relationship to meaning, a failing that can be overcome only by Bergman's fantasy of a pre-, nongendered realm that nonetheless is gendered as male.

The film's impulse toward nongender is also manifest in its use of voyeurism, of dominant cinema's notion of spectacle and woman as the object
of spectacle. *The Silence* conjoins issues of voyeurism and gazing in ways that
both disrupt and reinscribe the equation that constitutes a male viewing
subject and a female viewed object. Like Desirée in *Smiles of a Summer
Night*, the female protagonist Ester has a certain visual authority, but, when
she is viewing sexual scenes and objects, that authority seems pruriently voyeuristic. In many of the frequent shots from Ester's vantage point, she is
represented as spying on Anna, one of the most obvious instances of which
occurs in the scene when she goes to the room where Anna and the waiter
are having sex and, in a shot reminiscent of early film's use of voyeurism in
hotel corridors, listens by the keyhole and then crosses the threshold into the
room, the threshold that divides the subject from the object of the look.
Once inside, Ester is punished for her voyeurism when Anna upbraids and
humiliates her. As Doane suggests, "The woman's exercise of an active investigating gaze can only be simultaneous with her own victimization"
("The 'Woman's' Film" 72). But elsewhere in the film, too, Ester is seen
spying on Anna, watching her wash herself and later put on make-up before
she goes to the theater. And, on her return, the spectator sees her from Ester's perspective through a partially closed door. We see the dirt on the back
of her dress as the camera dollies in on her, probing, prying. Ester enters
Anna's bathroom, ascertains her sexual escapade, expresses her disapproval,
and departs. Both here and earlier, however, we note that the voyeur Ester
does not maintain the distance so critical to the viewer's pleasure; on the
contrary, both times she transgresses that distance by crossing thresholds, her

actions constituting a disruption of the boundary between viewer and viewed so central to male voyeuristic convention.

Interestingly, however, the view through a partially closed door is precisely the same composition in which the spectator viewed Ester moments before. Furthermore, Ester's voyeurism is associated with that of the spectator; while it may be sexually implicated, it also leads to a kind of connectedness, a movement across boundaries and into the space of the other. The connotations of prurient sexuality in Ester's (and the spectator's) voyeurism are further undercut by the fact that she is sexually ambiguous.

Ester's voyeurism is extensively identified with that of the spectator. The camera frequently positions us as voyeurs looking through half-closed doors and across head- and footboards. Even the camera movement is voyeuristic in its dollying and tracking shots after receding figures. Typical are first, the shot in which Anna leaves her room and walks away from us down the corridor to meet her lover, the camera following after her, and second, the shot shortly thereafter when she enters the room with her lover and the camera dollies after them as it continues its voyeuristic probing. After a cut to Johan at the door, the camera returns to Anna, who looks up straight into it with a defiant expression on her face. This instance of defamiliarization by returning the look coheres with two instances of her looking directly at the spectator through mirrored surfaces, to acknowledge and denaturalize the sexual quality of spectatorial voyeurism.

Thus, as in *Smiles of a Summer Night*, the voyeur is exposed and humiliated, but here that exposure extends to the cinema spectator. Voyeurism is further problematized by the fact that visual authority is ambiguously gendered in both Johan and Ester, who embody and transmit the film's redeeming values. Ester's voyeurism is differentiated from traditional male voyeurism in that she does not maintain the distance between observer and observed so essential for the pleasure of the voyeur. On the contrary, she repeatedly attempts to cross that space, to transgress the boundary between seer and seen. While reaffirming the female body as object of spectacle, the film acknowledges (and thus deconstructs) the alignment of the gaze with the masculine and flirts with the idea of a look that is sexually ambiguous if not androgynous, a gaze beyond gender. Such an interpretation is also reinforced extratextually by Bergman's increasing awareness of the ways in which all vision is sexually implicated, with his desire to achieve a less gendered mode of expression.

Tellingly, then, Anna, as the embodiment of body, is rarely shot looking at anything other than her own body, a fact that suggests both the limits of her authority and the genderedness of looking. One of the few occasions when Anna bears a significant gaze occurs when she picks up the waiter. The look she gives him (and that he returns) is powerful and sexual. But this gaze is problematic, as Kaplan points out:

> The so-called "loose" woman *can* gain a degree of subjectivity, . . . but only paradoxically, through manipulating the very position of erotic object conferred on her by patriarchy. Thus the control is bounded by the terms of the system that defines the woman as "loose," and her existence continues in the service of men (i.e. to depend on men economically through the selling of the self to them). (*Women and Film* 58-9)

Thus, Anna's subjectivity is limited by her "looseness." Her gaze is powerful only for expressing her own victimization and objectification. The film suggests, then, that gazing is coded for sexuality in our culture at the same time that, in Ester, it tries to deconstruct that coding through sexual ambiguity.

In the quest for a world beyond gender that deconstructs the boundaries between self and other, screening surfaces are prominent throughout *The Silence*. As Mayne has pointed out, film screens can be important metaphors for spectator/text relations, since they "are figures not only of spectacle . . . but [also] of the intersection of spectacle and narrative. For the screen is both surface and passageway, mirror and obstacle," and the cinematic viewing experience entails the "transgression of the boundary line separating two spheres" (*Woman at the Keyhole* 31). Metz has observed that the cinema is unlike the theater, where the stage and the audience, despite the boundaries that exist between them, constitute a single space: "[The] space of the film, represented by the screen, is utterly heterogeneous, it no longer communicates with that of the auditorium . . . . For the spectator the film unfolds in that simultaneously very close and definitively inaccessible 'elsewhere'" (64). Baudry, pointing to the other aspect of the film screen, sees it as a space of "regressive fantasies of fusion," "a return to a relative narcissism, and even more towards a mode of relating to reality which could be defined as enveloping and in which the separation between one's own body and the exterior world is not well defined" (56). Thus, Mayne argues that the screen has an ambivalent status insofar as it both positions and obscures simultaneously. Drawing on Stephen Heath, she notes:

> How the cinema "holds the subject" between "negativity and coherence, flow and image." [Heath] observes that the 'screen' in various Lacanian diagrams has a similar kind of ambivalence; locus of a potentially ludic relation between the subject and its imaginary captation, and the sign of the barrier — the slide — across the subject and object of desire. (*Woman at the Keyhole* 41)

Mayne then holds that "the screen bear[s] witness simultaneously to the necessity of the fiction of completeness and wholeness and to its impossibility" (41). An examination of the treatment of screens in *The Silence* as sites of enriching ambivalence can illuminate the complex issue of spectator/text relations in the film.

Although not nearly so prominent and overt as they will become in later films, screens of various kinds appear throughout *The Silence* and are of four types: black blank frames, windows, mirrors, and head- and footboards. The film begins with a listing of white credits on a black screen while an indeterminate ticking is heard on the soundtrack. This ticking sound and the credits call attention to the screen as a site of inscription, a barrier between the spectator and narrative, a threshold to be crossed. For, as Johnston points out, defamiliarization can serve a feminist function: "The work of the woman's discourse renders the narrative strange, subverting and dislocating it at the level of meaning" (*Dorothy Arzner* 6). This black screen reappears later in the film, after Anna and her lover enter their hotel room observed by Johan, and after the long take in which Ester, emerging from a confrontation with her sister in the same room, watches the dwarf troupe file slowly down the corridor. Between these two shots another black screen appears; Anna, hearing Ester outside the door, turns off the lamp and then, as Ester enters, suddenly turns it on again, revealing a tableau of passion that she has arranged specifically to hurt her sister. The dark screen created by the extinguishing of the lamp is linked with the other black screens as an image of boundary between subject and object and of sexuality. All these senses of the screen conjoin in the tableau that Anna illuminates for her sister's consumption. In all three cases, the black screen is associated with sexual desire. Like the black screens in *Persona*, these surfaces are images of opacity, of the difficulty of transgressing the threshold between self and other, at the same time that their association with sexuality designates the female body as impenetrable to the spectator's gaze, as a barrier to the world beyond gender that the film seeks.

The sense of the screen as both permeable and impermeable, transparent and opaque, is especially evident in Bergman's treatment of windows. An analysis of how windows are used to represent women's experience is also useful, since, as Doane points out, "The window is the interface between inside and outside, the feminine space of the family and reproduction and the masculine space of production. It facilitates a communication by means of the look between the two sexually differentiated spaces" ("The 'Woman's' Film" 72). The transgression of these sexually differentiated spaces is effected by both Ester and Johan. As the film opens, Johan awakens and rises directly into the foreground of our field of vision, facing the camera and thereby establishing his enunciating status in the film. In this extreme frontal close-up, he rubs his eyes and blocks the two women from the spectator's view, a further reinforcement of his function as mediating consciousness. After this direct confrontation with the viewer, Johan turns and walks deeper into the frame, where, on the opposite side of the train, he looks out, just as he had looked out "our" window a moment before. This action forces the spectator to realize that s/he was just now looking through a window at them, that the black impenetrable screen of the credit sequence has now been rendered invisible. The window functions, then, as an elaboration of the cinematic screen, transparent yet impenetrable, a screen that both invites and indicts the spectator as voyeur.

Windows both on the train and in the hotel further elaborate this metaphor of barrier and threshold. The baroque engraved design on two of the train windows demarcates these screens again as both permeable and impermeable, boundaries between the self and the other. They separate Johan (the film's privileged consciousness) from the women, and the window-screen is posited through the engraving (and the sign in the foreign language) as a site of potential but frustrated permeability. Subsequent reverse shots of Johan at a train window looking at the tanks and landscape position the spectator on both sides of the glass, alternately sharing the boy's visual field from a position behind his shoulder and situating him as the object of our vision. The fact that one of these shots shows the boy's hand pressed flat against the window surface (an image repeated in both *Persona* and *Fanny and Alexander*) reinforces the sense that these images concern the transgression of boundaries. The sequence concludes with a high-angle shot of Johan behind the window as his mother comes and stands behind him, the outline of the city that they are entering dimly reflected in the glass in front of their faces. Throughout this sequence, then, Bergman's use of windows stresses a fusion of spectator and spectacle. But the image of Johan together with his mother is also important insofar as the screen is a site of sexual inscription, and the film charts Johan's disavowal of the mother's body. By and large, Johan's windows, while referring to impermeability, are permeable. He and the spectator whom Bergman identifies with him are capable of transgressing the boundaries between the self and the other.

Window screens continue prominent once the family has arrived at the hotel. A high-angle shot from Johan's point of view of a city street, where men are bustling about noisily in the merciless sunshine, reinforces the notion of the window screen as a boundary at the same time that its transparency allows the intrusion of outer reality, of the other. The shot shortly hereafter when Ester looks out her window into the street below further supports the connection between Johan's pregendered identity and Ester's position of sexual ambiguity, a connection that is reaffirmed later when Ester and Johan are sharing a moment of connectedness in her room and the sound of a tank rumbling through the streets interrupts them. Cuts reveal Johan at the window, a point-of-view shot of the tank in the street, and a shot from outside the window of both Johan and Ester. This deployment of shots, while implicating the spectator as voyeur and aligning him/her with the hostility of the tank and the invasiveness of public male reality, also associates, through the reversal process, the spectatorial experience with the achieved intimacy behind the window. For, immediately after this shot, Johan and Ester establish a connection through a piece of theater, a Punch and Judy show that Johan performs for his aunt. The simultaneity of distance and closeness, the fusion of object and subject are associated with the window and also with the puppet show, a connection that defuses the obvious sexual threat from without. The transgression of boundaries is associated with both invasion and intimacy.

The tank and window images are also appropriate as a transition between this scene and the next with Anna and her lover in the hotel room, for both scenes address issues of sexuality, screens, and appropriation. Anna stands alone at a window, looking down into a yard where white-uniformed men carry buckets. The high-angle shot of the yard and a low-angle one of a patch of stark sky at the top of the air shaft impart a sense of vertigo to the subsequent alternating shots of Anna and the waiter on the bed. He is, we observe, paying attention to her bracelets rather than to her, an image that suggests that he completely objectifies her. Whereas the experience of the screen produces connectedness for Ester and Johan, it results only in objectification and appropriation for Anna. Both segments concern the transgression of boundaries, but Anna's objectification by the male and her grounding in the biological body prevent her from experiencing the more positive aspects of ambivalence embodied in the screen. The only other time she appears at a window occurs immediately after their arrival at the hotel, when Ester invites her to open a window and Anna refuses, rejecting an opportunity to transgress the boundary the window embodies.

Windows in *The Silence*, then, function ambiguously for both Ester and Johan, pointing to the ways in which both are vulnerable to appropriation and yet imbuing them with visual authority. For Anna, however, windows refer to opacity, to resistance to appropriation, and yet also to a sense of the body as imprisoning. Johan's and Ester's sexual ambiguity, an ambiguity projected onto the spectator by point-of-view shots, is reinforced by the ambivalence of the window screen, whereas Anna's confinement in the body prevents her from achieving this ambivalence.

Other screen surfaces in *The Silence* are, however, also galvanized to problematize these issues, supporting Mayne's observation that "the figure of the screen [can] emerge as the embodiment of ambivalence, as the site at which cinema both resists and gives support to the representation of female agency and desire" (*Woman at the Keyhole* 51). Mirrors figure prominently in this screen complex. Ester is associated with them twice: once we see her reflected in profile in a mirror as she tries to communicate with the waiter and once when the waiter hands her a mirror to help her comb her hair. On the latter occasion, after a few strokes of the comb, she absentmindedly puts the mirror down. In contrast Anna is repeatedly seen in the mirrors above the bathroom sink, over her bureau, and on the door of her wardrobe. We also see her on several occasions looking into a small hand mirror. In all these instances she is putting on make-up, arranging her hair, testing a dress, or in some other way speculizing the self and the body. Anna is engaged in her own objectification here, but, in objectifying her own desire, she also destroys it. By living through the body and allowing herself to be appropriated by the male, she cuts herself off from connection. While Ester's mirrors are associated with an attempt to cross boundaries and achieve connection, mirrors consistently point to Anna's objectification of the self, to the kind of narcissism that psychoanalytic criticism designates as characteristic of the prelinguistic, presymbolic, "imaginary" phase of child development. But on two occasions Bergman undercuts this simple equation. After awakening from her nap, Anna washes in the bathroom sink, looks up, and stares straight at the spectator who is positioned where the bathroom mirror is located. And later, when she is sitting in the cafe looking for a pick-up, an over-the-shoulder shot shows her looking into a hand mirror and engaging our gaze. These two instances of "returning the look" disrupt objectification and emphasize her potential as enunciator (if a very frustrated one), even as they posit the viewer as an "other" across or behind a screen. Ester's mirror imagery, then, concerns the transgression of the boundary between the self and the other, while Anna is associated with resistance to the penetration that the screen also embodies. In brief, Ester is associated with the energizing ambivalence of windows, and Anna, despite her two instances of "returning the look," more with the objectification and narcissism of mirrors. Ester's sexual ambiguity and Johan's position beyond gender allow them to cross boundaries and thresholds while Anna's confinement in the body and acquiescence to the male sexual order entrap her in sexual differentiation.

But some of the most interesting screens in the film are the constantly recurring head- and footboards on beds that connote the sexual nature of the image of the screen. The beds in Ester's and Anna's rooms have head- and footboards of different types: Ester's bed has vertical, tubular railings through which both air and light circulate while Anna's has a solid screen connected to a tubular frame with only several inches of space between the two. Ester's screen is, then, more "permeable" than Anna's. But the bed in which Anna and her waiter have sex also has vertical metal tubes like Ester's. Certainly this bedstead appears at a point in the film when Anna is at her most vulnerable, but it might also suggest that she too partakes of Ester's ontological despair, that her promiscuity and Ester's repression are both responses to the crisis of the body in male sexual ideology. Although permeable, these two screens are also imprisoning barriers both for the women behind them and for the spectator who looks through them. They are obstacles that problematize vision both intra- and extratextually.

That these bedstead screens function as images of boundary and of threshold to overcoming binary subject/object relations is apparent in recurring compositions in which two characters are separated by a head- or footboard, struggling to achieve contact with the person on the other side. Significantly, these images are paralleled by numerous shots in which the camera is positioned behind a head- or footboard focusing on either Anna or Ester in bed, thereby establishing a parallel between the boundary between these women and that between film and spectator; both are images of impermeability.

In this context, one instance of this imagery in the film is especially interesting. After shouting forth her revulsion at "erectile tissue and mucous," and implicating her huge, oppressive father, Ester succumbs to another attack, which is shot from behind her headboard. The barlike railings through which we see this and other shots make of this screen an imprisoning boundary associated with both the female body and the physical and emotional infirmity of the father and his sexual order.

While window screens generally associate Ester with permeability and Anna with impermeability, both women are implicated in the barrier effect of head- and footboard screens, their degraded sexuality finally preventing them from moving past the body into the authoritative subjectivity beyond gender. But Johan is not thus constrained. The shot that places him outside the door his mother and her lover have just entered is instructive. While the first shot of him watching them locates him at some distance, the second shows him right at their door and then cuts to the interior of the room. Such cutting would seem to imply that, although he does not literally see what is happening in the room, it is nonetheless within his field of vision; after all, the corridor shots up to this point in the film have reflected his point of view. His subjectivity is aligned with the crossing of thresholds. After seeing his mother and the waiter enter their room, Johan returns to the foot of Ester's bed. Confronting this boundary, he places his hands on top of the brass railing; despite the frightening sound of Ester's convulsive gasping, he comes around to the side of her bed to stand by her face, to acknowledge and connect with her. In this scene and others Johan, the film's pregendered, privileged subjectivity, is capable of transgressing the sexual boundary posed by the screen, is willing to connect with (and appropriate) the frightening reality of the other.

The final transgression of the screen boundary posed by head- and footboards takes place as the film draws to a close. After railing against "the monstrous powers" of sexuality and implicating the father in this monstrousness,

Ester draws a sheet over her face, as if welcoming death. But Johan refuses to allow her to die. A pan shows his progress past the footboard to the side of Ester's bed, a position like that of the child beside a bier in the old waiter's photographs. When he draws back the white sheet (another screenlike surface) from Ester's face, it seems almost like a reprieve from death. But, while the waiter's experience of death results only in the perpetual mourning of loss embodied in the photographs, Johan's exposure to Ester's death points to futurity and rebirth, to a new kind of subjectivity beyond gender, one that acknowledges loss but can create out of it the new order intimated in the last scene of the film.

Both the waiter's photographs and the picture Johan draws for Ester are visual representations that address the boundary/threshold metaphor. The photographs take as their subject events of which the boy and the spectator know nothing, an impossibility of knowledge exacerbated by the fact that the waiter and Johan do not share a language that might transgress this barrier. The compositions depict people posed self-consciously for the camera, a spectacle inscribed on a screening surface. But Johan's picture, while just as "unreadable" (it depicts a frowning monster with excessively long ears), is executed as a present for Ester. The photographs not only perpetuate loss, they also suggest that the waiter is trapped in a subject/object relationship with the world, while Johan's artistic practice represents a crossing of boundaries between subject and object, a crossing paralleled by the creation of the film itself. Alexander notes that this drawing

> and the Punch and Judy act are projections of his own feelings. They also record the world he sees about him. They symbolize the tanks and soldiers, the tension and cruelty between the sisters, and the general hostility and fear in his environment. To transform these feelings and observations into art, however, is not to translate them into bombs, is not to take them on as identity. (31)

This disturbing picture, then, may also refer to the film before us — while not "pretty," it is nonetheless an attempt at transgressing the boundaries posited by dominant culture, at moving toward a new allusive, less hierarchical practice.

Most of the screening surfaces in *The Silence*, then, are intratextual and refer to the characters' experience of the self/other dichotomy. But the aspect of spectator/text relations embodied in the images is implicit in the three black screens and will become a prominent feature of *Persona* and *Cries and Whispers*, in which Bergman extends his filmic practice to incorporate a treatment not only of the transgression of boundaries, but also of the notion of this transgression as appropriation both intra- and extradiegetically.

But the sense of space as both boundary and threshold also extends to the relations between interior spaces. *The Silence* represents the beginning of

Bergman's radical use of space that will culminate in films such as *Persona* and *Cries and Whispers*. Adjoining hotel rooms are photographed through each other, the other room separated by a doorway that is a threshold to the experience of the other. As Houston points out, such depth shots suggest that "though the rooms are continuous and can be seen as one, those who dwell in them are separate and apart, isolated in the space that could unite them" (118). These thresholds are, however, susceptible to transgression; the sexually ambiguous Ester attempts to cross these boundaries in a way that leads to connectedness and the destruction of binarism while the promiscuous Anna is associated with closing doors, rejecting transgression and connection. But, significantly, the last door-closing in the film is effected by the hotel waiter, who thus isolates Ester from her departing sister and nephew. His, rather than Anna's, closing the door foregrounds him as an estranging force; as a representative of the patriarchy's present absence, he erects barriers. His refusal to acknowledge loss (as represented in the photographs), specifically the loss of male cultural potency, aligns him with boundary and obstacle.

Not surprisingly, the spatial feature with which Johan is most frequently visually linked is the labyrinth of hotel corridors that he explores throughout the film. Throughout all these corridor scenes, both perspective and scale emphasize Johan's isolation and vulnerability, and we twice see him in long shot at the intersection of two corridors, standing in the center of a circle in the pattern of the carpet, a metaphor for the sexual crossroads at which he finds himself. It is out here that he meets men. He begins by playing hide-and-seek with some hotel workmen until, from a very sharp high angle, we see him take a toy gun and shoot the man repairing the chandelier, an action that reinforces the burden of the film as a kind of sexual drama of both initiation and repression. In an attempt to move beyond gender, he must both kill the father and, as we shall see, disavow the sexually threatening mother.

Both spatially and diegetically Johan is repeatedly designated as a mediator between his mother and his aunt. While the two women listen to Bach on the radio, Johan sits against the doorjamb between the two rooms. A moment later, he enters Ester's room to get some cigarettes for which his mother has asked and then takes them to her, clearly serving as a go-between. This scene is especially interesting in light of Claudine Hermann's comments on the female experience of time and space: "Masculine system has until now required women to assume material continuity — of daily life and the species — while men assume the function of discontinuity, discovery, change in all its forms, in essence, the superior, differentiating function" (ctd. in Mayne, *Woman at the Keyhole* 57). Johan, it would seem, is connected with both material continuity (his function as mediator and association with corridors linking spaces) and discontinuity (his various acts of discovery and his overall development in the film). His ambivalence in this regard is also the ambivalence of the film and of the filmmaker.

The conclusion of the film is dominated by the legacy of the sexually ambiguous Ester. The shot in which she is viewed writing "To Johan" locates her paper in exactly the same diagonal position in the frame as was occupied by the photographs the old waiter earlier showed to the boy; Ester has replaced the impotent male waiter, and her legacy of life and connectedness supersedes his legacy of repression and loss. While both the photographs and the letter are artifacts of culture, one pretends to be an accurate rendering of a "photographable" reality and is only partially permeable to meaning since the two viewers share no language, while the other, an oblique, allusive representation of a representation (or sign of a sign), renders a paradoxically more concrete reality (the words "kasi" and "hand") and is consequently more permeable to meaning. This allusive representation is furthermore analogous to Bergman's new filmic practice that strives for fluidity, suggestiveness, and connectedness rather than linearity and hierarchy.

After Johan throws himself on his aunt in a last embrace and his mother tears him away, Bergman cuts to a profile of Johan now on the train with a window in the background. A pan across the compartment shows Anna sitting on the bench opposite. This shot contrasts with the opening of the film, in which Johan first sat next to his mother, looking up at her adoringly, and then followed her when she moved over to the other bench; they are now separated — he has grown away from her in some important way. A pan back to Johan shows him taking the letter from his pocket, and then the film cuts to a close-up of the letter itself and Johan's hands holding it. As his mother comes into the frame, she asks to see what Ester has written to Johan, as if suspecting her sister of trying to set the boy against her. When she sees that it is only a few words of the foreign language, she hands it back to him indifferently, saying, "That was nice of her" (143). Anna then opens the window and bathes her face in the rain, still absorbed with the body, a sense of her that is underscored when, tired and disheveled, she caresses her face and neck. She looks down at her son, who returns her look coolly and distantly and then gazes down at the paper. The final shot of the film is a zoom-in close-up of Johan as he moves his lips while reading the words of Ester's letter.

The letter from Ester to Johan is, then, posited as central to the meaning of the film. Like many women, Ester lives in a silent world and writes in order to escape that silence. The letter is a private communication, a sign of intimacy and connection, of an attempt to transgress the boundary between the self and the other. It is what Roger Duchêne calls "a true letter . . . the spontaneous direct expression of lived reality written for the benefit of a privileged other" (ctd. in Hayes 205). Bergman too has emphasized how pivotal the letter is: "The important thing is that Ester sends a secret message to the boy. That's the important thing: the message he spells out to himself.... Ester in all her misery represents a distillation of something indestructibly human which the boy inherits from her" (Björkman *et al.* 183). The connection between the sexually ambiguous Ester and the pregendered Johan during their meal (that most important of social occasions in Bergman) points again to a movement beyond gender as the film's central focus.

But the letter is important also as a cultural artifact; while so much of Ester's life has been spent transmitting the culture of the (male) other, here she generates her own text, creates something all by herself. Her letter provides her with a way of expressing herself and is, as such, a protest against the silence to which male culture would consign her. But we notice that she does not compose a work of belles lettres, of "art," perhaps because, like so many women in male fiction, she is incapable of it. Despite her empowering sexual ambiguity and her association with connectedness and the transgression of the boundaries, she is still implicated in a corrupted sexual order that prevents her from achieving Johan's nongendered subjectivity. The fact that the letter is not a narrative, is instead simply a list of words in the foreign language and their translation into Swedish, indicates that, while language is ultimately affirmed, it is a different kind of language, oblique, fluid, devoid of hierarchy and of the false connections that narrative entails, a language beyond gender like that which the filmmaker seeks throughout the rest of his production.

The letter becomes then a kind of screen on which Ester's life experiences are written but which Johan can penetrate and appropriate. It furthermore becomes a screen that defines the space between his mother and himself, as does the water-streaked train window that she lowers in order to bathe her face in the rain. But, just as importantly, it motivates an exchange of looks between Johan and his mother that define her as trapped within the body and him as a "bearer of the look," with all that implies in terms of achieved subjectivity. Both the screen and the look he achieves are associated with Ester. Like her, he now looks disapprovingly at Anna. Of this realignment, Bergman says that Johan "starts seeing his mother a bit more objectively, but there's nothing inherently wrong in that. If he sees her clearly for the first time, it's because he sides with Ester" (Björkman *et al.* 188). Thus, his drama of initiation culminates in an alignment with sexual ambiguity and with maleness. His development entails a rejection of the mother and the female body and an embracing of an albeit radically different paternal force, in a trajectory that identifies the viewer with Johan's point of view. Thus, Johan's position outside of gender is, to a certain extent, compromised by the film's tendency to blame the mother. Ester's legacy to Johan linguistically, visually, and sexually is a connection that transcends gender by disavowing it.

Given the film's impulse to move beyond gender and its challenge to the assumptions underlying patriarchal culture (a culture that of course deeply informed both Bergman's childhood and the rest of his life) and that culture's appropriation of female experience and sexuality, given its radical treatment of the screen metaphor, of voyeurism, and of language, and its assertion of ambiguous sexuality, it is difficult to find this a pervasively misogynist film, as other feminist critics do. It represents gender and binarism as factors that prohibit connectedness and, through its valorization of this connectedness, subverts the notion of fixed subjectivity. At the same time, the movement beyond gender is predicated upon a view of the female body as inherently corrupt and is furthermore aligned with the (albeit pregendered) male who appropriates female experience in the development of his radically alternative subjectivity, just as the filmmaker himself appropriates female experience by projecting the failings of masculine culture onto female experience. In the present absence of the patriarchy, Bergman seeks to isolate meaning that is both gendered and nongendered. In short, the film is a testimony to the experience of a male director who is deeply ambivalent about the masculine. His cameo appearance as one of the soldiers into whose compartment Johan peeps also suggests this ambivalence. That he casts himself as a soldier, a participant in and contributor to the terrible war that impinges on the lives of his characters, might indicate an implicit awareness of his anomalous position as a male creator of a female reality and a perpetuator of a hostile male culture. Finally, *The Silence* seeks both mediation and discovery, both connectedness and differentiation, mergence and mastery.

# 6: *Persona:* The Deconstruction of Binarism and the False Mergence of Spectator and Spectacle

*Persona* (1966) occupies a singular position in film history, long acknowledged as one of the "great" films of the Western tradition. Michel Cournet considers it "a prodigy of the spirit, through which cinematic art, after seventy-five years . . . has felicitously found one of its promised forms" (ctd. in Sadoul). Simon acclaims it in an equally laudatory tone: "Experiment raised to the level of calm assurance, radical individualism bending tradition toward itself, modernism becoming classical before our very eyes" (215). The seminal nature of the film is also apparent in Bergman's statement that *Persona* is "Opus 1, the beginning of a new phase" (Oldin), "a breakthrough, a success that gave me the courage to keep on searching along unknown paths. For several reasons that film has become a more open matter" (*Images* 28). The film, then, is grounded in ideological collapse and the subsequent unraveling of traditional concepts of both subjectivity and the genderedness thereof, and of art. The experimentation and radicalism of which Simon speaks function as resistance to the norm, to the ideological systems and cultural values of Western society, and thus can serve as a locus for a potentially feminist experience. The film denaturalizes the dualism between self and other, spectator and spectacle, in both human and cinematic relations and then examines mergence both as an alternative to the male model of fixed (and gendered) subjectivity and as a fantasy (both intra- and extratextual) of a dissolution of the self/other dichotomy, a fantasy that entails both appropriation and violence.

Consistent with a view of *Persona* as embodying a certain feminist potential is the movement within the film from a series of stable oppositions to mergence, and then to deconstruction. "Breakdown . . . is both theme and form . . . it is experienced both by the characters and by the artist, the 'formal' collapse acting as a means of communicating the sensation of breakdown directly to the spectator" (Wood 145). But breakdown and collapse are not restricted to the characters within the narrative and the artist behind it; they are also manifest in the viewer's experience of that narrative. By subverting the spectator/text relations that have prevailed in dominant cinema for at least the last half-century, relations in which we believe that film gives us a voyeuristic access to unaltered reality, Bergman challenges traditional cinema and the dominant masculine ideology it historically serves. Images of permeability and impermeability, transgression, and containment abound and cohere finally in a deconstruction of these categories. As the film pro-

ceeds, dichotomy is superseded by dialectic and then by an explosion of dialectic. An examination of the introductory montage and its screening surfaces, of the two women protagonists and their (and the film's) experiences
of subjectivity, language, mergence, and difference, of spectator/text relations, and of space and other screening surfaces in the film suggests that
Bergman deconstructs first the stable oppositions between perceiver and perceived, representer and represented, and then the synthesis of these oppositions, to privilege a spectator experience that constitutes a challenge to
dominant cinematic practice. Working against the kind of suture and character identification that is at the heart of dominant cinema and that feminist
criticism finds so suspect, Bergman strives to create a "passionate detachment" in the viewer through a variety of distancing techniques. If Kristeva's
argument holds that "the ties of the avant-garde to the underground offer a
model for women to break through the limits of traditional (phallocentric)
language and forms" (ctd. in Kaplan 95), then Bergman's practice coincides
with the feminist project. For, as a criticism of dominant cultural practice,
*Persona* accords with her view that since "the category woman is even that
which does not fit into *being* . . . women's practice can only be negative, in
opposition to that which exists, to say that 'this is not it' and 'it is not yet'"
("Interview" 166). In *Persona* Bergman creates a film that opposes dominant
cinematic convention and seeks a new form of representation that is attuned
to complexity and difference and is more open to a meaning that is not
structured by the male symbolic order and that argues the simultaneous impossibility and necessity of discourse. *Persona*, then, foregrounds the dualism
and mergence of cinema and the ideology in which it is grounded. By constantly manipulating the spectator between positions of involvement and
distance, Bergman encourages the dispassionate involvement so productive
for the feminist enterprise. This vacillation works to undermine the artificial
naturalization of most dominant cinema as well as to resist the ideology behind that naturalization.

The very title of the film embodies these concerns. Bergman initially intended to call the film "Cinematograph," a clear allusion to the importance
in this work of a treatment of the nature of representation (the status of the
image, of the word, of action, of the film medium itself). Thus, both the
working title and the final title challenge the classical cinema that works toward making itself invisible, toward presenting itself as pure reality and
thereby erasing the subject/object dichotomy. The persona of the title may
refer to the mask actors wear in the Roman theater, the individual subject, or
the concepts of identity promulgated by the theories of Jung, Mauss,
Bataille, or existential phenomenological psychology and Gestalt therapy.
But these sundry senses of the term cohere in the title of Bergman's film, for
they all address a conflict, an essential tension between self and other, the

subject and culture, that within the film is presented as an issue of gender. By depicting this tension as one experienced specifically by women, Bergman problematizes the position of woman as other and acknowledges not only that this conflict is part and parcel of women's experience and that society inscribes upon them roles and identities essentially foreign to their subjecthood, but also the ways in which the position of women in dominant culture is informed by binarism.

The connection between self and other, spectatorship, subjectivity, and spectacle in *Persona* is immediately apparent as the film opens. It begins with a set of ostensibly disconnected images whose cumulative effect is so radical that Koskinen suggests that the prologue "constitutes a visual attack on the audience" (228). The film develops from a group of seemingly random and static images, to image clusters with common subjects, to a complex narrative line as images are projected into the language of narration. Differentiation is displaced by mergence. But, as Bergman reminds us at several points, the film can at any time be interrupted and broken down into its constituent parts. The film, then, alternately fragments and coheres in an effort to make the spectator conscious of the susceptibility of artificial constructs, both cultural and personal, to deconstruction.

The first shot of the film is one of a completely dark screen. This darkness is the director's canvas, upon which he arbitrarily imposes images and which suggests the depths of human experience that cinema strives to represent. At the same time that the dark screen functions like the curtain on a stage, separating self from other, spectator from spectacle, connoting the sharply delineated separateness of this film, an otherness subsequently experienced by the two women protagonists, it is also an extension of the darkness of the theater and as such embodies the mergence of spectator and spectacle that the film both exploits and deconstructs. Thus it also prefigures the film's deconstruction of the fantasy of mergence both intra- and extradiegetically.

The next shot shows two bright points of light, blurred, surrounded by black. As they swell and glow more brightly, it becomes clear that they are the ends of the carbon and tungsten rods in a 35-millimeter projector. They continue to grow until they merge and the whole frame is filled with an intense and brilliant light. Just as the rods merge to form energy, so too does differentiation give way to mergence in the two protagonists and between spectator and spectacle, instances of mergence susceptible to breakdown. The synthesis of these components also prefigures the tension between Alma and Elisabet insofar as both situations result in an intense fusion characterized by nondifferentiation. This image, then, speaks already to the mutability of identity — cinematic, psychological, and cultural. Thus, the white screens are also images of synthesis and represent, as do the black screens, the mergence of spectator and spectacle.

As the prologue continues, all black frames are quickly intercut with frames showing the mirror behind the tungsten rod in different positions. An image of the projector lens then alternates with both black and white screens, following which we see the "Start" that traditionally begins a reel of film, the black leader with the "Z" for focusing, and the numerals of the leader in descending order from 11 down to 3. These numerals are interspersed with black frames, and some of them are shown in extreme close-up, off to one side, or upside down, as though the camera were examining them from different angles. As the film proceeds, a shot of the rectangular gate of the projector with a strip of film running through it suddenly freezes. This freezing reinforces the idea that image and persona are inherently unstable, subject to breakdown and deconstruction, a point that is all the more ironic, since the film, while depicting stasis, continues to run through the projector at its usual pace.

This sequence of the film has several functions. By stressing the technical and mechanistic nature of his medium, the film encourages in the spectator a critical distance to the film, an awareness that s/he is observing a constructed artwork; we see the celluloid but look through it so that we see only the persona of the film. The image becomes the persona of the artwork as surely as celluloid and light are the film itself. But this persona is essentially constructed, as are the personae of the two women in the narrative. They are all constructs imposed upon a subject — the celluloid or the subjectivity of the individual women — by an external authority. And it is a recognition of the falseness of these constructs that the film privileges. By revealing the machine behind the illusion, the prologue also disrupts Bergman's authority as a narrating presence and therefore calls into question authority in general. The film presents the theme of dualism and its opposite, mergence, a concern that is central to the film.

If the first part of the prologue concentrates on the external apparatus upon which the film medium is dependent and foregrounds the relationship between spectator and spectacle, the second part continues this foregrounding by presenting a kind of ontology of film that exposes the conditions of the medium. A cartoon of a woman washing her hands appears, upside down (this image would, of course, appear right-side up after it had passed through the projector lens). The film posits, then, the female body and the speculization thereof as a historical condition of cinematic practice. From this image, Bergman cuts to a frame showing a reel of film turning very quickly followed by a shot of a child's hands rubbing each other, and a white screen. Juxtaposed with the cartoon, the hands seem "real," but are only real-seeming artifice. The contiguity of these images suggests not only that beside reality art is fundamentally false, but also that cinema speculizes the body, a speculization that demands deconstruction. The development from cartoon to photographed "reality" further emphasizes the increasing sophistication and transparency of the film medium. The following shot from Pathé continues this ontology of film, in which Kawin observes that the image is constructed "from scratch, historically, as well as ontologically 'beginning at the beginning'" (108). In the representation of this ontology, the film itself is posited as a site of authority at the same time that this authority, because it is a synthesis and subject therefore to deconstruction, is problematized.

A completely white screen separates the vaudeville segment from the next part of the introductory montage, which begins as a spider slowly takes shape in the frame. The next images are of a man's hand grasping sheep's wool, a zoom into a knife moving towards a sheep's eye, a hand in sheep entrails, and finally three shots of a human hand being held down while a nail is driven through it. All these shots are interspersed with blank white screens and can be read as allusions to other Bergman films (Blackwell 19–21) and/or as sadistic impulses that are designed to activate the spectator (Törnqvist 72). But they might also be seen as a kind of synthesis of religions, charting a development from the rapacious "spider God"(*Through a Glass Darkly*), through the ancient Greek custom of prophesying the future by reading the entrails of slaughtered animals, to, finally, the cruel and victimizing Christian God who is linked with crucifixion and human sacrifice (symbolism that challenges the Christian patriarch and appears in both *The Seventh Seal* and *Wild Strawberries*). The association between these random images and those depicting the cinema's conditions of production and its historical development suggests that these cultural institutions are grounded in a self-validating authority and are artificial constructs, products not of some immutable universal order but of specific cultural and historical circumstances.

These images of religious violence merge into images of harshness and sterility. The first shot in this series is of a flat, indeterminate brick wall (accompanied by church bells on the sound track, an aural reminder of the pernicious present absence of God), which dissolves into a shot of a landscape with trees. A spiked wrought- iron fence, located diagonally within the frame, cuts to a long shot of snow piled in front of the same fence. The initial surface blankness suggests a kind of impenetrability that gives way to the verticals of the trees, which are in turn replaced by the diagonals of the fence. These are then finally supplanted by the undulating contours of the snowbanks. As an extension of the earlier ontology of cinema and its association with the questionable authority of religion, the film now presents an ontology of form: from two-dimensional surface, to single-axis verticals, to diagonals, to the three dimensions of the snowbank. Thus, the screen surface, both boundary and threshold, represents a three-dimensionality that seems to merge with the three-dimensional space of the spectator in the theater at the same time that it remains pure surface. Formally as well, the film becomes increasingly sophisticated. As Kawin points out:

> The sophistication of these fragments, then, has grown to include not only the sequential cutting . . . and such optical devices as the fade-in on the spider, but now both montage and live sound. Taken as a whole, the opening sequence is, of course, itself a montage, but it is important to notice that a grammar of film techniques is maturing — on an *interior* level — from fragment to fragment. (110)

This sophistication process constantly reminds the spectator of the status of the filmic image as both synthesis and persona. This development highlights the "constructedness" of that persona, its false authority, and thus its susceptibility to breakdown and deconstruction. The film's movement toward the coherence and mergence of narrativity and its constant reference to the arbitrary nature of the constructed image, of the persona, and the false authority behind them are linked with the individual's attempt to merge with the other, to effect an erasure of the self/other dichotomy, at the same time that both these activities are compromised by their attempt to "interpret" and thus appropriate the subject. But this mergence is not only morally suspect, it is also ultimately impossible because the personae that constitute subjectivity, cultural and psychological, are themselves false constructs, syntheses prone to deconstruction.

The shot of a snowbank in front of a fence is followed by an extreme close-up of the mouth, chin, and nose of a corpse in profile. It is backlit with a translucent light that imparts a surreal effect to the image. This image looks less like a human face than a landscape, a fact that links it with the preceding segment. A series of related shots follow, close-ups of the heads, faces, hands, and feet of what appear to be dead people until an upside-down shot of an apparently dead woman's face cuts to a shot of her with her eyes suddenly wide open. These images, like similar images in *The Silence*, fragment the human body and have a potentially fetishistic effect; but the eye-opening shot suggests the impossibility of the containment for which fetishism strives, and the drastic angles foster both uncertainty about and critical distance to the onscreen images.

The final section of the introductory montage depicts a young boy whom we see in profile lying on what looks like a bier. The sound of a telephone ringing seems to waken him and he sits up. As the boy awakes, the space around him begins to take on form and shape. He turns toward the camera but does not acknowledge it, instead focusing on something below frame right. Putting on his glasses, he picks up a book, *The Hero of Our Times*, and begins to read. The preoccupation with faulty vision is one that recurs throughout *Persona* and speaks to the film's concern with issues of specularity. Alma dons sunglasses after the eruption of violence in her relationship with Elisabet, and the actress's husband also wears them. The equation between Alma and these two males, then, strengthens the impression of Alma's attraction (sexual and otherwise) to Elisabet. At the same time that the boy's eyewear improves his vision, the sunglasses allow Alma and Vogler to look out without the other being able to look in and thus function as another screening surface, linking voyeurism and gazing with both sexuality and the (im)permeable boundaries of the subject-object dualism.

The boy in the prologue is the same actor who played Johan in *The Silence* (and they even read the same book). In both films he is as an object of identification for both the spectator and the director in a search for a meaning that transcends gender, but here that moment occurs less for purposes of appropriation and disavowal than in order to arrive at a more nuanced understanding of subjectivity, gender, and spectacle.

When eerie electronic music stops on the soundtrack, the boy looks around him, sits up, and stares directly into the camera, his hand reaching towards it and blocking out part of the image. He then moves his hand back and forth across the lens as the camera reverses so that it now is behind the boy, who is in exactly the same seated position on his bed, his hand still outstretched. He is now reaching toward a large, indistinct image, a strange white screen on which gradually appears an ambiguous image that appears to be the rear-projected face of a woman, against which the boy is silhouetted. He seems to be touching a surface, a surface analogous to the film's two-dimensional screen surface. The image does not respond to the boy's touch and appears to be beneath the surface he is touching; it disappears for a moment and becomes all white, but the boy keeps touching it as if to coax it back. The face reappears, and, as the boy traces its features, it alternates nebulously between images of Bibi Andersson or Alma and of Liv Ullmann or Elisabet — we do not know whether they are represented as characters or as the actresses who will assume these roles. The last image cuts to a medium close-up of the boy looking directly into the camera and then cuts to the title *Persona*.

The place of this boy within the narrative is, I suspect, deliberately obscure. Kawin sees him as Bergman, "dizzy and bedridden, nagged by associates and afraid that he [will] never be able to work again" (111). Simon too maintains that the boy "must surely be an image of Bergman himself, a hero of our time, forbidden the luxury of crawling back into the womb of non-existence" (238). But his relationship to the female image(s) also suggests that he might be either Elisabet's son or Alma's aborted fetus, or an amalgamation of the two. Lucy Fischer argues that he "seems the *implied* protagonist of the narrative, the central consciousness through which the drama is formulated. It is his Oedipal view of women that we must witness, his complaints that we must hear. In this sense, Alma and Elisabet (as women) are only the 'pseudocenters' of the filmic discourse, despite their omnipresence on camera" (77). But the reverse between the boy's reaching out to us and then reaching to a screen could support an interpretation of him not only as an embodiment of the director's and the spectator's presence in the film, but also as a foregrounding of the spectator's attempt to "read" and appropriate the experience of the elusive protagonists. I would suggest, however, that all these sundry interpretations cohere in a way that sustains the film's concern with both the deconstruction of mergence and the mutability of identity, gender, and spectacle. This argument for cohesion is supported by the segment's extradiegetic mergence in the image of the women on the screen. The undulating, almost imperceptible shifting between the two faces and the constant presence of the boy come to be firmly entwined in the spectator's consciousness and to merge into a kind of collective unity, foreshadowing the merging of consciousness that occurs between Alma and Elisabet and between spectator and spectacle. While the film may posit this boy as Baudry's archetypal spectator, as one who "expresses an infantile longing for symbiosis, 'for the world of the imaginary'" (Fischer 77), it also problematizes and denaturalizes that impulse.

The reverse shot is pivotal to this segment. It destroys the illusion of the film as reality because the boy's reality intrudes on the spectator when he tries to reach out and touch us. It privileges a self-awareness that is fundamental to an understanding of this complex film. The boundary between the boy and the image is the boundary between the spectator and filmic events. We are confronted with the reality of the film as film, of the characters as actors, reminded of our position as voyeurs on the narrative, and prompted to consider how all this implicates us. Interestingly, this is the only male gaze in the film; by and large voyeurism occurs between two women. While this might be read as an instance of male disavowal, the fact that the female gazes are bracketed by instances of males gazing at females (the boy with the screen and the camera crew at the end of the film) would seem to indicate that voyeurism itself is an aspect of male hegemony, and the false mergence of both is deconstructed.

The image of *Persona* itself is equated with both the surface the boy touches when he reaches toward us and that of the women's images. This vacillating screen promises something behind the screen, a reality that can be penetrated at the same time that the inability of the boy to move beyond the surface demonstrates its essential impermeability. There is a kind of threshold between film and its audience, a membrane that is only partially permeable, the complete mergence between self and other false. The gender aspect of this screen is obvious, for the film, as Mayne points out, exhibits a "fascination . . . with the female body as both image and screen" (43). Like the shot of Johan in *The Silence* with his hand against a transparent screen, this image not only addresses the attempt to transgress the boundaries embodied in the screen between self and other and the mergence between the two, but also designates those boundaries as specifically gendered ones. The face on the screen is furthermore both a duality and a unity, corresponding to the duality and unity of the two points of light that began the film. The film and its screen are again equated with both separateness and mergence.

The credits appear on the screen accompanied by wooden bangs, electronic music, and sharp tones from a xylophone. Intercut with these noises and the credits are kinetic images of the characters in the film and shots of different subjects — a cut from the Pathé fragment, the wooded winterscape from earlier, a pair of lips shown sideways, a monk immolating himself, rocks on a seashore, and a picture of what appears to be dense barren branches on a pale grey background. We notice, however, that the title cards are on the screen long enough for us to process them, while many of the interposed images are of such brief duration as to be "unreadable." The credit sequence functions, then, as a transition between the seeming "impermeability" of the random images of the prologue and the "permeability" of the narrative with its false mergence of spectator and spectacle.

All-white frames follow, and a line develops along the bottom of the frame, which slowly forms itself into a rectangle — pure form. A door materializes out of the whiteness. Then slowly the door opens, and Alma walks through it; the story begins. Differentiation gives way to mergence, both intra- and extradiegetically, but, because this mergence is a false construct, it is essentially unstable and susceptible to breakdown. The creation of narrative is then equated with the emergence of Alma as spectacle, as a body to be read, interpreted, and appropriated by the spectator, at the same time that this spectacle, precisely because it is constructed as an image of false mergence, can be deconstructed.

As indicated, screens prominently "embody" the spectator's complex relationship to this film in particular and film in general; throughout *Persona* they function as both a frame of vision and as barriers that resist penetration. The black and white screens are, however, not restricted to the film's specifically and overtly self-conscious moments. After the introductory montage, white screens appear on four more occasions: when the celluloid seems to crack and burn two-thirds of the way into the film; when an extreme close-up of Elisabet fades to a white screen after Alma makes love to Elisabet's husband and shouts out how cold and indifferent she is; when the composite picture of the two women as one face fades to white; and when, after Alma coaxes Elisabet to say "Nothing," the screen fades first to a shot of Elisabet stroking back Alma's hair and then again to a white screen. The white screens occur, then, primarily at the beginning, middle, and end of the film in conjunction with moments of filmic self-consciousness or blatantly "fantastic" sequences, as images of the deconstruction of the fantasy of mergence. Because they are blank, these screens emphasize the contradictory nature of the cinematic experience. These "white, innocent, transparent [and] image-less" (*Images* 55) screens, themselves syntheses of spectator and spectacle, are associated with the film's subjectivity and with impenetrability and interject a distancing effect, privileging an insight into the separateness of self and other, spectator and spectacle. But, tellingly, all these white screens are preceded by a repression of emotion and desire — Alma's repressed anger toward Elisabet for her betrayal, Elisabet's indifference to Alma's pain and adultery with Vogler, Alma's cold analysis and judgment of Elisabet's behavior in the repeated monologue, and Alma's attempt to control Elisabet's voice and Elisabet's subsequent impassivity in her utterance. These screens are associated, then, with a repression of emotion and the body, with control and disavowal; they are linked with the luminous white light of the film, generated in the prologue by the two arc lights and suggestive of spectator/spectacle mergence, images of a dispassionate, controlling authority that we might designate as that body-which-is-not-one, as nonbody.

The black screens are equally prominent. From the first shot in the film, through the prologue and the narrative, they recur as contrasts with the white screens. The black screen appears when Alma, disturbed by her first encounter with Elisabet, turns the light on and off in her room and rubs cream on her body; when she cries out, after confessing the beach orgy and subsequent abortion, "It doesn't make sense . . . . How can one be? . . . How can one one and the same person [*sic.*]" (57); after the first occasion of the fantasy (?) image of Elisabet stroking back Alma's hair; and after Alma has torn Elisabet away from sucking her blood. The black screens, then, are also images of the deconstruction of false mergence, of a resistance to mergence and the appropriation and violence it entails. But they are all preceded by allusions to the female body and its frustrated desires — Alma's caressing her body to assuage her agitation about her first meeting with Elisabet, the memory of the orgy, the recounting of it, and her physical appropriation by Elisabet, an appropriation rendered in metaphors of vampirism. The black screens, in contrast to the white ones that denote noncorporeal subjectivity, are linked to the female body, its desires and its vulnerability to appropriation and violence. It is significant that the image of Elisabet brushing back Alma's hair after the orgy narration should fade into black while the same image after the "Nothing" sequence dissolves into white. Both images deconstruct the fantasy of mergence, but the former is imbued with a sexual tension carried over from the orgy narration while the latter suggests an attempt to control desire, to assert the mind over the body. While both screens deconstruct the fantasy of mergence, the white screens connote mind and pure surface; the black ones, themselves a mergence of the depth of the film and the darkness of the theater, connote body and pure depth, a false dualism the synthesis of which is also posited as false, susceptible to deconstruction, just as the mergence of black and white that constitutes the film's images is also susceptible to deconstruction into its component parts.

As the screen is a metaphor for the female body, Bergman tacitly challenges the sexual ideology of dominant film practice, which positions female experience as either pure surface, on which male culture inscribes itself and its desires, or pure depth, the "dark continent," the mystery to be penetrated and mastered. In foregrounding the tension between the two-dimensional surface of film (equatable in dominant cinema with the female body) and the three-dimensional depth it feigns (the being behind and inside that body), Bergman points to the ways in which film positions the female body and the spectator. *Persona* consistently foregrounds and subverts both this dualism and the mergence of its poles. The screen becomes simultaneously a site of sexual inscription and an acknowledgment of the impossibility of that inscription.

The sense of spectacle both as the separation between the self and the other, the male subject and the female object, and as a fantasy of mergence that is deconstructed is both implicit and explicit in this film written and directed by a male but in which men are severely marginalized, displaced by two women who resist the attempts of society, of the director, and of cinema itself to position them as objects. The tension between woman as subject and woman as object, as both spectator and spectacle, is central to *Persona*, as it subversively investigates the roles, masks, and dichotomies that inform women's lives and create their personae, personae that are themselves instances of false mergence between body and mind, self and other. The film goes on not only to examine the dissolution of those personae, but also to deconstruct the false mergence of them. In search of authentic subjectivity, these two women negotiate the subject/object dichotomy in a way that illuminates issues of both authority and spectatorship. By depicting the search for authenticity as one undertaken by women, the film also rejects the notion of female specificity, the idea that women can be confined within gender.

One of the clearest ways in which these two women challenge masculine culture's definition of what it is to be a woman is their recognition of the emptiness of the roles, the false selves they have to adopt in that culture, a recognition that has an obvious feminist import as it privileges a similar recognition in the spectator. Both the women protagonists, then, are represented as confined within false personae that are themselves instances of false mergence between mind and body, self and culture.

The personae that have circumscribed Elisabet's life are primarily those of actress, mother, and wife. The doctor points out that her embracing of muteness is a rejection of these roles. Significantly, the males in the film, her

husband and son (through his father), try persistently to undermine her
muteness so that she will resume those roles — witness the husband's enclosing in his pleading letter a picture of the son, presumably a ploy (however
unconscious) to induce guilt in Elisabet for neglecting her pitiable little boy.
Men, then, are depicted as attempting to subvert this woman's quest for
authenticity.

It is, of course, not happenstance that Elisabet is an actress. Her profession underscores her connection with the self/other, spectator/spectacle dichotomy, for, as Haskell points out, "In one sense, the actress merely
extends the role-playing dimension of women, emphasizing what she already
is" (*From Reverence to Rape* 243). A woman who seeks to merge the dichotomized roles foisted upon her by society is, as Irigaray describes it,
caught up in the "masquerade of femininity" (84). The extreme theatrical
make-up Elisabet wears as the film flashes back to a shot of her onstage is a
grotesque and specifically feminine mask that renders her an object of spectacle. As Johnston has pointed out, "The star system as a whole depends on
the fetishization of women . . . . [It establishes] the star as the focus for false
and alienating dreams . . . . What the star system does indicate is the collective fantasy of phallocentrism" ("Women's Cinema" 136). She is clearly depicted as a kind of sexual icon, a body on which male culture inscribes its
narrative, at the same time that the repeated instances of her confronting the
spectator's look imparts to her a powerful female gaze. It is interesting, then,
that Elisabet as an actress and as such an object of male fetishization is consistently associated with voyeurism. For instance, during the orgy monologue
Elisabet lies staring at Alma, voyeuristically objectifying her, the sexual implications of which are apparent in Bergman's observation: "If you look at Liv's
face, you'll see that all the time it's swelling. It's fascinating — her lips get
bigger, her eyes darker, the whole woman is transformed into a sort of
greed . . . . Equally important [as Bibi's tale], equally important erotically in
that scene, is the woman who listens to her; the receiver, she is bombarded
and stimulated" (Björkman *et al.* 208). Elisabet lies on the bed, listening to
this story "as if absorbing the narrated sexual experiences into her own body"
(Simon 274). Just as she has been consumed and appropriated by male culture and its voyeuristic mechanisms, so too does she vampirize and appropriate Alma, simply stepping into a male position of power, deluded into
thinking that she can control this voyeurism and appropriation.

But her work as an actress playing the role of Electra, the doctor tells us,
was not what broke Elisabet; on the contrary, it helped her to go on precisely
because it was such a blatant bit of role-playing, one that did not pretend to
be reality as did the other roles of her life. The self/other, spectator/spec-
tacle dichotomy was secure; only in life does it become problematic for her.

The personae projected onto her by her family, however, pretended toward reality and were therefore unbearable.

Elisabet's rejection of these roles takes the form of a self-imposed mute-ness. When we first encounter her, she has been hospitalized for her refusal to speak, an indication that society deems her actions to be those of an ill woman and defines the rejection of otherness that is at the heart of her muteness as abnormal and somehow "sick." But, in contrast to the many classical Hollywood films that depict an ill woman nursed back to health and to her "proper" role in society and the family by an omniscient male doctor, she is being cared for by a doctor who is a woman, one who, although rather self-satisfiedly smug, clearly understands her situation. Thus, *Persona* seems to challenge male convention. While we might see Elisabet's condition as part of dominant cinema's "almost obsessive association of the female pro-tagonist with a deviation from some norm of mental stability or health, re-sulting in the recurrent investigation of psychical mechanisms frequently linked with the 'feminine condition' — masochism, hysteria, neurosis, para-noia" ("The 'Woman's' Film" 69), Elisabet's and Alma's crises are linked less to their bodies than to their culture and the "human condition." The doc-tor's diagnosis of Elisabet is extremely informative:

> The hopeless dream of *being*. Not seeming but being. And at the same time the abyss between what you are for others and what you are for your-self . . . the continual burning need to be unmasked. Every tone of voice a lie, an act of treason . . . . The role of wife, the role of friend, the roles of mother and mistress, which is worst? . . . Keeping all the pieces together with an iron hand and getting them to fit? Where did it break? Where did you fail? Was it the role of mother that finally did it? It certainly wasn't your role as Electra. That gave you a rest . . . . She was an excuse for the more perfunctory performances you gave in your other roles, your "real-life" roles. But when *Electra* was finished, you had nothing left to hide behind, nothing to keep you going. No excuses. And so you were left with your demand for truth and your disgust. Kill yourself? No — too nasty, not to be done. But you could be immobile. You can keep quiet. Then at least you're not lying. You can cut yourself off, close yourself in. Then you don't have to play a part, put on a face, make false gestures. Or so you think. But reality plays tricks on you. Your hiding place isn't sufficiently water-tight. Life starts seeping in everywhere . . . . Elisabet, I understand that you're keeping quiet . . . . I understand it and admire you for it, I think you should keep playing this part until you've lost interest in it. When you have finished playing this part, you can drop it like you drop your other parts. (42)

The diagnosis the doctor provides is especially significant not only because she pronounces it in a coolly objective, authoritative tone, but also because, as Treichler has pointed out, "diagnosis [can be used] as a metaphor for the voice of medicine or science that speaks to define women's condition. Diagnosis is powerful and public; representing institutional authority . . . . It is a male voice that privileges the rational, the practical, the observable" (65). That this authority belongs to a female character and is furthermore used to indict the cultural confinement of women indicates but one of the ways in which this film challenges dominant male discourse.

But Elisabet's search for pure "being" is also analogous to the filmmaking process; Kawin observes, "Elisabet's search for 'being' is comparable to a photograph's attempt to become unfiltered, undefined light — as it is comparable to the artist's desire to be profound, and the protestor's insistence on perfect virtue" (120). Both Elisabet and the film strive for a dispassionate, unmediated subjectivity beyond the body. Her rejection of the otherness of role-playing, of the false mergence of personae, of the speculization of her body that her profession encourages, is linked to the film's attempt at authenticity, even as both can only intimate that subjectivity because the subjectivity of nonbody is not so much "pure" as a site of the binarisms and mergences of dominant culture.

Elisabet's strategy is especially interesting in the context of dominant cinema's treatment of muteness in women (*Shock, Possessed, Johnny Belinda*, and *The Spiral Staircase* to wit), in which the female voice is effectively repressed. But muteness in *Persona* is not repression but a strategy of resisting domination. Whereas muteness could serve to discount the woman as subject, in the larger context of the film Alma's repeated monologue and the female doctor's verbal diagnosis impart a female voice to the female body. Thus, silence is used in *Persona* in a way that violates cinematic convention, as an aspect of a search for authentic subjectivity. But the doctor makes it clear that the muteness is also another role that Elisabet ultimately will cast aside, for language is both impossible and necessary. Muteness is an attempt at dispassion, noninvolvement, like the film's striving for the "pure" luminous light of a subjectivity beyond the body. As Kawin points out, Elisabet's muteness can be equated with the white screens: "The nearest the mindscreen can come to confronting itself . . . is to reduce itself to white: the visual equivalent of perfect, articulate silence" (126). Both the white screens and Elisabet's muteness connote the body-which-is-not-one and subvert dominant cinema's use of both spectacle and sound to appropriate and contain the female.

But silence is both a rejection of male discourse and a reification of the gender dichotomy: both a protest against an ideologically corrupted language and a surrendering of language and its power — a resistance and an acquiescence to the male symbolic order. This understanding of muteness itself as a role, a relinquishing of authenticity, accounts for the cinematic equation between Elisabet and the carved wooden statue of a woman outside the summerhouse. This statue appears twice: when Alma, frustrated over her inability to extract speech from Elisabet, begins to scream at the statue in the foreground and when, at the end of the film, a shot of Alma departing the house lingers on a close-up of the statue's face and then cuts to a close-up of Elisabet in her Electra make-up. Silence is death and language is, again, both impossible and necessary.

Elisabet's decision to remain mute is based on a fundamental recognition of the inability of language accurately to reflect subjectivity, "being." The gender implications of this decision are manifest in the fact that it is two males who are most pointedly excluded from her search for being, while she remains in touch, however marginally, with both her female psychiatrist and Alma. Both the hackneyed language used by Elisabet's husband in his attempt to reclaim his wife and Alma's growing linguistic frustrations demonstrate the bankruptcy of this hierarchical mode. Language in *Persona* is, as Sontag observes, "an instrument of fraud and cruelty . . . of unmasking . . . of self-revelation . . . of art and artifice. *Persona* demonstrates the lack of an appropriate language, a language that is genuinely full. All that remains is a language of lacunae, appropriate to a narrative strung along a set of gaps in the 'explanation'" ("Styles" 146). As Alma's mergence with Elisabet is being deconstructed by its inherent violence and appropriation, she says, "When it should happen. It didn't as a failure. Yourself where you are, but I ought to do so. Not anything, not no. The collected advises others. A desperate perhaps. Take, yes, but what is nearest. It's called what. No no no no no. Us, we, me, I, no. Incomprehensible pain, throw" (93), a speech that reveals the inadequacy of language for accurate expression, an inadequacy linked with the collective judgments of the other and with the subject-object dichotomy. Bergman's insistence that this linguistic failure "is not a matter of psychology" (Samuels 189) is important; while one might argue that he is simply associating woman with incoherence, reinscribing the view that the world of logic and causality is male and the cognitive mode of women is irrationality and nonlogic, that formless utterance reflects formless mind, such an argument founders on the insistence that this incoherence is based not in Alma's psychology but rather in language's cultural implication in meaninglessness.

As Alma increasingly comes to feel merged with Elisabet, that fusion is expressed as an eradication of certain linguistic features associated with gender. When she cries out after her orgy confession, "Can one one and the same person" (57), and when she begs Elisabet to forgive her for the glass shard incident, she cries out, "You won't forgive me because you're proud! You won't condescend! I won't — I won't!" (81), her speech effects a displacement of the subject/object dichotomy on which language is constructed. Too, when Alma is trying to separate herself from Elisabet, trying to reestablish the self/other dichotomy ("I'll never be like you, never. I change all the time. You can do with me as you will. But you still won't change me"), subject-verb agreement returns to her speech but is expressively ineffective, and the nurse begins hitting and pounding a table in frustration. On the radio Alma hears, "Cannot speak, not listen, not understand, on the whole," which contrasts with the radio earlier in the film that produced only clichéd, melodramatic declarations of heterosexual love, indicating that language itself "cannot speak, not listen, not understand" and emphasizing Alma's breakdown as symptomatic of a larger cultural ideological breakdown. Both cinematic and verbal discourse are binary in structure and yet are predicated upon a false mergence, the illusion of permeability and coherence, the dissolution of the subject/object dichotomy.

This same language issue appears in the "mindscreen" part of the film, when Alma shouts, "Defend nothing. Cut a light. A sort of another. Warning and without times. Uncalculated." The unconventional use of subjects and verbs is again significant; the coordination of these two parts of speech is one of the basic ordering (hierarchical) elements of language, those elements that consequently are most gender-implicated. But this statement is also interesting insofar as it can be read to refer to film in general and *Persona* in particular. The camera "cuts a light," refracting it into a spectrum of images. Film itself is "a sort of another," embodying false dualism and mergence. *Persona* is, in some sense, a "warning" about dualism, mergence, subjectivity, and specularity, about conventional categories of experience and expression. And the film occurs both inside and outside time, insofar as it is a temporal artifact of specific duration for the audience, and yet the spectator feels that "real," outside-the-theater time is suspended during the showing. Finally, ironically, the images before us can seem "uncalculated," but are of course carefully constructed, the mergence they "embody" false.

The representation of the dualism and false mergence of cinematic discourse is also apparent in the "breaking" in the middle of the film. As Alma waits for Elisabet to step on the glass, suddenly the film skips, cracks, breaks, and burns. Simon argues that it is as though the intensity of the emotional content were too much for the film to bear (292), thus establishing a parallel in terms of inadequacy between verbal and cinematic representation. The deconstruction of discourse here also surfaces in the strange noises on the soundtrack that are actually speech (the doctor's query to Alma, "What is your first impression?") recorded backward (as was first observed by Peter Ohlin). Kawin, however, also suggests that:

> the issue is one of . . . an emotional overload as well as an indirect confrontation with the fiction's own logic . . . . At this moment and for the first time, all the masks are off — Alma, no longer a nurse or a chatterbox, has let down her own and ripped off Elisabet's pose of harmless, passive superiority — and the film image itself is accordingly unmasked. (125)

Verbal language and filmic language are but false constructs informed by dualism and yet pretending toward mergence, the breakdown and stripping away of which reveal the film's white screen, another instance of mergence, but now between spectator and spectacle, in the illusion of the body-which-is-not-one.

Elisabet's resistance to language, her muteness, is, then, an act of resistance to all her roles, her false selves, but especially those of wife and mother. That she rejects the role of wife to her maudlin and desperately needy husband is understandable, but her refusal to accept the role of mother is more complicated. Bergom-Larsson severely upbraids Bergman for his depiction of "the woman's death wish towards her child, a woman's rejection of the fundamental human relation between a child and its mother" (143). But while Elisabet certainly does reject her son, both the doctor's statement and the association in the repeated monologue between Elisabet's denial of the child and her friends' confinement of her within the role of the glowing "devoted" mother indicate that Elisabet is also resisting society's norm of maternal behavior, its imposition of otherness. The rejection of the child is also very much a rejection of the role of mother as defined and enforced by society. Elisabet's fear of and hostility toward her child, exacerbated by his desperate love and need for her, may seem like evidence (from a male perspective) of some monstrous feminine abnormality, but they also derive from her recognition of the inauthenticity of this role. While this facet of Elisabet's character may center on a deterministically biological view of women that criticizes them for their refusal to embrace their natural roles as childbearers, it also recognizes the ways in which society has used this biological fact to restrict women to roles that serve the larger androcentric culture. For the first time in his production, Bergman steps back (however tentatively), from his biological definition of the mother as a function of the needs of the male child to consider mothering as a sociocultural activity.

But, if Elisabet rejects societally imposed roles engendered by self/other binarism before the film begins, Alma learns the lesson of otherness during the course of the diegesis. While Elisabet tries to reject her personae so as to reveal her deeper, more authentic self, Alma clings to her masks, the embodiment of which is her uniform. Her participation in role-playing is apparent the first night after she meets Elisabet. From Elisabet's softly lit hospital room, Bergman cuts to a severe foreshortening of Alma thrashing about, unable to sleep. Ironically, the patient in her care is drifting peacefully off to sleep while Alma, the ostensibly healthy one, is unable to do so.

Once they arrive at the summerhouse, Alma reiterates her dedication to roles and society's expectations; she confesses that she wants to be like the old nurses where she trained, to live for her work, wear a uniform all her life, believe in something so much she can devote her whole life to it. With the bleak landscape at the center of our visual field, we sense the vacuity of her words, of her desire to "serve mankind." Alma is dedicated, then, not to self-actualizing, but to self-image (as Fritz Perls puts it), to the roles of mother, wife/lover, and caring professional that society finds appropriate for her.

The film charts the breakdown of her belief in this role system, deconstructing both binary relations and false mergence. Alma, the nurse, becomes the patient as Elisabet strokes, caresses, and comforts her after the orgy confession, and the nurse ends up threatening and tormenting the woman in her care. The narrative also charts Alma's disillusionment insofar as her role as potential mother is concerned. Both the abortion she had after the beach orgy and the repeated monologue in which she identifies with Elisabet's rejection of her son make her question herself as a mother. But the narrative also subverts her image of herself as lover. The orgy confession engenders a realization that she cannot fulfill the role of faithful lover and fiancée, an awareness reinforced when she later steps into Elisabet's role as wife to her husband and collapses into incoherence, shouting out, "Give an anaesthetic. Throw me away. I can't. I can't go on. Leave me alone. I'm cold, rotten, and indifferent" (89). The interchangeability, and hence invalidity, of these roles is evident throughout the film. The otherness inherent in role-playing is repeatedly subverted and deconstructed.

But the two women are not alone in wearing masks in this film. *Persona* can, as Kawin suggests, "allude, in words and images to the fact that it is a mask — can in fact directly dramatize the nature of the mask — but cannot *directly* present the mind behind the mindscreen, the metaphysical intelligence that here masks itself. . . . It is up to the viewer to intuit the consciousness behind the mindscreen; the most the film can do is to draw attention to its own 'awareness' that it is a mask" (126). This the film does on several occasions, one of which occurs after the "breaking" of the film when Elisabet goes outside to look for Alma. She is outlined against the hills with the setting sun at such an angle that it blocks our vision and blinds us until Elisabet steps in front of it, allowing us to focus on her features. She steps aside and again we are blinded by a screen of white. Masks and personae, both cinematic and psychological, prevent an acknowledgment of and a confrontation with the body-which-is-not-one; they are false constructs susceptible to deconstruction. The film repeatedly, then, denaturalizes the binarism of subjectivity and role, self and other, and investigates mergence both as a subversion of monolithic subjectivity and as a false fantasy (both intra- and extradiegetic) of the dissolution of the self/other dualism. Dualities and mergence are constructed only to be deconstructed.

While the female-female relationship between these women certainly suggests the lure of a retreat from the patriarchal community, it is clear that male power relations still infect it and the attraction between them. Male-female binarism is deconstructed by this relationship, and yet the mergence posited in its stead is also deconstructed. The female-female bonding they experience is so intense that the boundaries between one woman and the other give way and they become a single character energy. Sontag points to the theme of "*doubling*; the variations are those that follow from the leading possibilities of that theme (on both a formal and psychological level) such as duplication, inversion, reciprocal exchange, unity and fission, and repetition" ("Styles" 135). This mergence can serve feminism by rejecting the notion of fixed subjectivity (and gender) and, I would argue, works rather like the kind of doubling described by Kaplan in *Marianne and Julianne* as "not a mere externalization of an inner split . . . . It functions rather on an altogether more complex level, revealing, first, the strong attraction that women feel for qualities in other women that they themselves do not possess, [and] second, the difficulty women have in establishing boundaries between self and Other" (*Women and Film* 107).

While von Trotta's film and Bergman's are vastly different, this description of the representation of doubling might apply to the relationship between the two women in *Persona*, a relationship that through mergence deconstructs the false dualism of male culture, and then is itself deconstructed. The attraction Elisabet and Alma feel for each other and the absence of any remotely viable male sexuality in the film cohere with their identification with each other and the permeability of boundaries between the self and the other to create a doubling that is at the heart of the film and that reveals the "multiple, shifting, self-contradictory identity" of which de Lauretis speaks, a notion of identity that undermines male ideology. The representation of identity mergence suggests, both intra- and extradiegetically, the possibility of a subjectivity that includes the other (thereby undermining masculine dualism) but then rejects that mergence as itself an illusion. Koskinen is right, I think, to argue that the film intimates that "the spectating subject is not sovereign and independent, but rather emerges in relationship to the other — the 'you' — which here is the same as the film screen" (130). Bergman is fascinated by the idea of the mutability of identity, of its potential in the development of a radically other subjectivity, at the same time that he undermines it not only because he rightly sees identity mergence as an ideologically implicated aspect of the cinematic experience based on vampirism and appropriation, but also because, I suspect, he fears the complete dissolution of fixed male identity. As throughout his work, Bergman's fascination with the mutability of identity is both a progressive figuring and a regressive impulse toward mergence with the mother.

This theme of mergence and doubling surfaces early in the film in Alma's statement that she went to see one of Elisabet's films and was struck by the thought that they were so much alike (the subtitles are misleading when they render her statement as "We look alike" — the Swedish implies both that translation and "We are alike"). She goes on to say, "I could probably change myself into you. If I really tried. I mean inside myself. . . . And for you it would be no trick to change into me" (58). But one of the most obvious instances of doubling is the two women's dress during the first two-thirds of the film. In the mushroom-sorting scene they are both wearing light-colored summer clothing and wide-brimmed straw hats, similar except for the fact that Elisabet's is light in color while Alma's is dark. That this scene foreshadows the doublings so central to the film is evident not only in the fact that Elisabet picks up Alma's hand and compares it to her own, but also in Bergman's statement:

> The moment I saw that picture [of Bibi and Liv] I thought: My God, how alike they are! In a strange sort of way, they resembled each other. Afterwards . . . the resemblance began going round and round in my head. I thought it would be wonderful to write something about two people who lose their identities in each other; who are similar in some way. Suddenly I got the idea of them comparing hands. And that was the first image — of two women sitting there comparing hands and wearing big hats. (Björkman *et al.* 196)

This doubling appears throughout the early part of the film when, on the day(s?) Alma confesses to Elisabet, they are both dressed first in similar bathrobes, then in dark sweaters, and finally in white nightgowns. The scene by the window when they are in dark sweaters visually prefigures the negative aspects of this doubling, for it is difficult to tell where one body ends and the other begins (Simon 272). One shot shows the two women's heads touching, as though they were one person, and in another we see a strange torso with two heads. Yet a different shot shows Alma blocking out Elisabet's face, but not her arm and shoulder, an image of a strange distorted figure, two arms of dissimilar size, an oddly turned chest, and Alma's head. Later, when Alma turns, the image takes on two heads, but still has only two arms and one chest. Because they conflate false selves, mergence and fusion become distortion and deformity.

After Alma learns through the letter to the psychiatrist that Elisabet has betrayed her, this similarity in clothing ends (except for the repeated monologue scene when both are wearing dark turtlenecks). Thereafter she dresses so as to differentiate herself from the actress by wearing a shirtwaist that resembles her uniform and finally the uniform itself. The straw hats, an early image of intimacy between the two women, appear later in the film but not in the same scene; Alma wears hers ironically enough when she leaves a glass shard for Elisabet to step on, and Elisabet wears hers on the patio while she refuses Alma's desperate entreaty to speak. These hats, however, also have another association, for Alma mentions that she and her friend were wearing large straw hats before the orgy on the beach; the pleasure each of the two women derives in watching the other have sex is transferred onto Elisabet.

While Alma's clothing early in the film suggests identity mergence and sexual attraction, her later resumption of role-specific clothing indicates both her rejection of that appropriating mergence and a reassertion of the false selves that constitute her life. Dress, then, as the body's persona is susceptible, both as differentiation and as mergence, to deconstruction. The film's treatment of dress reinforces its suggestion that only false selves can merge; mergence conflates false selves, not real subjecthoods.

This mergence is also represented in a close-up of the two women's heads next to each other as Elisabet gently strokes back Alma's hair. This erotically charged image of doubling (for Elisabet is imitating Alma's repeated gesture of stroking back her hair) associates identity mergence with intimacy and a positive transgression of the boundary between self and other and reappears later in the film immediately after a dissolve from Alma's mouth and Elisabet's downcast face as she says "nothing," and also when it is superimposed on a shot of Alma toward the end of the film, when, just before her departure from the summerhouse, she again strokes her hair back in a mirror. The image suggests both mergence and, with the superimposition, its deconstruction and the reassertion of the false autonomous self associated with Alma's uniform. But this shot is not one of the actresses themselves but rather of their reflection in a mirror, as we know from the fact that Alma's hair is parted on her right, whereas during the rest of the film it is parted on the left. This double-mirror effect is also, then, linked with the assertion of the spectator's self that, by association, is also problematized as potentially false.

But the repeated monologue is perhaps the clearest example of the mergence of these two women. When Alma finds Elisabet hiding the photograph of her son, she sits down opposite her and proceeds to tell how Elisabet became pregnant after being taunted for not being maternal, but soon began to hate and fear her child (even though her friends complimented her on how beautiful she was during her pregnancy!), a dislike that grew as the child was born and developed a desperate clinging attachment to her. During the first recitation of the monologue, Bergman photographs Elisabet's face over Alma's shoulder in nearer and nearer close-ups (that again position the spectator as voyeur) until the scene concludes with an extreme close-up and a loud, dissonant chord of music. Exactly the same monologue is repeated in a reverse shot of Alma's face over Elisabet's shoulder. Both sequences conclude with the actress in a close-up like that on the boy's screen at the beginning of the film that may "tie [the shot] to the perspective of an infant, for whom the maternal visage is grand, awesome, and grotesque" (Fischer 74). At the same time the infantile impulse toward mergence (ever terrifying and alluring for Bergman) is denaturalized by the fact that both women confront the look of the camera in an instance of direct address to the spectator. The identity mergence of the two women is conflated with the undermining of the conventional narrative mergence between spectator and spectacle; our mergence with the narrative is disrupted when their mergence occurs.

Finally, the scene climaxes with a composite picture, the left half of which is Alma's face and the right half of which is Elisabet's. The right half of the composite picture fades into complete blackness, a gaping lack of light replacing Elisabet's side of the image as Alma cries, "No, I am not you. I don't feel like you. I'm Sister Alma. I'm just here to help you. I'm not Elisabet Vogler. You are Elisabet Vogler. I want. I love. I don't have" (97). The composite picture returns with renewed strength and impact and finally fades to white. The freezing of this remarkable image and the aural emphasis on it privilege it as an epiphanic moment; its image of false, destructive mergence, mergence as violation and appropriation — both psychological and cinematic — is underscored. As Koskinen suggests,

> [Alma's and Elisabet's] aggression is simultaneously directed, through [their] look, out towards the camera — as if the spectator — or more correctly *the gaze of the spectator* — were an accessory to that which has happened. And the question is if that is not precisely what it is; the gaze of the spectator allows itself willingly to be deceived by an infernal photographic trick. It sees — and yet doesn't see — and contributes thereby to the creation of this repulsive hybrid; it is the co-creator of the image — and accessory. (133)

The repeated monologue is probably (but not certainly) Alma's mental event, an attempt by her to appropriate aspects of Elisabet's identity and demonstrate to her how much better she can act the role of mother, live up to social expectations of maternal behavior than can Elisabet. But in attempting to appropriate the other through mergence, one loses the self. It is the nurse's recognition of her mergence with Elisabet as both vampirism and loss of self that creates the horror of the composite face.

As Livingston argues: "This moment of doubling is not merely a formal operation: the dramatic context suggests that beneath the seeming differences between Alma and Elisabet lies a fundamental similarity, an identity involving the same kind of relation to others" (212), a relation expressed as the "sacrifice" of another. The vampirism/voyeurism they share is expressed as an assertion of the self at the expense of the other, a relationship to the world that also corrupts mother/child relations. But Elisabet's feelings of disgust and loathing toward her child are extreme indeed. A view of this scene as essentialist misogyny would also seem to be supported by Bergman's claim that the composite is a combination of the two actresses' less attractive sides (Björkman et al. 203) and by Bergman's numerous references to his mother's rejection of him ("I thought that I was an unwanted child evolved out of a cold womb and given birth to in a crisis both physical and psychological. My mother's diary later confirmed my idea: my mother was violently ambivalent to her wretched dying child" [*Images* 17] and "My . . . heart was consumed with a dog-like devotion [for her]" [*Magic Lantern* 3]). We note too that the whole issue of the destructive maternal is the central focus of the play in which Elisabet is acting the title role, that *Electra* enacts a narrative of matricide. Not surprisingly, Bergom-Larsson finds that "the form of inner destructivity that is most brutal and most contrary to nature in Bergman is the woman who hates her child and pushes it away from her" (66). Thus, *Persona* conforms to patriarchal ideology in its criticism and victimization of women characters who exercise their right not to be a mother, either by consciously choosing not to have children or by obtaining an abortion, at the same time that it represents a rejection of motherhood as part of a larger subject/object dualism. While this doubling and identity mergence might be read as essentialist, as defining both these women in terms of their rejection of motherhood and their reproductive function, such an interpretation is also undermined by the earlier implication of dominant culture and its norms of motherhood.

Furthermore, the technique with which this mergence is depicted subverts a male reading. The two faces have become one, their fusion reflected in the fusion between viewer and viewed at the same time that the direct address and composite picture disrupt both fusions. Both Alma's and the spectator's attempt to appropriate the other through mergence, to read the other's body, is represented as violence and violation. False mergence engenders deconstruction. Alma's rejection of this identity mergence is an assertion of the authoritative false self that is undermined by her linguistic stumblings. She literally loses her voice in the mergence process. While the film presents the mergence of identity as an alternative to the male model of a fixed (and gendered) subjectivity, it also investigates the false mergence of the spectator/spectacle relationship of appropriation and deconstructs it (a deconstruction that may also reflect Bergman's fear of mergence with the mother). Both binarism and facile synthesis are denaturalized. The dissolve to a blank white screen further suggests that such mergence is inherently unstable and must produce breakdown, even as the white screen that denotes nonbody is also deconstructed.

This same visual fusion takes place in the next scene when Alma, confused and frustrated, says, "How can I cope with it?" after which Elisabet lowers her head to a black profile against white and Alma's head bends down to join hers, producing a remarkable image in which the bottom half of the screen is completely white and the top half occupied by a heavy black mass, formed by the joining of the two women's profiles facing downward. We have here then another image of mergence, even more abstract, more false.

As the false mergence of body and nonbody intensifies, the self is completely dissolved, appropriated by an other.

The sense of mergence as disintegration of the self is also apparent in the next scene. When Alma speaks incoherently to Elisabet, the latter is seen in extreme close-up, Alma's face behind her. As Alma moves forward, her face behind Elisabet's head, the right side of the actress' face and all of Alma's are in shadow so that the shot appears to show a face one side of which is twice as large as the other. This image of grotesque fusion is followed by a visual instance of fission: a cut from Alma's left-facing profile to Elisabet's right-facing one, both outlined against a white background. These conjoined profiles figure dualism, rigidity, and differentiation at the same time that they are an image of abstract, false mergence. Mergence threatens and encroaches upon, rather than enriches, subjectivity, and the dichotomized false subject reasserts itself.

The displacement of mergence by a reasserted false self is represented as fusion engendering fission, doubling generating splitting. The image of Alma by the lake is a case in point. After reading Elisabet's letter, she is photographed by a lake in an extreme long shot, doubled by her reflection in the water. Her fusion with Elisabet is both appropriation and personality dissolution. Appropriation produces fragmentation. This shift from close-up to long shot is a structuring principle in this film; as Stig Björkman has pointed out, "*Persona* is almost exclusively built up around close-ups and wide long shots, and the form is entirely congruent with the content. In the relations between the women there are these strong vacillations between closeness and distance, intimacy and reserve. The narrative technique is of course consciously intended" (206). The extreme close-ups that are especially prominent later in the film can produce in the viewer, as Arnheim has pointed out, a sense of uncertainty and dislocation. Juxtaposed with extreme long shots, they create a sense of distance not unlike that occasioned by the shot in which Elisabet takes our picture. Camera range consistently denaturalizes voyeurism; permeability and fusion are appropriation and violation.

The last third of the film portrays fusion engendering fission as Alma consistently pulls herself back, away from Elisabet (visually as well as figuratively) in an attempt to reassert autonomy. Elisabet's voyeuristic objectification and appropriation of Alma is, in the context of the film, morally reprehensible. Her "studying" of Alma and her later attempts at appropriation are acts of vampirism, a vampirism graphically delineated when Elisabet literally sucks Alma's blood. Alma then usurps Elisabet's position as voyeur when she stands behind a window staring past a curtain to watch the actress step on the glass and also when she comes to Elisabet's room and stares down at her asleep in bed. The extent to which voyeurism is an attempt to control the viewed subject is apparent in the fact that in the latter scene she upbraids

Elisabet for her puffy face, her scar, and her wrinkles. Identity mergence and the appropriation of the other are linked with specularity insofar as Alma's voyeurism is represented as an attempt to reclaim the powerful self by objectifying and vampirizing the other.

This overall movement from mergence to breakdown is also paralleled by the structure of the film itself. While the earlier part of the film frequently shows the two women within the same frame, the latter part presents them almost exclusively in separate shots or in shots denoting fusion and the transgression of boundaries as appropriation and violence.

The deconstruction of appropriating mergence is also evident on the extradiegetic level in Bergman's treatment of viewpoint. The unitary point of view posited by dominant cinema, according to which the spectator identifies with a monolithic (male) authority is systematically subverted in *Persona*. The film speaks the truth of Barthes's contention that "the opposition of the sexes must not be a law of Nature . . . both the meanings and the sexes must be pluralized" (*Roland Barthes* 69). If, as Gentile argues, the feminist potential of a film is directly linked to multiple viewpoints because of their ability to engender "critical subjectivity" and a "plurality of vision" (70–73), then Bergman's film would certainly seem to participate in this potential. Not only is the spectator in a very overt way allowed to experience each of the protagonists through the eyes of the other, but the whole issue of viewpoint is extensively problematized by the prologue, the "breaking" segment, and the conclusion of the film. In addition, however, to the posited viewpoints of "cinema spectator," the boy in the prologue, Elisabet, Alma, and the camera crew at the end of the film, with all of whom we experience alternately identification and separation, Bergman further problematizes the issue of viewpoint by presenting scenes and events that can only with great difficulty be located in a particular individual consciousness. After the "breaking," the film no longer presents the real-seeming artifice of the first part but instead depicts action in such a way that we are uncertain as to where and how it is happening, thereby undermining the implicit mergence between film's perception of itself and the spectator's perception of it, the naturalization for which dominant male cinema strives.

As Sontag has pointed out, "Causal connections operative in one part of the film are flouted in another part; the film gives several equally persuasive but mutually exclusive explanations of the same event" ("Styles" 125). At times the images before us appear to be Elisabet's, at other times Alma's. For instance, even if it can be argued that Elisabet does in fact speak to Alma the night of the orgy monologue (Blackwell 70–71), the impression remains that the spectator is confused on this point. David Boyd has treated this issue in some detail, finding that in *Persona* "the interpreter's identification *with* the interpretant is repeatedly subverted by his uncertainty about the identification *of* the interpretant" (13). Pointing to our inability to ascertain whether or not Elisabet actually speaks to Alma and whether or not she comes to her room, Boyd goes on to chart how the viewer begins by identifying with Alma in her attempt to interpret Elisabet but then transfers identification to Elisabet when she becomes the spectator surrogate while listening in the darkened room to Alma recount the orgy. He further points to Alma's position as a "text to be read" by Elisabet (14) (as the letter to the psychiatrist makes clear). Thus, the "impossibility of interpretation" for which Boyd argues coheres with Bergman's treatment of these women and their bodies as screens into and behind which the spectator would penetrate for purposes of appropriation. The foregrounding of these issues and Bergman's consistent frustration of the spectator's attempt at interpretation constitute a criticism of dominant cinema and a resistance to the ideology on which it is based. Pure subjectivity cannot be represented, expressed, or interpreted.

Questions centering on interpretability arise with even greater urgency in the last third of the film when Elisabet's husband comes to visit his wife and makes love to Alma and when Alma seems to be able to read Elisabet's mind during the repeated monologue sequence. While these two scenes suggest that Alma is being increasingly appropriated by aspects of Elisabet's subjectivity — her experiences as actress, wife, and mother — the film nonetheless does not locate them in a particular consciousness and thus encourages a critical questioning of authoritative viewpoint. The film also refuses to provide a clear, cogent ending to the events of the diegesis. Unlike the classical cinema, *Persona*, Bergman's most anti-narrative film, resists closure and explanation, fostering instead intellectual activity and speculation, developing a spectatorial "critical subjectivity."

The deconstruction of male discourse also surfaces in the absence in the latter part of the film of any objectified moral scale according to which we can judge the characters and their actions as good or bad, moral or immoral. This absence of a moral center culminates in the scene when Elisabet, coaxed by Alma into speech, utters the single word "Nothing." But the film embraces less nihilism than a view that only by challenging and subverting traditional categories of language, experience, and art can one forge a new cultural and social practice.

Deconstruction also pervades time-space relations whose "natural" coherence is subverted. The prologue, the interpolation into the credit sequence of the characters from the narrative, the "breaking," and the ending of the film all violate conventional time-space relations, as do the scenes of fantasy or mental event that largely comprise the last third of the film.

Indeed, the film's treatment of space deconstructs both the false dualism of self and other and the fantasy of mergence on which dominant cinema is predicated. While there is no clear-cut separation between male and female space as in *The Silence*, it is clear that Elisabet (and Alma with her) has retreated to this tiny island in an attempt to separate from the two males who threaten her with their needs. While the male tradition posits female communities as exiled, for Bergman this exile is his own, the place where he finds himself. He is engaged less in the confinement of women than in an exploration of their position as both self and other. Thus the film problematizes the traditional masculine treatment of space that designates range as masculine, confinement as feminine by emphasizing the interconnectedness of the two.

Not surprisingly the deconstruction of both dualism and mergence is represented in the film's various screening surfaces that foreground the interior/exterior, self/other dichotomy. In addition to the literal screens that constantly reappear in the film, Bergman proffers a variety of other screening surfaces in the form of windows (frequently only partially obscured by transparent curtains and draperies) that are positioned as intersections of transgression and containment, mergence and differentiation, and that are further elaborated by a series of doorways and corridors that reinforce the motif. As the interface between feminine space and masculine space, windows can highlight gender issues, and not surprisingly they recur throughout *Persona* as images of threshold and barrier. Shortly after their arrival at the summerhouse, Alma and Elisabet breakfast in front of a window, separated by a mullion, the bleak rocky seascape visible outside. They are furthermore both dressed in heavy bathrobes: while visually separated one from the other, they are together on the same side of the screen, warm, cozy, protected. As the day wears on, they move next to each other, the hostile outer world now curtained off by transparent, gauzelike draperies. Still later at night, Alma curls up in a corner of the room against large black windows to recount the orgy on the beach, and windows recur the next morning when Elisabet types a letter in the foreground as Alma appears outside the window, enters, and takes the letter for mailing. We note, then, that as the film progresses, the two women stand on different sides of the window screen. It is interesting, I think, that Alma is increasingly associated with the space beyond the window screen, for it is her mind and her body that are objects of violation and transgression; she is the screen to be permeated, the text to be read, just as she is linked with the black screens of body, penetration, and appropriation.

That this transgression is incomplete, the appropriation not fully effected, is apparent in the use of gauzelike draperies over the windows in Elisabet's hospital room, over the expanses of glass throughout the summer-house, and even in doorways separating rooms and entrances to closets. The shots of Alma pulling back the curtains in Elisabet's hospital room to let light in, of Elisabet performing the same action in order better to scan the horizon for the missing Alma, and of Alma drawing back a drapery to watch Elisabet cut herself are all eloquent images of an attempt to penetrate behind the screen, to know and thereby master the specifically female reality lurking there. Furthermore, we twice see Elisabet emerging through these drapes — when she enters Alma's room, holds her, and strokes back the girl's hair and when, immediately after the film "breaks," she approaches the spectator. In both cases, her approach to "this" side of the screen is erotically charged, promising accessibility and knowledge. Neither opaque nor transparent, these curtaining fabrics embody both permeability and impermeability, the simultaneous impossibility and desirability of moving behind the screen that represents both false mergence and separation.

But space is also deconstructed when we see an extreme long shot of Alma jumping about on the rocks by the shore, and Elisabet suddenly pops up from beneath the screen, facing the camera, to take a picture of us. She snaps, turns around, and then walks toward Alma. We observe her taking a picture of Alma, following which she again turns toward us and takes our picture. This scene is all the more striking because we have just been focusing our attention deep within the frame to ascertain what Alma is doing so far away, and our perceptual field requires rapid readjustment when Elisabet pops up before us. Bergman is manipulating his spectator in terms of visual field and in terms of viewer expectations of a consistent fictional posture; he deconstructs the false mergence of both space and narrative.

This deconstruction of space continues with Bergman's use of a telephoto lens in the mental event sequence when Elisabet's husband comes to visit. The scene begins with a hand reaching out to Alma from the camera's position; it seems in some sense to be coming from the spectator, a strategy that merges the spectator's sense of space with that of the diegesis and yet disrupts the fantasy of mergence by foregrounding it. The background to this scene consists of tangled, dense, barren branches and vines, but the choice of lens makes the background seem to lurch forward and to exist on the same plane as the characters. Since the effect of depth is almost negligible, the objects within the image, the people and the background, seem superimposed one upon the other, a technique that deconstructs space as a site of both dualism and mergence.

The two letters in the film also serve as screens that deconstruct dichotomy and mergence; they are pages on which desire is inscribed, that both invite and resist penetration for, as Terry Eagleton has pointed out, "Letters concede and yet withhold intimacy in a kind of prolonged teasing, a courtship which is never consummated" (ctd. in Epstein 139). Letters are an extremely negotiated form of communication, embodying both mergence and separation. Both the letter from Elisabet's husband to her and the one from Elisabet to her doctor connote an "intimacy never consummated," the former because it is written by a rejected husband and the latter because Elisabet refuses to speak. Both pieces of communication are deeply compromised, the first by the husband's hackneyed language and the latter by its confession of appropriation. Both letters, then, focus on the scanning of the female body, the attempt to penetrate into it and master, even as they acknowledge such appropriation as morally suspect.

The photographs of the film also function as screens that deconstruct mergence. The first appears when Elisabet watches television in her hospital room, and we see a newsreel showing a priest immolating himself in protest against the Vietnamese government. These shots are intercut with ever nearer close-ups of Elisabet's shocked and horrified reaction to what she sees, and the mergence between viewer and viewed is foregrounded by the repetition of the immolation segment, at the same time that the repetition subverts the mergence of spectator and spectacle by deconstructing it.

Two other photographic images appear in the film: the picture of Elisabet's son (which appears twice) and the photo of a young boy in the Warsaw ghetto being marched away at gunpoint by Nazi soldiers. When we first see the picture of Elisabet's son, it is shot in the foreground with the actress behind it, as though the spectator were offering it to her, a positioning that again deconstructs the cohesion between spectator and naturalized narrative. She looks at it for a moment, an expression of fear crosses her face, and she tears it in half lengthwise, destroying this screening surface just as she tries to deconstruct her own persona. It later surfaces when Alma sees it hidden under Elisabet's hand, a discovery that precipitates the repeated monologue scene. The self/other dualism and the false mergence implicit in both the photograph and in Elisabet's relationship with her son are problematized and deconstructed.

The photograph of the Jewish boy would seem to be a kind of synthesis of the two other photographic images: public political events as they impinge upon the subjectivity of a young boy. While Bergom-Larsson finds Bergman's equation between, on the one hand, the Holocaust and Vietnam, and, on the other, Elisabet's private problems as a kind of bourgeois subjectification (143), the issue is not quite so simple for Roller, who observes that feminist novels "do make reference and connection with [world political] events . . . . [But] the emphasis is . . . put [not] on the events in these novels but on the impression the event makes on the mind of the character" (104). The power of this image is apparent in Elisabet's visible distress, but the deliberate fragmentation of this picture (after a shot of the entire photograph, we see close-ups of small sections of it) and that of Elisabet's son would seem to challenge the image's ability to communicate wholeness. At the same time, these images are depicted as possessing great authority. Bergman comments, "My art cannot melt, transform, or forget that boy in the [Warsaw] photo . . . or the man who set himself on fire for his faith . . . . I

can never get past those images. They transform my art into tricks, something indifferent, whatever" (*Images* 58). While one might associate the
authority of the photographs with the fact that all have male subjects, they
also address both the mergence and the separation of the subject and the
spectator, a separation of time as well as space, as well as the futility of art in
the face of "reality." They remain screens that mark the fusion and the separation of viewer and viewed. Their authority combines with the separation
between spectator and spectacle to reinforce the fundamental tension in
screening surfaces between permeability and impermeability. Like the photographs in *The Silence*, these images do not invoke nostalgia; on the contrary, they assert the death of structuring authority, the impossibility of
containment, and create an absence effect that overshadows photography's
implicit presence effect. If these photographs function as fetishes that strive
for containment and appropriation, the fetishism is subsequently undermined
by the destruction and fragmentation. Again, both stable oppositions and
mergence are deconstructed.

As the film draws to a close, we see Alma, suitcase in hand, leaving the
summerhouse and a lingering close-up of the wooden statue of a woman,
which then cuts to a close-up of Elisabet in her Electra make-up, staring into
the camera. This instance of direct address again forces the spectator into an
awareness of his or her own voyeurism. Cuts reveal Alma walking along the
shore to the road and a low-angle shot of Bergman and his cameraman Sven
Nykvist, high up on a crane. This insertion of himself and his own body into
the narrative continues the self-consciousness implicit in the prologue and
works very much like Bergman's disembodied voice-over that we hear on the
soundtrack while we see a long tracking shot of Alma and Elisabet behind a
stone wall at the beginning of their stay at the summerhouse. This voice simply tells us of their arrival at the house, imparting no information that could
not have been incorporated into Alma's speech and seeming very much like a
intrusion into this female world. While it might be argued that this voice-
over functions to reassert Bergman's (male) primacy and control over the
world of these women, it might also be seen as serving to establish as male
the larger public world by which the female world of the film is circumscribed. This interpretation of the voice-over as ironic is further buttressed by
the fact that this voice, unlike that in most dominant films, imparts no de-
finitive interpretation of events, no authoritative view; it is narrationally and
interpretively "empty." The "emptiness" of the voice-over, the very fact that
it does seem an intrusion, and the film's persistent and wide-ranging thematics of self and other point, then, to a reading in which this is but another
of the film's distancing devices, one that specifically foregrounds and criticizes the role of male authority in defining and constricting female experience.

As the camera through which we are seeing rises up to meet Bergman and Nykvist, we see in their viewfinder an upside-down shot of Elisabet/Liv Ullmann looking out at us, her hair spreading luxuriantly around her. Cuts show Alma climbing on a bus, a shot of a film set where Elisabet is posing, and a shot of the bus' departure panning down to gravel superimposed upon which is the image of the boy touching the screen from the prologue. A white screen is replaced by shots of the inside of the projector, concluding with the extinguishing of the two arc lamps, which leaves the screen black. The ending is the same as the beginning but inverted, as though in a mirror, establishing only the most highly negotiated kind of closure. The spectator is given no authoritative knowledge of how this story ends, of what becomes of these women or how the events they have shared will impact upon them; the only closure possible, Bergman demonstrates, is the imposed closure of art, of cinema, a closure compromised by the ideological systems in which the apparatus and male culture are grounded.

The return of the image of the boy is important to the conclusion of the film, for he was posited in the prologue as a potential interpreter, a reader of the female body. Even if we identify him as a Bergman surrogate, the effect here is, as Boyd points out,

> not to ground the fiction in a sense of immediate authorial presence, but rather precisely the opposite, to dispossess the author of his own text. For the boy is presented from the very beginning as a fellow-interpreter, trying to make sense of images on a screen, as he was last seen in *The Silence* struggling to puzzle out the meaning of words in the foreign language. And an interpreter he remains to the very end, never even vaguely approaching the authorial control that Fellini's surrogate, for instance, belatedly assumes at the end of *8 1/2*. (17)

Bergman further undermines his own authority by filming himself and his cameraman, by rendering himself visible and discrete. He points up the divided quality of a narration composed by a man about women, stressing that male authority brackets this ostensible rendering of female experience and that appropriation is male-gendered. The woman remains trapped as an image on a screen in the male artwork; she is a fetishized icon, her luxuriant hair and provocative glance invoking a sexuality that is firmly embedded in the male imagination, her gaze challenging the spectator to admit complicity in this sexual system. Thus, the film demonstrates that it promotes the imaginary coherence of the male rather than the female subject. The fantasy of mergence between spectator and diegesis is totally deconstructed, and the black screen suggests both the otherness of the film and its connection/mergence with the spectator's space of darkness in the theater.

We have, then, in *Persona* a film authored and directed by a man about women, a film that instead of reinscribing the domination of the male describes the complicity between gendered ideology and representation, that acknowledges the appropriation of women by the codes of cinema, and that deconstructs masculine cultural values and systems. Both images and narratives, the film suggests, are constructs, instances of false mergence, like that which occurs between Alma and Elisabet. While it is true that the film represents women as subscribing to the male model of human relations as rooted not in sympathy or fellow-feeling but in power and authority, that it depicts the mutability of identity as threatening, it also indicts dominant cinema's fantasy of mergence for its appropriating strategies. This "use" of women by a male artist serves, then, less to reinforce patriarchy by appropriating them as a means of satisfying homosocial desire, than to criticize that appropriation and to criticize the patriarchy and its ideology by demonstrating the implosion of the artificial categories it imposes for its survival and supremacy. The "screen test" (to borrow a coinage from Judith Mayne) of this film manifests ambivalence and contradiction on a whole series of interconnected levels, but resists "the dual traps of co-optation and recuperation, on the one hand, [and] endless circulation within and attendant containment by the field of binary opposition, on the other" (Mayne, *Woman at the Keyhole* 83). In this respect, the film represents a significant advance over *The Silence*, which while questioning nonetheless still reinforces that binary opposition. For one could argue that *Persona*, like several of the films Mayne examines,

> explore[s] the limits of the interface between spectacle and narrative, and in so doing seek[s] to "investigate" the elements that are repressed, marginalized, or otherwise displaced in classical film narrative. The metaphor of the screen serves not to replace one sense of "screen" (what is made invisible) with another (the luminous, white space of consciousness) but to produce a kind of narration that can account for both. To "account for both" does not mean to establish a static duality, but rather to account for their interdependence and the tension between them. (*Woman at the Keyhole* 86)

The pleasures that this film offers the spectator are not, then, centered around homosocial desire, those of voyeurism and fetishism; on the contrary, the film indicts these activities as reprehensible. Instead, it gives us radically other pleasures, those of contradiction, of piecing together a story, of awareness. The film refuses any space of "unitary subjectivity" (Kuhn 171) for the spectator, striving instead with every technique available in its cinematic arsenal, through the deconstruction of cinema's fantasy of mergence to foster in the viewer the "passionate detachment" necessary for social, sexual, and artistic growth.

7: *Cries and Whispers:* The Repression
of the Sexual Body and the
Reification of the Maternal

Like Bergman's other women films, *Cries and Whispers* (1972) addresses issues of female subjectivity. The male critical response to the film has been almost exclusively laudatory, of which Mosley's sentiment is typical: "Bergman has never shown more absolute control of his material; the photography is exquisite, the acting impeccable; his direction is imaginative, rigorous and precise, creating a fluid interplay of exterior and interior, past and present, sound and silence" (157). This fluidity is paramount for Bergman, as he attests in the introduction to the "story" (rather than screenplay) of the film: "What it most resembles is a dark flowing stream: faces, movements, voices, gestures, exclamations, light and shade, moods, dreams. Nothing fixed, nothing really tangible other than for the moment, and then only in an illusory moment . . . . Everything must be beautiful and harmonious. It must be the way it is in a dream" (69). This description is, of course, not unlike the director's earlier definition of "chamber film" — this again is a work that devalues plot in favor of "the significant motif" and an impressionistic fluidity of characterization and visual rhythm that have the potential to contribute to a feminist reading.

But the feminist response to the film has been far from enthusiastic. Mellen finds it inauthentic and suspect as well as politically repressive (312). Haskell also sees in the film "a furtive misogyny, a hatred that dares not speak its name" (38), and Ann Morrisett Davidson argues that it is characterized by "outrageous manipulations" (70). Among feminist critics, Constance Penley also criticizes the film's representation of female experience. Starting with Bergman's 1956 statement that he makes films in order "to illuminate the human soul with an infinitely more vivid light, to unmask it even more brutally and to annex to our field of knowledge new domains of reality. Perhaps we could even discover a crack that would allow us to penetrate into the chiaroscuro of surreality" (205), Penley argues that "in this expression of his obsession to expose, to unmask brutally, to annex, to penetrate, [he] uses the language of rape to describe his filmmaking. The experience of seeing Bergman's latest film *Cries and Whispers* is one of being emotionally and psychically raped, as once again, a man uses women driven to the edge of experience as sacrifices for his own salvation and then calls it Art" (205). Penley goes on to reproach Bergman for creating female stereotypes (woman as victim, temptress, evil incarnate, and earth mother) in a film that constitutes "a crash course in objectification and alienation. It is *the* filmic paradigm of woman as Other, of woman as nothing but the projected fears and desires of men, of women, as cosmic victim" (208). Mellen extends this argument, as well as one put forward by Pauline Kael, to conclude that "seeing woman as 'different' and 'Other' amounts in Bergman's films to their utter dehumanization" (301) and that he "provides one of the most retrograde portrayals of women on the contemporary screen" (312). Thus, while there are women critics who praise his film for its experimentation and others, avowedly feminist, such as Gail Rock, who praise him because of his "belie[f] that women possess some mysterious power of the psyche" (ctd. in Penley 208), the feminist critical consensus is that *Cries and Whispers* stands as a monument to the male appropriation of female experience.

But this reaction may seem surprising in light of the film's similarities in its rendering of female experience to *Persona* and *The Silence*, with their questioning of dominant male ideology, psychological, social, and cultural, for many of the same concerns, structures, and techniques surface here, and, like them, it treats the dissolution of the boundaries between self and other and the possibilities of woman as subject. This chapter, then, will investigate not only the potential of this film for creating a feminist viewing experience, but also the changes in Bergman's perceptions of the genderedness of human and aesthetic experience. *Cries and Whispers*, while privileging female subjectivity and using many of the same disjunctive strategies that encourage a feminist reading of *Persona*, ultimately disavows the role of masculine ideology in the corruption of the self, locating that corruption instead in the female body and in the mother in particular and furthermore strives for precisely the kind of appropriation and false mergence that *Persona* rejects. The film first destroys and erases the evil mother's body as sexual and then reifies the body of the all-nurturing, self-abnegating good mother.

As in both *The Silence* and *Persona*, this film deals almost exclusively with a world of women, the male all but absent from the narrative. God is a destructive, alienating force, as the priest indicates in his speech over Agnes's corpse, when he describes the plight of humanity as "left here on the dark, dirty earth under a empty and cruel heaven" (75), thereby intimating that God is responsible for human misery and alienation. This concept of the masculine is reflected in all the male characters in the film. Marginalized and unidimensional, the men have no real depth or breadth of experience or insight; they are never fully developed and we never understand their minds or their motives. They are furthermore pitiable, corrupt and/or repulsive as lovers and husbands and impotent as spiritual leaders. Haskell rightly observes that "all the men in the film — the pompous, self-satisfied doctor, the sardonic, sadistic husband of Karin, and the weak, pallid, plump husband of Maria — are pathetic figures, less physically vibrant then the women" (303).

Bergman depicts his men as professionally ineffectual and personally repugnant. The doctor's examination of the dying Agnes is "perfunctory," and he cannot cure either Anna's child or Agnes. He is further represented as cold and calculating in the scene in which he verbally excoriates Maria for trying to seduce him. And he twice rejects her advances with indifference and scorn. In the scene in the doctor's bedroom, he holds a mirror for Maria and describes the calculation, hunger, indifference, and indolence in her face while an ironic sneer is visible on the doctor's mouth in the background. When Maria then says that it is not in her that he sees these things but rather in himself, she would appear to be speaking the truth of the film. He implicitly agrees with her when he suddenly exclaims, "Selfishness. Coldness, indifference" (79); the two of them, he says, are "so alike." This is, then, a classic instance of male projection; after attempting to project his own qualities of character onto Maria and failing, he then holds, as a desperate last stand, that both of them have these qualities. While he may be right in his assertion that they are alike, his attempt at projecting his own failings onto a woman is a strategy typical of male domination. The fact that this encounter takes place before a mirror links it with the screening surfaces of *Persona* and again implicates the cinematic mirror as a site of appropriating mergence. But in this mirror metaphor Koskinen tellingly finds "a reemergence of the [naturalized] boundary between the spectator and the film fiction" (148); the foregrounding of the relationship between spectator and spectacle has been (at least temporarily) abandoned.

Significantly, both he and the other repulsive male in the film, Karin's husband, are shown eating in a distinctly unattractive manner. It is not merely that they eat as Europeans do that makes them seem to be shoveling food in their mouths greedily and rapaciously. They also smack their lips and make disgusting noises while they eat, either ignoring their fellow diners or regarding them coldly and indifferently.

Like the doctor, the other male character who is specifically identified with a profession is inept and repugnant. The pastor who presides over Agnes' funeral does not provide comfort to the mourners but rather uses the occasion to confess his own lack of faith, his own despair, and to ask Agnes to intercede with God on our behalf, "to free us from our anxiety." He exhorts her to ask God "for a meaning for our lives . . . plead our cause" (75). The minister's professional ineffectuality is underscored by the fact that Bergman casts Anders Ek in the role, for his face always has something of the grotesque about it (witness his roles in both *Sawdust and Tinsel* and *The Seventh Seal*).

This scene is, I think, pivotal in the development of Bergman's ideas on both gender and subjectivity. There is a resounding absence of the father in this film. *The Silence* depicted a world in which the Father, both religious and familial, was a destructive present absence, and the film charted the devastating legacy of that patriarch. But in *Cries and Whispers* no mention is ever made of the sisters' father; while implicating God as an alienating and destructive force that infects the lives of these four women, their legacy of coldness and despair is laid at the feet of the mother; in erasing the father, Bergman implicates the mother. In a rather skillful bit of ideological sleight-of-hand, Bergman posits God as the corrupter of female experience but then largely ignores the impact of masculine ideology on that experience, simultaneously blaming Woman and seeking reconciliation with the lost mother.

While men seem marginalized to an unprecedented extent in this film, male absence here seems to suggest a desire more effectively to "penetrate" into and appropriate the world of women; by removing the onscreen observer, the film eliminates the distantiation effect created by the boy, the camera crew, and the metacinematic footage in *Persona*, an effect that contributes in the earlier film to the development of "critical subjectivity" on the part of the viewer. Thus, while the negative representation of God and certain male characters might seem to contribute to a potentially feminist experience of this film, the absence of the problematized bracketing male perspective and the designation of metaphysical malaise as female subvert that potential.

At first glance the film does look like something of a feminist project, one that investigates women's ways of articulating their selves and their position as narrating subject and object. The protagonists are all clearly and subtly defined as the director strives to give them a voice. He expresses the anger, boredom, and internalized pain that characterize their lives, stages their loves and hatreds, the frustrated attempts at sharing that make up their reality. There is depth to these women, and they achieve substantial narrative authority in the first-person sequences. But one must question the extent of that authority, as Haskell does in her argument that these women are "parody-composites" whom Bergman "controls like puppets, abusing them for what he has made them," concluding that they are mere "projections of his soul (as well as his sexual vanity)" (315). Mellen echoes this view:

> Women are indeed frequently so significant to him as symbols of the dilemma of alienated suffering human beings that Bergman employs them as spokeswomen to express his personal world-view. . . . His women characters sometimes serve Bergman to express his agony over our ultimate inability to derive meaning from life except in rare moments of sensual ecstasy which are soon contaminated by disgust over the bodily processes in which all experience is rooted. (297)

The extent to which these charges are true can only be verified by a detailed analysis of the film, of the individual women in it, and of the cinematic structures — specifically those of screens and of voyeurism and fetishism —

that inform the viewing experience. Thus, a consideration of these issues as well as of the role of disease, masochism, fantasy, sexuality, female bonding, and motherhood can illuminate the workings of this film and the development of Bergman's representation of gender and ideology.

Because the film centers around four women and is structured so that each is presented separately, first in a brief "reality" segment and then in a first-person sequence, a separate examination of them as individuals is warranted. Each of these women is defined by certain clothing (this film embraces a fetishism of clothing and costuming to a degree virtually unparalleled in Bergman), specific objects and activities, various physical movements, and particular camera treatments and on- and off-camera sounds, as well as through her responses to sexuality, female bonding, and pain, and all these strategies cohere and culminate in the character's first-person sequence.

The character of Agnes in many respects functions as the emotional center of the film and the destruction and erasure of her body its major action; it is she who begins and ends the film and she whose subjectivity is first explored in any depth. It is furthermore because of her ill health that the other sisters have gathered at their childhood home, and it is through their reactions to her illness and death that the spectator comes to know who her sisters are.

Throughout the film Bergman emphasizes Agnes's innocence and denial of self, a characterization that is reflected even in her wardrobe. She is seen in ascetic white nightgowns and once in a pale peach robe. The fact that she almost always appears in white reflects the film's persistent association between white and innocence, virginity, and the repression of the female body. The objects with which she is linked reinforce this idea. Early in the film Agnes sits down at a beautiful inlaid desk with cloisonné ink pots on a small marble stand. A close-up of these objects establishes a physical environment for the character, one in which beautiful objects of a past age — these items, elegant little clocks, and white lace — all link her with a kind of cultural legacy that partakes of beauty and grace. All these "feminine" objects serve to define this character as part of a cultural legacy. She is the owner of the estate, the only sister still living in the family house, and consequently is the bearer of the family legacy, as well as of "feminine" tradition and culture. That she is riddled with disease and dies during the course of the film invites an interpretation according to which this tradition must, for Bergman, be destroyed.

Agnes is also twice visually linked with white roses, with their traditional connotations of innocence and ephemerality. This ephemerality is also underlined by the clocks that circumscribe her existence and that derive from Bergman's childhood memory of his grandmother's apartment in Uppsala (*Magic Lantern* 21, 26). The prominence of clocks suggests that time is either running out or standing still. And such is the case — time is running out for Agnes because she is dying, and time stands still for all the women both because they have returned to the home of their childhood and because they are locked into patterns of behavior that will not allow them to grow and develop. That these patterns of behavior are the legacy of the mother implicates her also as the prime mover responsible for the destruction of forward-moving, progressive time.

The activities in which Agnes engages substantiate an interpretation of her as bearer of a "feminine" cultural legacy, for she primarily occupies herself, when feeling well enough, with painting and writing. Significantly, the subject of her painting is a white rose that again suggests her innocence — she is after all a virgin. But her writing also takes place within a traditionally feminine framework as does her painting, for she writes not books for publication but rather personal impressions in her diary, a kind of composition that by definition is a private activity undertaken for the benefit only of the self. Agnes is, then, confined to the kinds of cultural activity that the patriarchy has traditionally allotted women, activities sanctioned by male ideology precisely because they are private and do not encroach on the masculine realm of professional progress and culture for business. As Jensen points out, "To extol women's natural gift for epistolarity amounts to confining women's writing to letter writing and, moreover, limits their letter writing to its social practice. The male theoretician thus asserted man's exclusive right to literary letters" (41). We note too that the character of Agnes is one of the few representations in Bergman's forty-year career of an artist who is also a woman. But the nature of that artistry is very much circumscribed by biology; Desirée in *Smiles of a Summer Night*, Elisabet in *Persona*, and Alexander's mother and grandmother in *Fanny and Alexander* are actresses engaged in a profession that emphasizes interpretation, not autonomous creation. Acting furthermore speculizes the female body for male consumption. Even the Ingrid Bergman character in *Autumn Sonata*, although a pianist, is an interpreter whose authority is undercut by her failure as a mother. Thus, Bergman condescendingly dismisses Agnes's artistry by saying, "She has vague artistic ambitions" (*Four Stories* 60). Indeed, one seeks in vain in the canon for a fully autonomous female artist who creates on the same conditions and the same level as Bergman himself does. Agnes is thus a kind of perpetuator of certain cultural traditions, but only those designated as "feminine."

Agnes, as a representative of a feminine cultural tradition and as a personification of the diseased body, is also defined by the physical rhythms of the shots in which she appears. Her own movements are alternately soft and gentle (when she walks around in her room at dawn), and sharp and abrupt (when she thrashes about in pain). And the camera reiterates these rhythms:

she is visualized in zooms, high angles, and panning shots. Close-ups frequently portray her in undulating diagonals, drastic foreshortenings, or sudden verticals, all of which emphasize the grotesque and are visual metaphors for the illness wracking her body and align her with the distorted and grotesque.

The sounds associated with Agnes also emphasize the grotesque. She screams and howls in pain, and shots of her are frequently accompanied by an eerie rasping breathing on the soundtrack, an aural leitmotif of horror and desperation throughout the film. Even her writing in the diary is associated with an unnaturally amplified sound of the pen scratching across the paper. The entire characterization of Agnes is grounded in her pain and illness. We see her grimacing time and again in close-up as her brow is knit, her teeth clenched in an effort to fight off the pain that wracks her body. In the first Agnes segment, we see her eyes wide open in terror and her brow knit in obvious pain, her face a grimace as she tenses her body against a new onslaught of pain. A terrible gasping rips through her body as clenching noises are emitted from her throat. Finally she is able to weep, take a drink of water, and relax. This entire shot lasts fully two minutes and is thus privileged in the film as aligning her with pain.

In this same sequence, a cut to the diary in which she is writing shows the words "it is early Monday morning and I am in pain" (63). She underlines the word "pain." The juxtaposition between a statement of her pain and one in which she simply tells what time it is contributes to a sense of what Mosley calls "her almost casual resignation to a life-long isolation" (158) at the same time that she seems a kind of martyr to forces beyond her control. Even her name associates her with the lamb of God, with ritualized Christian martyrdom. But Agnes's martyrdom is complicated by the fact that, despite the priest's contention (and Mosley's) that she "submitted to [her pain] patiently and uncomplainingly" (75), she does no such thing. On the contrary, she often wails and moans, screaming her defiance of pain. But that Bergman sees her in these terms is apparent in her death scene when a long shot of her shows a light from the window that shines on her more and more brightly, a shot reminiscent of Raval's death in *The Seventh Seal*; a beneficent stream of light descends to signify a passing into peace. Her function as ritual sacrifice is also reiterated in the minister's speech at her funeral when he begs her, as an innocent victim, to intercede with God on mankind's behalf. Of this event, Mellen argues, "The individual woman Agnes is sacrificed . . . in a primitive ritual (again explaining the omnipresence of the color of blood) in the hope that this time God will answer" (307).

This victim who is asked to intercede for us is clearly a Christ figure, as is also clear from Bergman's statement that her name is "hommage à Strindberg" (*Images* 88), a reference to the protagonist of *A Dreamplay* (also

called Agnes) who, like Christ, is sent to the human world in order to investigate the plight of humanity. But this Christ figure is a woman who reiterates the director's continuing identification with women as victims, at the
same time that this film, unlike *The Silence* and *Persona*, locates women's victimization not in social and ideological structures, but in their biology.

· Those aspects of Agnes that must be sacrificed are clearly her body and
her sexuality, which Bergman links with disease. Her body, with its vomiting,
convulsions, and gaspings, is posited as a text to be read, interpreted, consumed, and thus erased. Agnes's body, more than that of any other character, is visually fragmented in close-ups. In her sickroom, hands flutter in and
out of the frame — an arm is lifted, Agnes's feet are isolated against the footboard — the fragmentation of the female body, a traditional filmic strategy
for controlling the threat posed by female sexuality, and the persistent designation of Agnes's bed as a site of illness also associate disease with female
sexuality. In recurring close-ups we see her writhing and almost vomiting,
screaming and sweating, gasping for air and biting her chapped swollen lips.
As Mellen argues:

> The full ugliness of the body dominates. Bergman's disgust becomes ob-
> jective and aesthetically repellent to the subject herself, adding to her mal-
> aise. Stripped of its cumbersome and portentous metaphysics, this portrayal
> reveals in Bergman a man for whom not only sexuality or its intimations of
> need are vile, but most particularly, the female functions. (301)

The red blood of her illness, like that of Karin's genitals, is metaphorically
splattered all over the walls of the manor house; the equation between female
illness and female biology, as so often in male discourse, infects the entire diegesis.

Significantly, the illness from which Agnes is suffering is cancer of the
uterus, a point that links her disease with childbearing. Bergman states that,
although emaciated, "her body is swelled up as though she were in an advanced state of pregnancy" (61); while Agnes's swollen abdomen would
normally indicate pregnancy and be linked with fertility and fecundity, it is in
reality the symptom of a sickness eating away at her. Mellen thus rightly argues that "[Agnes] is dying of cancer of the womb, at once the disease of
being a woman and of not fulfilling a woman's function of bearing a real
child" (302). The female womb becomes in this film a site of disease, the
original source of pain and suffering. The graphic detail with which Bergman
charts Agnes's illness speaks to an obsessive need to link motherhood with
physical and spiritual disease. If *Persona* reveals Bergman's refusal to relinquish the myth that motherhood is the biological destiny of women, we find
here, as in such later films as *Autumn Sonata*, a further ramification of that
refusal. Not only is the rejection of motherhood psychologically destructive
for the individual woman, but the womb itself and female biology become

the source of all evil. Bergman is here projecting the failure of the Patriarch that he had previously extensively chronicled in so many films onto women in a variant of blame-the-victim in order to "save" the father so that there might be a possibility of reconciliation between father and son.

This projection, this attempt to "save" the father, is motivated, I suspect, by the fact that on April 29, 1970, Bergman's father died. He and his son had achieved a kind of reconciliation, and in the hospital a few days before he died, he suddenly invoked the Christian benediction. "A dying father calling down God's blessing on his son. Everything happened very swiftly and un-expectedly" (*Magic Lantern* 277). Bergman's reaction to his father's death — "the yearning for something at last to touch me, to give me grace" (*Magic Lantern* 278) — helps to explain why, in his next few films, he re-treats from his criticism of the patriarchy and instead castigates the mother. Tellingly, *The Touch*, the only film between his father's death and *Cries and Whispers*, features prominently a wooden madonna that is being devoured from within by insects that have remained dormant for five hundred years but that now, exposed to air and light, are activated to consume the icon of the mother. Haunted by guilt over his callous treatment of his father, Bergman projects the failings of the paternal onto the maternal that he might preserve the possibility of ultimate reconciliation with the male parent. As Zern observes, Agnes describes her mother in terms very similar to those used for Ester's and Anna's father in *The Silence* (202). The faults of the fa-ther are transferred onto the mother.

But the Father is, as noted, conspicuously absent from this film; personal interaction takes place under the sign of the female and specifically the mother. Thus the relationships between these women are especially informa-tive. Lonely and isolated, Agnes has relationships only with her sisters and her servant and even these are, despite the final scene in the film, deeply compromised and inadequate. During Agnes's attacks, Maria cowers in the background, Karin bustles about ineffectually, and Anna is the only one who offers real help. The biological sisters by and large relate to Agnes only in terms of their own fears. There is no genuine connection, no attachment of the kind that Ester feels for Anna in *The Silence*, the reason for which be-comes apparent in Agnes's first-person sequence, in which the mother is posited as the source of Agnes's anguish.

Agnes's first-person segment concerns her and her sisters' childhood and concentrates on their mother. This woman (played by Liv Ullmann, who also portrays Maria) is first shown in a barren autumnal garden; the sad, mel-ancholy expression on her face, combined with the information given us over the soundtrack by Agnes's voice, paints a portrait of a woman very much like Maria, childlike, sensual, but given to moods of despondency and despair. Agnes, like Bergman (*Images* 17), feels a deep love for the mother who is "cold and indifferent" to her child (66). She is a woman very much like her daughters, plagued by "ennui, impatience and longing." Even the occasion of a childhood Christmas party when Aunt Olga entertains the children with her magic lantern (another Bergman childhood memory [*Magic Lantern* 24]) brings no joy to Agnes, who feels cut off and isolated from maternal affection. The only moment of true communication between her mother and Agnes occurs when they share a feeling of despair as the mother reaches out and touches her daughter, sharing with the little girl her own pain. All that unifies mother and daughter is suffering.

There is, however, another function to this segment in that it characterizes all three sisters as products of an ongoing maternal heritage of loneliness, alienation, and despair. (One thinks of the many Strindberg characters who are described as "will-less" or "born without a backbone" because they were unwanted by their mothers.) There are, then, two mother figures within the film, Anna and the sisters' biological mother, who correspond to the two archetypal figures of the good mother and the evil mother. The biological mother cannot give her daughters any support or prepare them to face adulthood, because she is gripped by an anguish and melancholy that incapacitate her. When Agnes and her mother do finally connect in their despair, soft piano music is heard in the background, for music again functions in Bergman's world as a kind of metalanguage, a superior form of communication and connectedness. Agnes's, and later Anna's, first-person sequence speaks to Bergman's longing for reunification with the mother, for the reconciliation he so longed for in childhood (*Images* 17), to the refusal throughout his production, however informed it otherwise is by insight as to the genderedness of subjectivity, to relinquish the myth of the mother. Alternately blaming her for his despair and longing for reunification with her, Bergman is never able to demystify the maternal or perceive of motherhood except insofar as it mirrors his own needs. It is in this androcentric projection that *Cries and Whispers* is anchored.

The next daughter whom the spectator encounters is also defined in terms of the maternal legacy, for Maria's difficulty in accepting the responsibilities of adulthood is attributed directly to the mother's failings. Because Maria is played by the same actress who plays the sisters' mother and they are described as being very much alike (66), the film locates Maria's failures in the mother and also projects the daughter's inadequacies back onto the mother, positing the mother as the same spoiled child Maria is (61). The film indicts, then, the mother for Maria's sexual irresponsibility and equates Maria's sexual activity with her destructive neglect of her children.

The film's first post-prologue shot reveals Maria with her eyes closed, the left half of the frame in shadow. She has white lace around her neck, and her delicate hand is lying by her throat as though she were caressing herself. The lace, her childlike hand, and the slightly puffy but sensual cast of her face while asleep establish already the most important aspects of her character, even as the darkness at the left of the frame hints at the "darker" side of this self-preoccupation. She also wears clothes that indicate both self-indulgence and sensuality: low-cut, diaphanous gowns in soft pastels or bright red, with lace at her breasts and jewelry at her throat. The opening shots also link her with a harpsichord, a mirror, wall sconces, an elegant desk, and various gilt chairs, thereby suggesting that she, like Agnes, is a part of a larger cultural tradition of beauty that, as the film progresses, is revealed as a terribly destructive force.

The objects with which Bergman associates her substantiate this impression. In the "reality" segment that introduces Maria, the first shot shows a dollhouse through which the camera pans, revealing a man and woman in the dining room (an image that will later contrast ironically with the scene between Karin and her husband in the dining room) and then the bedroom and kitchen. A close-up of Maria shows her hand at her mouth as though she were going to suck her thumb, with lace around her neck and hand, her hair streaming across the pillow, a doll next to her. Maria is, then, a veritable paradigm of childlike self-absorption and of sensuality. Subsequent shots of the dollhouse reveal a maid at the stove in the kitchen (reminiscent of Anna in her capacity as servant and nurturer), a blond woman beside a bed (Maria is, of course, the only blond woman in the film and is consistently associated with sexuality), and a blond man with mutton-chop whiskers in the dining room (Maria's blond husband sports the same kind of whiskers). It is noteworthy that earlier pans through the rooms of the dollhouse are replaced by cuts, suggesting that however graceful and sensual Maria may appear, she suffers from the same fragmentation of subjectivity as do her sisters. During these shots a music box plays softly, a noise that again associates Maria with childhood objects.

A further series of dollhouse shots is equally connotative: we see a dining table completely set, but with no people around it, a twisted birdcage, and a soldier together with a blond woman. A cut to a detail of a painting shows Maria's mother gazing out to meet the eye of the beholder; the features are Maria's but her hair is black like Karin's and Agnes's. The reference to her mother reinforces an impression of Maria as a child as does the next cut to Maria on the bed next to her doll. While images of birdcage and dollhouse function elsewhere in the Scandinavian artistic tradition as occasions to reflect on the stifling domesticity imposed upon women (the birdcage in Strindberg's *Miss Julie* and Alf Sjöberg's film of the play and the dollhouse, of course, of the Ibsen play by that name), such is not the case here; here they are not problematized, they merely reflect the character's childishness and irresponsibility, her refusal to accept adulthood.

The visual rhythms that define Maria reinforce this spectator impression. She seems to flow in and out of the film frame, gently and smoothly, primping at mirrors, her touch a bit flirtatious. Maria is almost always shot in languorous diagonals and horizontals. We note here too that Maria is twice photographed asleep and is unable to stay awake during her vigil over her sick sister, a manifestation of her self-absorption as well as of her languor and irresponsible passivity.

This self-absorption also prevents Maria from effectively bonding with her sisters. She either evades Agnes's needs or else recoils in horror from her illness. But the extent to which her life (and by extension the mother's) is ruled by self-indulgent sensuality is apparent not only when she tries to seduce the doctor who has come to examine Agnes, but also in her first-person sequence. In the former instance, the one we also see first chronologically, the camera alternates between close-ups of him and medium shots of the two together taken over his right shoulder. This camera position privileges spectator identification with the doctor, and we see her with his eyes as temptress. The spectator experiences female sexuality through an objectifying male, not a female, perspective. For Maria (as for, by extension, the mother) female sexuality is a matter not of sharing but of self-indulgence. The extent to which that female sexual self-indulgence is implicated as irresponsible and destructive becomes apparent in Maria's first-person sequence.

It begins as the doctor attends to Anna's daughter, who is sick. The next cut to Maria in a bright red, low-cut dress at the dinner table sipping red wine implies that she exploits this child's illness to seduce the doctor. Thus, Bergman establishes another link between female sexuality and the destruction of the child. A close-up of the doctor eating shows Maria predatorially watching him as she invites him to spend the night. After the scene shifts to the doctor's bedroom and he upbraids Maria for her coldness and selfishness, it concludes with a long shot of them behind a seemingly enormous white bed, as the film again associates female sexuality with narcissism.

A cut to the next morning shows Joakim, Maria's husband, at breakfast, returned from his trip. The next shot of Maria with her little girl reinforces the identification between Maria and the child-like, at the same time that the spectator is asked to condemn her as an irresponsible and bad mother who neglects her child for her own selfish whims. After she tells her husband about the doctor's having spent the night, he gazes into her eyes and observes that she looks downward, apparently unable to bear his scrutiny. Then Maria follows him to his study, and a long shot shows Joakim at his desk with a dagger in his chest turning to the camera and pleading for help. Maria recoils in horror as she exclaims, "No!" following which the scene fades to a red screen. Maria's first-person sequence concludes, then, with a restatement of the equation between female sexuality and narcissism, as the film erases the female body as morally reprehensible.

Karin's character and personality are delineated through the same techniques. She wears high-necked, constricting, dark-colored dresses of stiff, formal fabrics, and the activities in which she is engaged suggest rigidity as well as a certain cerebral quality. We see her working on what look like the household accounts when the pen suddenly drops from her hand in a movement expressive of despair. At this point a long shot shows her at a heavy wooden desk, against a window through which cold rays of sunlight seem to sear and expose her. Her head drops onto her hands until she suddenly with apparently great effort pulls herself erect with a sharp jerk that is reminiscent of Agnes's similar jerky motions and thus suggests that both women suffer from the same spiritual disease. This whole sequence of images describes a woman struggling against a power too strong for her, a woman whose rigidity is a defense against forces that threaten to engulf her. We note too that Karin's hair is the same color as her mother's and is worn the same way, further linking Karin's frigidity and the maternal legacy.

Karin also occupies herself with an extremely intricate bit of lacemaking. When approached by Bergman about doing the role of Karin, Ingrid Thulin purportedly agreed to wear a black wig but drew the line at reading a book for her stage business, so that Bergman compromised on her doing lacework instead. Although the reference is less obvious, the lacework indicates Karin's detached, cerebral character as surely as Maria's primping intimates her vanity and narcissism. Karin's rigidity and inflexibility are further suggested by the way she speaks to Anna, imperiously giving orders and addressing her in the third-person singular. Her lament that she is "freezing" indicates (in Swedish as well as in English) that she is physically (and emotionally) cold and that she perceives herself to be freezing, petrifying into a kind of living death. The rhythms with which Bergman defines Karin strengthen this impression. She moves awkwardly and stiffly and sits absolutely erect. While Agnes is often seen foreshortened and in diagonals or sudden stark verticals, all of which emphasize the grotesque, and Maria is depicted in languorous diagonals and horizontals, Karin is usually shot in a completely vertical posture, stiff and unmoving.

The reason for this rigidity is dramatically shown in her first-person sequence, an intense and powerful vision of the extent to which, from a feminist perspective, she has internalized male violence. A long shot shows a very formal scene with the husband and wife at table separated by a large candelabra; Karin is seated in front of a black Chinese screen, a massive carved black chest, and a lamp, Fredrik against a formal marble fireplace, flanked by two tall globed lamps. He is, then, associated with rigidity and formality while she is surrounded by black two-dimensional surfaces, a background that again suggests her subjectivity. This scene uses more than twenty straight cuts to build up a tension between these two characters, the only bond between them their common biological need for food and sleep.

During their stilted conversation, the husband appears pinched and mean and eats and drinks gluttonously, while Karin is nervous and distressed. Despite the fact that her husband "is repulsive to her physically and mentally" (61), Karin tries to play the role of the good wife, the pleasant dinner companion who engages her husband in interesting small talk and plans their social outings. But, when he suggests that they go to bed, Karin's wine glass falls and breaks, an obvious metaphor for the fragility of that role and of her emotional health, which has been sapped by a sham marriage. As Törnqvist has observed, the feast of love is here replaced with a feast of hate (89). One might add, however, that cups and chalices are also an object symbol for the receptive, fruitful aspect of the mother; for Karin this aspect is distorted into an implement of destruction; tellingly, Karin, although she has five children, is described in the screenplay as "untouched by maternity" (61). Her misery, her "permanent rage against life" (61), and the "guilt" that so torments her are all associated with her rejection of maternality.

A quick succession of close-up cuts shows her attempt to hide her feelings and her husband's smug complacency. As he leaves the table, a final close-up shows Karin with a white rose in the frame. She is completely surrounded by the black carved chest but has now taken over the rose symbolism previously associated with Agnes. Both Agnes and she, through their repression of physicality, represent the film's valorization of the suppression of the body. As Karin's hand picks up the shard of glass her voice is heard on the soundtrack: "It's nothing but a tissue of lies" (69), an acknowledgment of the bankruptcy of her marriage and her life.

The scene continues in Karin's dressing room, where Bergman moves back to a slow long shot of her. As Mellen observes: "Undressing, Karin peels off endless layers of clothing, beautifully symbolic of the layers of convention hiding feeling . . . . The facade of false identity is represented by her elaborate clothes and is contrasted with the childlike closeness to her own feelings of Anna who helps her" (308). Dressed for bed in her white nightgown (which again associates her with Agnes), Karin gazes at the shard of glass and, as we watch her face, inserts it into her vagina. She bends forward in pain but then leans back with a smile on her face; the only pleasure she can know is the pain of sexual self-mutilation whereby she denies pleasure to the male. After she enters the bedroom, a cut shows her husband leering at her, and then a close-up reveals her spreading the blood from her wound on her mouth and smiling victoriously. But her smile soon disappears as she realizes that she has attained but a pyrrhic victory over her husband's loathsome advances.

Not surprisingly, this extraordinary sequence of female self-mutilation has occasioned some of the most severe criticism of the film by feminists, typical of whom is Mellen, who finds that Karin "revels in her own degradation and the degradation of her sex" (308). While Karin's rejection of her repulsive husband's sexual demands and her acknowledgment of her marriage as a "tissue of lies" might be read as privileging a feminist reading, the form her rejection takes certainly cannot, for it occurs as a mutilation of her own body. In a career distinguished by graphic renderings of the fantastic and the bizarre, this scene stands out as singular in its violence, its cruelty, and its purported anchoring in a specifically female reality. If psychoanalytical theory is correct in its view that dominant cinema galvanizes mechanisms of fetishism to counteract the threat of castration posed by the female body, Bergman's film goes even further: by locating castration in the female, it projects again a male fear onto the female. Furthermore, by reinscribing the Freudian assumption that in women masochistic fantasy replaces sexuality, this film participates in the male discursive tradition. The locating of Karin's (f)rigidity in her sexuality, in her biology, is again suspect, a projection of the ills of the world onto the female and her body.

The film posits, then, two kinds of female sexuality — promiscuity and frigidity, both products of the evil mother. As Mellen puts it, "For Bergman's women in general the body and its demands are insatiable. When bodily urges are unacknowledged, rage and frustration follow in the denial. When they are gratified, the mind and the sense of middle-class decency are outraged, possessed by feelings of disgust, low animality, and self-hatred" (300). She further argues, appropriately for this film if not for the whole production, that his men

> fail largely because their pleas go unanswered; his women are ensnared at a much more elementary level of human development. Their lives lack meaning because they are rooted in biology and an inability to choose a style of life independent of the female sexual role . . . . If [woman] refuses to be a woman as Bergman defines woman — instinctual, passive, submissive, and trapped within the odors and blood of her genitals — there is no place for her in the world. (298–99)

While the scene might be read as a feminist statement about the self-violence that society visits upon women, the fact that the film is unclear as to whether this scene is fantasy or not undercuts that potential. The issue becomes instead a matter of Karin's individual masochistic psychology. Bergman refuses to allow Karin to speak for something that goes beyond her own self, instead capitalizing on her pain to shock the spectator while refusing to situate her pain in a larger ideological context.

Appropriately, Karin has an intense aversion to female intimacy, manifested in her rejection of Maria's gestures of friendship and Agnes's demands on her, and in her recoiling from all human touch. But it is Karin, the protagonist who represses rather than expresses sexuality, who embodies the possibility for human connection, and, after Agnes's death, she becomes the authoritative presence in the film. Tellingly, although she has previously behaved imperiously toward Anna and slapped her, she asks the servant for forgiveness, thereby suggesting that she acknowledges the claims of others. And Bergman says of her, "She bears a gift for affection, devotion, and a longing for nearness" (61). As in *The Silence*, the hope for a shared subjectivity that transcends the dualistic parental legacy is located in the female who represses sexuality and disavows her body.

This hope is fulfilled on the evening on which Karin and Maria share a meal in the dining room. As before, Karin's background is a massive carved chest while Maria is seen against the Chinese screen, sitting in the same position as Fredrik during Karin's first-person sequence. Now both women share black backgrounds and are dressed in black. Too, the elaborate candelabra that separated husband and wife have been replaced by symbolic flowers and fruit. The fact that this encounter occurs in the same room where Karin eats with her husband invites a comparison between her behavior then and now. Then she engaged in small talk but was repressed, trembling with the sublimation of her anguish, while now she is more genuinely communicative, reaching out however tentatively to her sister. Karin confesses to all the hate she bears within her, to her thoughts of suicide, her guilt, her boredom, and her contempt for her sister, until she bolts up from the table and the camera pans after her. As Karin begs Maria's forgiveness, Agnes's bedroom is visible in the background, suggesting that this reconciliation is possible only because of the ritual sacrifice of Agnes. A close-up of both women in profile hugging, caressing, and speaking with each other is accompanied by poignant cello music that renders the sisters' speech inaudible. Thus Bergman, like various feminist filmmakers, stresses again that language is inadequate, that touch and music are alternative means of genuine connection. There is here a sense of female connectedness and intimacy from which the men in the film are excluded and which expresses itself in a kind of "mutual gazing" between the two women that works against the usual visual modes of domination and submission. It is important too that Bergman, in this and the predinner scene in which Maria tried to connect with Karin, uses pans extensively. Previously, pans were associated largely with Agnes and Anna, but Agnes's death functions as an event that unites all these women, and they enter into a state of grace engendered by the destruction of the female body. The camera is at its most fluid in this scene moving up, down, and around its subjects as though it were caressing them, touching them as they touch each other, a visual expression of the film's desire to connect with but also to appropriate and contain the female.

It is appropriately Karin who picks up Agnes's diary and reads about to-getherness and friendship, her voice reverberating over a long shot of Anna standing by Agnes's body. As Anna appears in close-up, Karin's voice reads, "And it is this which is called mercy;" Anna and the forces of commitment and maternality she represents are a secular form of "mercy." The fact that Karin's voice joins with Anna's image, however, also links the two of them, suggesting the possibility of Karin's entering into the mercy of which her sister writes and which Anna embodies. The conflation of these two charac-ters is also interesting in light of their names; Karin was the name of Bergman's own mother, and, when he wrote *Best Intentions*, a fictional ac-count of his parents' courtship and early marriage, he named the fictional mother Anna, two instances of naming that suggest again the extent to which this film centers on reconciliation with the mother.

The similarity between the two sisters' first-person sequences is striking. Obvious parallels include the fact that both are introduced by a male narrator and both present a dinner scene, a bedroom scene, and an act of bloody self-mutilation. But the formal symmetry of Karin's sequence contrasts with the looser asymmetry of the scenes between Maria and the doctor. Karin's scenes depict a frigidity of character while Maria's illustrate a childlike irresponsibil-ity. Thus, the two sequences can be seen as Bergman's attempt to represent the two sisters as only superficially different, as essential(ist)ly alike in their grounding in biology. The final major character in Bergman's visual drama is Anna the servant. The screenplay claims, "She doesn't speak; perhaps she doesn't think either" (62), a representation of her that is sustained through-out the film. Her clothing is muted; earth tones of grey, black, and brown predominate, and she is always seen either in uniform or in her nightgown, a fact that restricts her to the role of servant at the same time that the night-gown (like those worn by all the other women) hints at an essentialist female subjectivity grounded in sexuality. Anna is the stereotypical servant, scurrying about to serve others. In the opening of the film, after waking Maria and serving her breakfast, she makes up the morning fire, during which Bergman shoots her in profile, her face warmed by the flames; Anna is consistently as-sociated with light and fire, for she is, for Bergman, an elemental force, a woman of hearth and light.

Throughout the scene in which Bergman introduces Anna, she is linked, like her predecessors, with connotative objects. The iron bed railings indicate her confinement within the social role of servant at the same time that a can-dle radiantly illuminates her. Her humble prayer (this nonthinking uncritical woman still apparently believes in God), the vase of flowers, and the apple she eats all speak to the simple, earthbound qualities of this woman. Her room significantly is the only one in the house in which the walls are not red; rather, it is white, a color that links her with Agnes and the denial of the body. The picture of Anna's dead child (not problematized as were the photographs in *The Silence* and *Persona*), a close-up on a detail of the child's face, and the segment's final shot of an empty crib emphasize again Anna's maternality. The soft piano music transition to the next sequence with Agnes links Anna's maternal qualities (we first hear it over the photograph of her child) with Agnes, who, because of her victimization, her association with Bergman's childhood memories, and the fact that only she and the director himself are granted the authority of voice-overs, is also a representation of Bergman and his need for reconciliation with the mother.

Anna's activities àre those of a female servant — sewing, building a fire, caring for the ill, serving food, all nurturing activities traditionally allotted the mother of the family. That this is somehow "right," that Anna is in tune with "natural" forces and that Bergman is romanticizing rather than contesting the conditions of female servitude (almost all the servants whom he so idealizes — from *Smiles of a Summer Night* to *Fanny and Alexander* — are women) is apparent also in the fluid camera treatment she receives. As she responds to a voice calling, "Anna! Come here!" the camera pans with her in a smooth movement connotative of Anna's ostensibly instinctual relationship to life.

Bergman's idealization of the conflation of the mother and the servant supports Ellmann's observation that the mother is frequently aligned with the servant in male discourse in a combination of "uncritical obedience and respect combined (as these childlike qualities cannot be in children) with sexual maturity" (126). This positioning of women serves, as Bergom-Larsson points out, to mythologize not only "woman" but also the lower "serving" class: "To both the lower class and to woman is ascribed an original natural power that in some way can save the members of the bourgeoisie from the disintegration that threatens them" (70). Here as earlier in the canon, then, we observe Bergman's steadfast refusal to allow woman as mother any autonomy; she exists solely in relation to the needs of the (male) child and the extent to which she does or does not (as is almost always the case in Bergman) satisfy them. The film refuses to acknowledge that "the recognition a child seeks is something the mother is able to give only by virtue of her independent identity . . . . Indeed, as the child increasingly establishes his own independent center of existence, her recognition will be meaningful only to the extent that it reflects her own equally separate subjectivity" (Benjamin 24).

The representation of Anna's body conflates the maternal and plenitude, the heaviness of her body positing her as an embodiment of fullness and richness — "Everything about her is weight" (62). Interestingly, Bergman purportedly encouraged Kari Sylwan, who plays Anna and who was at the time a ballet dancer, to gain a great deal of weight for this role, and in *Images* he describes the character as "heavy, exhausted womanliness" (88). The representation of her body as maternal plenitude is further manifest when she twice frees her breast from her nightgown to comfort and caress Agnes. On the first occasion, Anna's kissing Agnes on the lips suggests, I think, the subliminal sexual aspect of the attraction to the mother at the same time that the positive aspect of the implicit lesbianism of this scene reflects Bergman's continuing fascination with the possibility of a sexuality not fragmented by gender.

It is furthermore telling that Anna is the only woman who escapes fetishization by the camera; while Agnes is fetishized through fragmenting close-ups of body parts, Maria through her seductive clothing, and Karin through the long shot of her naked body, both Anna's body and her clothing escape this male strategy of containment because she "embodies" maternal plenitude, the possibility for Bergman, once he has repressed the evil mother, finally to become reconciled and reunited with the good mother. Too, when the minister says, "May [God] let His angels disrobe you of the memory of your earthly pain" (75), the camera lingers on Anna, who, in her capacity as surrogate "good" mother, embodies the qualities necessary to redemption, reconciliation, and a forgetting of pain. The bodies of all these women, then, are sites of the inscription of male desire, a desire to erase the female body through repression (Agnes), containment (Karin), disavowal on moral grounds (Maria), or confinement within the maternal (Anna). As Butler observes, "The association of the body with the female works along magical relations of reciprocity whereby the female sex becomes restricted to its body, and the male sex, fully disavowed, becomes paradoxically, the incorporeal instrument of an ostensibly radical freedom" (12). By alternately disavowing and containing the female body, the male asserts his freedom from corporeality.

Anna's representation as maternal body is underscored by her first-person sequence, which begins in her room as the sound of a child's crying is merged with Agnes's raspy breathing, underscoring Anna's maternal relationship with Agnes and suggesting that even Anna is a failed mother who has transformed the guilt and grief over the loss of her child into a maternal solicitude for Agnes. As Anna enters Agnes's room, she finds a tear running down the dead woman's cheek. But only after her sisters have rejected her does Agnes turn to Anna, who, in a series of pans that contrast with the cuts used to portray the two sisters' reactions, tells us in a frontal close-up "You needn't be afraid. I'll take care of her" (89), and closes the door on Karin and Maria. Close-ups of Karin and Maria showing their fear and repulsion cut to a long shot of Anna holding Agnes in her lap in a pietá-like position, again with her breast bare as cello music swells forth; "Agnes sinks into her tenderness and grows calm; the hard tension in her tormented body softens

and relaxes. 'How good you are,' she whispers. 'You're so kind and good'"
(71). The maternal body is the source both of ultimate pain and of ultimate
consolation; the dying female Christ figure reposes in the arms of the good
mother, an image grounded, one suspects, in Bergman's feeling that his own
mother rejected him as an infant because he was mortally ill (*Images* 17).
This cello music, like that which we heard during Karin's and Maria's moment of intimacy, marks in both instances a fullness of experience and connection possible only when the sexuality of the female is repressed and
replaced by the maternal. But this portrait of intimacy and selfless love is
problematic, since Anna's love for Agnes is clearly a projection of the love she
felt for her dead child. Furthermore, this is no reciprocal relationship; Agnes
gives Anna nothing but her needs, for in Bergman's world the mother has
no needs of her own, no purpose except to nurture her children. This is also
born out by the pietá-like composition that ends this sequence, a composition that, through its cultural associations, again mythologizes the mother
and deprives her of subjectivity. *Cries and Whispers* represses the sexual female body in order to reify the mother as non-body and all-body.

Thus, despite Bergman's possible intentions to give women a voice, the
women's voices in *Cries and Whispers* speak only an anguish of biology
grounded in the failings of the mother. In terms of female sexuality, the only
alternatives the film posits are the polarities of repression and promiscuity.
The film's relentless binarism might be connected to the aforementioned crisis in Bergman's relationship with his parents, to Benjamin's observation that
"when the conflict between dependence and independence becomes too intense, the psyche gives up the paradox in favor of an opposition. Polarity, the
conflict of opposites, replaces the balance within the self" (50). No longer
does he present women such as Ester, Elisabet, and Alma, whose sexual ambiguity reflects their dissatisfaction with androcentric values and ideology. No
longer do deeply flawed but basically aware and thoughtful women struggle
to define themselves against a hostile culture that would contain them within
rigidly circumscribed roles. Instead, his women characters are cardboard cut-
outs, overdetermined by their specific sets of attributes — certain clothing,
certain objects and occupations, certain sounds, certain movements, and
certain camera treatments — as if Bergman had, before writing the filmscript,
set up a chart on which he gave each woman a particular set of characteristics
in all these categories. It all fits neatly together, reality "doesn't seep in" any-
where, and the spectator is left with a schematic (if pictorially compelling and
brilliantly visualized) chart of female stereotypes. Women become in *Cries
and Whispers* the "pseudocenters" of the filmic discourse.

But, if Bergman has jettisoned Ester for Karin, Alma for Maria, if he has
turned his back on the ambivalent and ambiguous women of his films from
the early and mid-sixties, he retains to a great extent the potentially feminist

filmic strategies from those films. The first-person sequences are a case in point. The four brief introductory segments (Agnes in her bedroom in the early morning, Maria with her dollhouse, Karin at the desk, and Anna in her room) are reiterated and amplified through the rest of the film as each woman has a more lengthy segment of interior monologue. The first four segments portray these women from the outside, while the second four demonstrate the "cries and whispers" that define their subjectivity. We note too that, while each of the introductory segments is devoid of speech (with the exception of Anna's prayer for her daughter), the second series points up the duplicity and inadequacy of verbal discourse. Language is still for Bergman deeply implicated, but now it is an expression of the maternal legacy of narcissism and despair, rather than as an aspect of male ideology.

The film privileges these first-person sequences as authentic through bracketing close-ups; except for Agnes's sequence, they all begin with a dissolve from the filmic present to a red screen and then cut to a close-up of the woman whose segment we will see. Another red screen then dissolves to the beginning of the sequence itself, all of which conclude with a reversal of the same series of shots: dissolve to red screen, dissolve to close-up, dissolve to red screen, dissolve to the filmic present. The recurring use of close-ups at the beginning and ends of the first-person sequences functions, then, to authenticate the interiority of the scenes before us as "pure" subjectivity.

The authenticity of these segments is also reinforced by the fact that the close-ups, like the clothing, objects, occupations, and movements of these women, are character-specific. In Maria's close-up her mouth is half-open, suggesting "an expression of discontent and hunger" (68), and we hear a remote sound like two people making love. Karin's close-up with her eyes and mouth open resembles several shots of Agnes in pain. This resemblance is significant because it is Karin who will assume Agnes's authority in the film and because the possibilities for redemption that they share are rooted in a denial of the self and the female body. The sounds that accompany her close-up are those of a remote whispering and weeping, again like that associated with Agnes. By contrast, Anna's face is quiet and "expressionless, impassive" (64), and the "cries and whispers" that reverberate on her soundtrack are those of a child weeping softly. The mother is linked again with inexpressivity, with a denial of the autonomous self. The film thus stresses the authenticity of these inauthentic representations of female experience. Whereas *Persona* employed devices to dislodge the female voice from the female image, the close-ups that introduce this film's first-person segments serve to reinforce the equation between female subjectivity and the female body.

This tendency in the film to deny the spectator any space for critical subjectivity is apparent also in the larger development of the four first-person sequences. Immediately after Agnes's segment we see her suddenly awakened by noises, an event that allows us to perceive of that which has gone before as a dream, the most conventional and readily-accepted of film's possibilities for interior monologue. But the following first-person sequences seem less and less tied to events in objective reality. Kawin points to another distinction when he argues that, in Karin's sequence, "The impression of self-knowledge is more intense. Whereas Maria's sequence is tied into the plot by a simple act of association (another attempt to seduce the doctor), Karin's appears not simply to explain but to influence her behavior during the second half of the film" (16). The whole question of subjectivity becomes more complicated as the film progresses, for, while Maria's and Agnes's sequences may be flash-backs to "real" events, the very extremeness and the intensity of the self-destructive impulse in Karin's sequence make us wonder if it is a flashback or simply a dream, a fantasy of revenge on her odious husband. If it is the latter, then the film is moving one step further away from palpable reality — from memory to fantasy — yet deeper into subjectivity. This explanation becomes all the more plausible when we witness Anna's first-person segment.

Anna's first-person sequence is in a number of respects different from those that precede it. Not only does Bergman contrast Anna's love for Agnes with the sham marriages that trap Karin and Maria, but the narrative tech-nique differs. The fact that both Maria and Karin stare comatosely off into space and, most importantly of course, that Agnes has somehow come back from the dead prohibits our ascribing to this scene the same "reality" that we could to the others. Bergman describes this segment as somehow non-real: "I don't quite know how to explain this. What is important is that everything in this situation appears natural — real and yet mysterious, in a tension" (85). The film has, then, moved deeper into interiority through its increasingly subjective modes of narration. Kawin rightly sees this increasing interiority as central to the film:

> Among these sequences there is a structure of ascending intimacy . . . . In response to the vastly differing capacities for openness . . . each woman pos-sesses, their subjective sequences achieve different degrees of intimacy . . . . It is in keeping with the film's apparent intent to suggest that increased in-timacy (in which Bergman has led the audience to participate) results not in isolation but in community . . . . Maria's [sequence] is a memory, Karin's a memory that may or may not shift to fantasy, and Anna's is an entirely cre-ated mental event. (15, 18)

By presenting Anna's first-person sequence as fantasy, Bergman forces the spectator to share her perception, to experience a kind of increased intimacy with the film itself. The film achieves, then, extradiegetically what characters achieve intradiegetically. The mergence of subjectivities and valorization of multiplicity and connectedness subvert the dominant masculine notion of fixed selfhood. But, if the film's representation of subjectivity deconstructs certain binaristic categories, it also deprives the spectator of the possibility of judging it critically. While Bergman may intend the obviously "non-objective reality" of Anna's first-person sequence to foster in the spectator the same kind of critical detachment that *Persona* engenders, to activate the same kind of alternative pleasure of puzzle solving, such a strategy is not an essential part of the larger structure; it is at odds with a content and a structure that posit the absolute knowability and concomitant appropriability of female experience, for, unlike *Persona*, *Cries and Whispers* unproblematically promotes the mergence of spectator and spectacle.

The first-person sequences and red screens are but two of the film's disjunctive strategies that both subvert and support a feminist cinematic experience. *Cries and Whispers* also adopts a clearly antinarrative stance; linear progression is exchanged for a fluid, associative structure. Indeed, one is reminded of Donovan's argument that women's texts, in order to be faithful to female experience, may have to use different narrative devices, devices that may appear like "plotlessness" or use a "webbed, networked . . . nuclear," rather than a linear, structure, "mov[ing] out from one base to a given point and back again, out to another point and back again" (106). Like these texts, Bergman's film seems to follow Virginia Woolf's call for "less 'system' and more sympathy." This associative quality is further enhanced by the use of vignettes, dream association, and somnambulistic movements. *Persona*, to be sure, deploys many of these same structural strategies, but there is, I think, a salient difference between the two works in that the earlier film opens itself up at various points to intrusions from "the real world" that call its fictionality into question, thereby allowing a space for what Kuhn calls "a radical heterogeneity in spectator-text relations" (*Women's Pictures* 171). *Cries and Whispers*, on the other hand, constructs a closed, internally coherent, fictional world and never questions its own status as a fiction or the conditions of its creation.

Like *Persona*, this film also galvanizes multiple viewpoints, thereby asserting pluralism and dispersing authority throughout the film rather than ascribing it, as is usually the case in classical cinema, to a single, usually male, consciousness. But the multiple viewpoints adduced in *Cries and Whispers* are, in reality, not multiple at all, for they all assert the idea that women are rooted in biology, that motherhood is the source of human evil and malaise, and that female sexuality exists only as repression or promiscuity. These multiple viewpoints also suggest that female relationships take place only within certain androcentric parameters — as substitution or consolation for faulty or aborted mothering. The film after all posits a single collective male consciousness despite the narrative technique. Thus, while the filmic structures of fluidity and association in *Persona* are grounded in a perception of the mutability of human identity, in a questioning of the absolute equation between gender and subjectivity, similar structures in *Cries and Whispers* are based in an understanding of women as all fundamentally the same, as all experiencing the same biological destiny. That these structures in the later film also serve to reinforce the male stereotype of woman as incoherence and formlessness merely compounds the problem.

Bergman's use of images of screening surfaces is equally problematic. As in *The Silence*, head- and footboards are a recurring image. Long shots from across the footboard or medium and close-up shots from behind the headboard reveal Agnes on her sickbed, and Anna is associated with rusted bed railings and her child's empty crib. For both Agnes and Anna, then, the head- and footboards are associated with internalized pain, with a need to repress sexuality, as they were for Ester in *The Silence*. But, while that film situates the source of pain and repressed sexuality in the father, this film locates it in the mother. And, whereas Ester possesses an acute awareness of her position, Agnes and Anna do not; rather, they are both described as blindly accepting in their submission to their pain even though that acceptance is, in Agnes's case, not consistent. Whereas Ester bequeaths a positive legacy of futurity to Johan, Agnes's legacy is one of acquiescence. Thus, these screen images, as metaphors for the female body, do not problematize the permeability/impermeability complex but rather are rendered as absolutely permeable for and absolutely appropriable by the male gaze.

The same can be said of the window imagery in *Cries and Whispers*, while both *The Silence* and *Persona* use window screens to address issues of the transgression of boundaries of subjectivity, and while the earlier of these films describes this problem specifically in terms of a hostile male world encroaching on a female one, by 1972 Bergman seems to have rejected this practice. Early in the film, we observe Agnes looking out a window into autumnal gardens stripped of their foliage. This world outside, unlike that in *The Silence*, is not characterized as specifically male; its barrenness is associated specifically with the mother, the only person (until the last moments of the film) whom we see in this landscape. The danger to the women in this house comes not from the male but from the female; the threat of encroachment and violation is identified with the mother and her legacy. This impression is strengthened when, shortly before Agnes's death, Karin rises and approaches Maria, only to turn and walk to a window. Both Agnes and Karin (who becomes the locus of spectator identification once Agnes dies) are associated with windows in contexts that speak to specifically female failure. While *The Silence* and *Persona* link the mutability of subjectivity with the gender of the protagonists, they also posit that subjectivity as a response to, and in constant conflict with, male subjectivity. They posit women as more likely to experience crises of subjectivity because of their cultural experience, whereas this film describes these crises as arising out of female biology.

The coloration of the film also warrants examination in terms of its function as a potentially disjunctive device. Blood-red dominates to an extraordinary extent in this film, calling attention to itself in every scene. The interior walls are (with the exception of Anna's room) all papered or painted this bright red and serve as a background for almost every scene in the film. These interiors derive from Bergman's view that the decor for this film should be "flexible, enclosing, elusive, and present, evocative without being obtrusive .... The bluntest but also the most valid [reason for the red] is probably that the whole thing is something internal and that ever since my childhood I have pictured the inside of the soul as a moist membrane in shades of red" (60). Years later, he says "When I was a child, I saw the soul as a shadowy smoke-blue dragon hovering like a great winged being, half bird, half fish. But inside the dragon, everything was red" (*Images* 90). The spectator may, however, have other associations with this bloodred color, which culturally connotes life and energy and yet is also the color of the loss of life, of death. The red may also suggest that the interior of the house is a kind of womb, an interpretation that would cohere with the film's persistent emphasis on the shadow the mother casts over the lives of the protagonists and with the pervasive "femaleness" of this environment and the fact that Agnes is suffering from cancer of the uterus. Thus, the red screens may also be seen as another aspect of the ideological substructure of the film that places women solely within the realm of biology and equates female subjectivity with the womb. The pervasive red can then be seen as a kind of colorative determinism whereby everything that happens is predestined by the color's biological associations.

Red screens like those bracketing the first-person segments appear throughout *Cries and Whispers* — behind the credits at the beginning, between the shot of Anna's face by the fire and the Victorian dollhouse, and after the words that constitute the penultimate shot of the film. But, if various screen images function in both *The Silence* and *Persona* as metaphors for a transgression of boundaries, a problematizing of female experience as permeable and impermeable, such would not seem to be the case here. They instead function as images of permeability, as fields that allow the spectator access to female "reality" without ever problematizing that access. These screens, unlike those in *Persona*, do not involve a questioning of the ethical dimensions of voyeurism and appropriation, of the attempt to "read" the female body. They do not question the permeability of female experience to the spectator's gaze; rather, the film posits it as a given. While the screens in both films implicitly challenge the spectator's complicity in the cinematic process, those in this film are bright red, a color that seems more palpable, more corporeal than the white and would seem to promote rather than to deconstruct the fantasy of mergence. In brief, screens in *Cries and Whispers* function to decrease rather than to increase the potential for critical subjectivity in the viewer.

The blood red of the film is vividly juxtaposed with white to create a persistent visual dichotomy. If the red connotes biology and blood, white is the color of innocence and nonbody (in the final scene of the film, all four characters wear white dresses). Large blocks of white occur in the sheets on Agnes's bed to reinforce the association between white and the repression of sexuality, as do, of course, the women's nightgowns. Thus, Mellen suggests that their clothing expresses the characters' "unconscious wish developed throughout the film to return to the virginal" (303). While the fact that all the nightgowns look almost identical might in isolation be read as a marker of female connectedness, what it instead indicates, I suspect, is Bergman's desire to subsume all women into one essentialist view, to see the female in terms of sexuality and biology.

The inclusion of black as a tonal accent reinforces the binary worldview of the film. While black is, of course, realistically appropriate to mourners, it is also a color that Bergman throughout his production associates with clerics and with Christianity — witness Raval and the flagellant priest in *The Seventh Seal*, Tomas in *Winter Light*, and the ministers in this film and *Fanny and Alexander*. There seems to be a sense, then, in which Bergman projects onto his female protagonists the failings of the patriarchy when he dresses them in black. Thus Anna's black garb, although appropriate to her servant status, also reinforces her as a source of alternative salvation in this film. The pietá position in which she holds Agnes during her first-person sequence and her maternal nurturing indicate that she is a redemptive figure. If Anna is the site of alternative redemptive religious values like Mia in *The Seventh Seal*, she is also inarticulate and unthinking, a subjectivity aligned with the maternal body. Thus the distantiation effect of the drastic coloration of the film is undermined by its unreflecting binarism as well as by its sexual and biological ideology. The schematic coloration reflects a schematic concept of the female. Although the coloring of the film might privilege "passionate detachment" on the part of the spectator, that detachment is subverted by its gender associations. Visually striking as this film is, it ultimately is an albeit very beautiful male seduction.

The deployment of silence too can, as feminist criticism has repeatedly pointed out, function as a criticism of male ideology and the language with which it empowers itself, as is the case in *The Silence* and *Persona*. The film tries, through the suppression of spoken discourse and the understatement of the diary entry in the opening segment, to communicate by image and nonverbal sound and thereby to emphasize the inadequacy of the spoken word. But silence in *Cries and Whispers* is presented less as protest or as a condition imposed upon women by male culture than as arising out of female experience, as part of the maternal legacy. Agnes's most cherished memory is of her silent moment with her mother. Indeed, the entire film might be seen as defining female space as belonging to Lacan's presymbolic, prelinguistic realm, a view that Bergman's use of music also supports, for while *Persona* uses nonnaturalistic music to encourage "passionate detachment" and to reinforce the film's insistence on the noninterpretability and inexpressibility of subjectivity, in *Cries and Whispers* music (especially in the scene of intimacy between Karin and Maria) underscores the inability of female experience to be articulated, the fundamental incoherence and formlessness of that experience. We note too that the priest speaks *for* Agnes; the film seems to suggest that only through male intervention and interpretation can women genuinely and truly speak.

A filmic delineation of space (and consequently of time), because of their gender implications for spectator-text relations, can also serve a disjunctive function. Most of the film, according to the screenplay, takes place in a manor house that "was built . . . as a retreat for a distinguished gentleman's cast-off mistress" (59). Not only does the setting and its coloration posit the house as a female space defined by biology, but, unlike *The Silence*, this film does not problematize space by acknowledging the traditional distinction between the female domestic sphere and the male public sphere. If there is a kind of "prison-nest effect" to this interior space, it does not occur in any kind of social or cultural context. That these women are trapped is clear, but the recognition that entrapment is the function of male authority is disavowed. Here there is no problematization of the traditional designation of range as masculine and confinement as feminine; instead, it is naturalized. The film creates a kind of architectural determinism; it designates the domestic sphere as female but also makes that space one of anguish and terror, revealing that "the paradigmatic woman's space — the home — is yoked to dread, and a crisis of vision" (Doane, "The 'Woman's' Film" 70).

This strategy coheres with a mobile camera that effectively removes the film's action from any conventional sense of space. The extensive use of pans, predominantly but by no means exclusively both in Agnes's death scene and in the depiction of Anna's character imparts a kind of dreamlike fluidity that Bergman presumably intends to privilege a spectator experience of the film as an amorphous flow of consciousness, but, because the content of that consciousness is so rigidly gendered, the technique hinders rather than promotes a potentially feminist reading.

The disjunction of time is one of the features of the film that is also troublesome from a feminist perspective. The introductory pans and cuts to various clocks indicating different times could function as a radical disjunctive strategy; Bergman says, "Time has ceased to exist in this house, in these rooms (but it is probably grandmother's apartment anyway)" (*Images* 88).

But the association of the clocks with Agnes and her physical dissolution develops an equation between time and biology as two inexorable forces. The film captures a sense of history and cultural tradition by focusing on objects of a lost age, but Penley rightly points out that this temporal scheme is problematic:

> You know it's a period piece, [but] you never have any temporal or historical perspective on the action, because it is never certain what the time of the film is, and the goings-on of the house are never related to anything in the outside world. (I guess that's supposed to make it more "universal.") In true bourgeois spectacular form the film does its best to prevent any critical interaction because of its seductive dream-like richness combined with the most outrageous emotional manipulations. (207)

The film does not allow the spectator to locate it in historical time, privileging an emotional rather than critical interaction with the text. The disjunction of time, then, perhaps paradoxically, hinders rather than promotes critical subjectivity in the spectator.

The treatment of voyeurism and gazing is also problematic in *Cries and Whispers*. If *Persona* radically foregrounds these issues, the same cannot be said of this film. While the camera's panning around Karin's naked body might serve to identify her crisis as one of specularity, this potential is thwarted by the fact that the individual doing the gazing is female — it is Anna who is looking at her in this invasive way, and Karin's rejection of her specular position is manifested as an anger toward the female. The scene in which Karin's husband leers at her while she smears the blood of her genitals on her face further identifies the female specular position with masochism. This problem is compounded when one considers the extent to which the spectator is encouraged to identify Anna's pervasive visual and auditory voyeurism. If her gazing were designated as powerful, as in some way authoritative, the film might be read as calling into question the powerful male gaze and its role in structuring meaning in cinema. But such is not the case; the owner of this female gaze is a servant, powerless, uncritical, and ruled by her biological impulses toward the maternal. Thus, this film does not, like *Persona*, challenge male voyeurism and its dehumanizing effects upon women; rather, *Cries and Whispers* "erases" male voyeurism and posits in its stead impotent female voyeurism.

The issue of auditory voyeurism is complicated by the use of voice-overs in this film. A male voice-over (Bergman's own) introduces both Karin's and Maria's first-person segments. In Maria's case, it simply sets up the sequence by telling us about Anna's ill daughter and Joakim's absence from the manor house, but in Karin's the voice has greater authority. When it says she "soon found out that her marriage was a mistake. Her husband, who is twenty years her senior, is repulsive to her physically and mentally" (61), it has moved beyond simply imparting factual information to an assumed omniscience about the female character's interior life. This use of male voice-over can, I think, best be understood in terms of Silverman's observation:

> The theological status of the disembodied voiceover is the effect of maintaining its source in a place apart from the camera, inaccessible to the gaze of either the cinematic apparatus or the viewing subject — of violating the rule of synchronization so absolutely that the voice is left without an identifiable locus. In other words, the voiceover is privileged to the degree that *it transcends the body*.... Insofar as the voiceover asserts its independence from the visual track, it presents itself as enunciator. It seems, in other words, to be a metafictional voice, the point of discursive origin. (*Acoustic Mirror* 49, 51)

Bergman's voice-over, then, locates him rather than the women characters as the site of discursive authority; it is *his* voice that supplies the illusion. Again a comparison with *Persona* is telling. The male narrator there functions as a part of the larger metacinematic structure that subverts male authority. It is a self-conscious bracketing of female experience by male authority that contributes to detachment on the part of the viewer. But in *Cries and Whispers* the authority of the male voice-over and the moral ramifications of the male appropriation of female experience are not problematized. On the contrary, voice-over functions rather as Kozloff describes:

> The spectator is placed less as a voyeur and more as an invited confidante. Since in many cases, the voiceover allows the spectator — and the spectator alone — access to highly personal information, it thus simulates the exchange between the closest of friends or relations (except that in this instance, the spectator is privy to another's secrets and not required to divulge any of his or her own). In sum, films that "speak" to us offer a close, mutually validating relationship. (129)

The use of voice-over, then, coheres with the other ostensibly disjunctive devices not to privilege critical subjectivity in the viewer, but rather to seduce him or her into an illusion of the mergence of spectator and spectacle, an illusion of shared "truth," the validity of which in this case is questionable in the extreme.

The conclusion of the film bears out this argument. In the penultimate scene Karin has promised Anna a memento from Agnes's belongings. She furthermore thanks Anna for her support during this difficult time and makes an overture of intimacy toward Maria. These changes in Karin set the stage for the last scene, in which Anna reads from Agnes's diary and her voice fades out and Agnes's takes over. Long shots show all four women dressed in white, tacitly embracing virginity and repressing the sexual body. Over this beautiful autumnal scene Agnes's voice recounts:

I closed my eyes and felt the breeze and the sun on my face. All my aches and pains were gone. The people I'm most fond of in the world were with me. I could hear them chatting round about me, I felt the presence of their bodies, the warmth of their hands. I closed my eyes tightly . . . thinking: Come what may, this is happiness. I can't wish for anything better. Now, for a few minutes, I can experience perfection. And I feel a great gratitude to my life, which gives me so much. (94)

A zoom in on Agnes's face flanked by the backs of Maria's and Karin's heads concludes the imagery of the film.

Because Anna's voice begins the reading and Agnes's takes over, this scene reconfirms the connection between the two women, an impression supported by the fact that, while Agnes is the narrator of the diary, it is Anna who is reading it. As Kawin argues, "Their private experiences have, as a fact of the image, conjoined" (18). This moment of warmth and tenderness occurs as Anna, the substitute "good" mother, rocks the three women in an outdoor swing that Steene calls "a cradle of nature" ("Bergman's Portrait" 103). Significantly, too, this final scene takes place outdoors; throughout the film we have observed all three sisters gazing out windows, longing for escape, and finally they succeed in breaking out of their isolation to enjoy freedom outdoors. The final shot, then, is a peaceful close-up of Agnes marking "a release from suffering, an expectation of harmony" (Cowie, *Ingmar Bergman* 280).

But the scene poses some problems for this interpretation. One might argue not only that the idyll of this scene is overshadowed by the brutality of the film, but also that the only one who has grown and developed is Karin. Maria is as selfish as ever, Anna is now without an object for her compulsive mothering, and Agnes has died a painful, agonizing death. But, most importantly, the moment of happiness and perfection of which Agnes speaks is illusory, because intimacy requires that more than one of the participants experiences it, and Agnes is alone in her perception of the connectedness of this moment. Too, as Mellen points out:

Agnes writes, ironically, not of Anna and her love, but of the sisters who will abandon and betray her and who will recoil when her need in death is greatest. And it is Anna and not her sisters who must read these words. . . . After all of Anna's devotion and Agnes's dependence upon her comforting, not a syllable registering her feeling for Anna is present in the diary. (311)

Thus, both visually and emotionally the escape into the lovely fall landscape is less an image of liberation than a repetition of the setting in which the failed mother was first photographed. Agnes's image of sisterly sharing is, both extra- and intradiegetically, an illusion, one that furthermore is not problematized as such by the director.

The image of the "good" mother rocking her charges may represent a wished-for resolution for the director, but it is ultimately inconsistent with the whole of the film. Bergman may long to posit Anna's ascendance over the sisters' biological mother (she is in some kind of tenuous control in this landscape associated with the biological mother) as a means of reconciling himself with the maternal, but all that this surrogate mother can preside over is, in the deepest and fullest sense of the term, an illusion.

The film concludes, then, with the words "And so the cries and whispers fall silent," followed by a red screen and a fade to a black screen. The film suggests that only through connectedness can one silence the tormenting cries and whispers, but this resolution takes place under the sign of the nonthinking, all-giving, self-abnegating mother. The final red screen privileges a spectator intimacy with the film that parallels the intimacy of the characters, but that intimacy is predicated upon the mergence of spectator and spectacle that Bergman so pointedly rejects in *Persona*. If critical subjectivity in spectator-text relations is grounded in "an involved but critical approach, a kind of detached passion" (Kuhn 172), this film can certainly not be said to encourage such a perspective. The "subject-effect" of the film is fundamentally misogynist.

Tellingly, even the circular structure of the film — it begins and ends with Agnes's interior monologues over shots of the estate's park — subverts an anti-narrative impulse by providing coherence and closure. While the circularity of *Persona* pointed to the film's status as a construct of the male imagination, circularity here provides unproblematized closure. The film is resolved in intimacy, isolation has been transcended for both the characters and the spectator, but both mergences figure delusion and appropriation.

Thus, critics such as Penley and Mellen, who take Bergman to task for his "narrow characterizations of women" for the fact that "this is not how we are" (207, 300), seem justified at least as far as this particular film is concerned. While he might argue that he is not trying to present women "as they really are," but rather to present a "soul-scape" in which he seeks a filmic representation of certain states of mind that are common to both sexes, the underlying structures of the film demonstrate that such is not the case.

*Cries and Whispers*, which may well be Bergman's most visually beautiful film, asserts female connectedness as a model for human relations, aligns narrative authority with the female voice, and further reiterates the inadequacy of hierarchical systems of language and subjectivity. It also includes vestiges of filmic techniques that privilege a feminist reading of cinema — the not-infrequent instances of direct address whereby the character confronts the spectator's gaze and the positing of Agnes's diary entry as a screening surface that problematizes her body and her subjectivity as texts to be read and appropriated. But the other potentially disjunctive devices that privilege a feminist experience of *Persona* are here galvanized to reify rather than subvert the male tradition's representation of women as the film strives for the containment of the female body. Through the fetishization, stereotyping, and destruction of that body, the film seeks a reconciliation with the nonsexual body of the mother and presents the spectator with multiple instances of the female "subject which is not one." Although Bergman throughout his career manifests an albeit sometimes grudging awareness of the complicity between ideological conceptions of gender and cinematic representation (motivated in large part by his identification with women as victims of dominant patriarchal culture), he never seems able or willing to demystify the figure of the mother, to see her with the same clarity of vision that he brings to the father. *Cries and Whispers* indicates the extent to which, because of his guilt over his father's death, he projects onto the mother the failings of the patriarchy. While much of the rest of his production is, I would argue, characterized by an illuminating, thoughtful, and energizingly ambivalent treatment of gender issues, this film stands as a monument to the limitations of that treatment, to the insight that, "best intentions" notwithstanding, all art is a product of the culture and ideology that produce it.

# Conclusion:
# Genderedness and the Imagination

Issues of gendered representation are a constantly recurring feature of Bergman's production and are manifest also in his perception of his own imaginative endeavor. In an interview he has stated:

> I am very much aware of my own double self. The well-known one is very much under control; everything is planned and very secure. The unknown one can be very unpleasant. I think this side is responsible for all the creative work — he is in touch with the child. He is not rational, he is impulsive and extremely emotional. Perhaps it is not even a "he," but a "she." (Kakutani 28)

The human imagination, then, would seem in Bergman's view to be aligned with the female. Thus, even though Bergman designates this female imagination as "unpleasant, child-like, and emotional," an investigation of individual acts of imagining from *The Seventh Seal* through *Fanny and Alexander* can illuminate the relationship between gender and representation in his production. Not surprisingly, a number of issues raised in previous chapters resurface here, but a reexamination of them from the perspective of Bergman's entire oeuvre may contribute to a more comprehensive assessment of Bergman's treatment of this relationship.

On the most elementary level, we observe a development through these films in terms of the gender of the imaginer. In the pre-trilogy works, not surprisingly the imaginer is male, while in the post-1960 films it is female, with the exception of Johan Borg and Alexander. This development coheres, of course, with the shift from androcentric quest films to gynocentric films of interiority. Even Johan's vision is at least partially shared by a female character. Furthermore, both of the later male imaginers are clearly functioning as directorial alter egos, both artists, either realized or incipient; hence, they partake of the imagination's ostensibly "feminine" aspect. Significantly, throughout his work there is a growing emphasis on the synthesizing and redemptive power of the imagination. Significantly, all the acts of imagining he enscreens disrupt binarism by addressing the impingement of external reality on subjectivity, the interconnectedness of subjective and objective, and the ways in which patriarchal structures invade and pervade human life. While Bergman increasingly merges ideas of female experience, childhood, the nuclear family, and the redemptive imagination with filmic techniques that privilege a feminist experience, ultimately his vision remains deeply gendered even as he struggles against patriarchal systems.

The apocalyptic choral music and a reading from Revelations that open *The Seventh Seal* immediately establish a connection between God and destruction. Accordingly, the film represents the Knight's vision of Death as a construct of the religious patriarchy. The binary coloration of the Death figure and the dissolve in the first sequence from the geometrically exact patterns of the chessboard to the plastic, asymmetrical surface of the sea suggest the divine patriarchy's imposition of hierarchy upon an amorphous reality, as does the dissolve to a rocky shore with a grey and desolate sky occupying fully two-thirds of the frame. For this film about God, males, and patriarchal authority questions the benevolence, the "rightness" of that authority (it is, of course, his belief in God that has so completely debilitated Block), even as the nature shots indicate how that authority, like one of William Blake's malevolent skygods, has rendered nature itself hostile, and the dissolves establish that authority as all-pervasive. But, while Bergman posits God-based male authority as somehow, ironically enough, causing the "fall," corrupting and infecting reality, he also undermines it, robbing, through a variety of camera techniques, even the figure of Death of the awesome force one might expect him to wield.

While the Knight's vision is of Death and a hostile God, male in all its parameters, Jof, whom Bergman calls "a visionary" (*Images* 238), has a vision of life, fecundity, and faith constructed around female values. His first vision is of the Virgin Mary teaching the baby Jesus to walk, an image that is literally iconized. But we note that in this holy family the father is absent. Given the malevolence of the father in Bergman's work, a functional family seems predicated precisely upon the absence of the father. We notice, then, that while the father is powerfully, palpably absent, a figure of simultaneous fear and longing for reconciliation, the mother is the stereotypical source of self-abnegation, blessing, joy, and connection, values represented in the film by Mia.

But Jof's final vision of the dance of death recoups him for the male forces of the film. Although consistently associated with Mia and the traditional female forces she embodies, with the simple, joyous belief in natural good, Jof for Bergman must still be aligned with the Father. Thus, Jof's final vision, in terms of coloration, composition, subject matter, and ideology, resembles the Knight's perception of Death, and Jof shares with Block an insight into the destructive legacy of father This is one of the earliest examples in Bergman's production of consciousness merging, a strategy of disjunction that can serve the feminist enterprise by calling attention to dominant narrative's attempt to naturalize its notion of immutable subjectivity. *The Seventh Seal* is ambiguous: while the female is idealized as a creative and generative force, authority and agency are still located in the patriarchy. This act of imagination then is rendered as a conflation of male and female values, but the conflation is self-contradictory since the imagination for Bergman seems to require the rejection of male values and ideology.

Although in many respects a vastly different film, *Wild Strawberries*, in its view of the human imagination and the family, also addresses patriarchal authority. The plot centers around a man who shares with Bergman his initials: Eberhard Isak Borg and Ernst Ingmar Bergman. Borg is himself a negligent father, of whom Bergman has said, "I modeled a figure who superficially resembled my father but *who was thoroughly and completely me*" (*Images* 20). After the initial nightmare sequence — a representation of Isak as dead though alive — Bergman through the subsequent dreams charts the reasons for Isak's failed life. The summerhouse fantasy concentrates precisely upon Isak's patriarchal family of origin. In it Isak is out fishing with his father, a union that takes place off-screen and is not visualized, and this allegiance is visually accompanied by other signs of patriarchal authority: the Swedish flag with its symbol of dominion over Norway is raised up the flag-pole(!), and the social and family structures are extremely hierarchical. Although this scene bustling with energy, joy, and order is linked with an alliance with the father, there is trouble within this patriarchal paradise, as we discover when Sara laments to her cousin that she just can't choose between Isak and his brother Sigfrid. This fraternal conflict, one Bergman himself experienced with his brother Dag (*Magic Lantern* 56), is patriarchally implicated when Sara says that Isak is morally aloof and consumed by issues of morality and sin, a religious obsession that, along with his intellectual bent, associates him with Antonius Block and a patriarchal position. God and the father are still envisioned in this film as distant and aloof, as malevolently negligent: witness Evald's hatred of his father, their cold and unfeeling natures, and Marianne's flashback where Evald stands against a bleak grey sky very much like that linked with the Knight in *The Seventh Seal*. Evald is also very much his father's son in his rejection of his unborn child. The father of reality is distant and negligent; only in fantasy does Isak find a loving, paternal figure.

But the figure of the mother in this film is very different from Mia. When Isak and Marianne go to pay his mother a visit, the previously clear sky becomes threatening, and she seems cold and indifferent to her children and grandchildren, as Marianne confirms when she comments on the legacy of coldness and death that has passed from mother to son to son. Isak's real-life mother, like his father, is distant and aloof; only in the imagination can he find the good mother Sara. This image of the rejecting mother clearly centers on Bergman's sense of himself as an unwanted child, on his belief that his precarious health as an infant can be traced to his mother's ill-health and rejection, a belief that leads to a mystification of the mother that pervades his entire production.

Almost all the women in the film cohere into maternality: even Agda the housekeeper nurtures her employer. The fact that the two Saras are both played by Bibi Andersson strengthens the impression that Bergman is here portraying not individual women but instead his concept of idealized Woman as Mother, an impression reinforced by the dissolves between Marianne's and Sara's faces. This issue also surfaces in the nightmare summerhouse sequence when the camera isolates a cradle from which Sara picks up Sigbritt's baby to comfort it. Indeed, the Sara both of Isak's past and of his present as well as Marianne are all three depicted in terms of motherhood, of their abilities to produce and nurture children. The female body is almost exclusively a site of potential or frustrated maternal plenitude for the male. That in *Wild Strawberries* the legacy of coldness and death, elsewhere in Bergman attributed to the father, is associated with the mother is a case of a projection of the failings of the father onto the mother in order to save the father so that the son might be reconciled with him.

There is, however, one important exception to this idealized image of Woman as Mother — Isak's wife. When he is confronted with his past failings in a nightmare, the film intimates that her infidelities are motivated by Isak's coldness and indifference toward her, that she and her life are victimized by a male destructive force. This scene, with its indictment of the masculine, surfaces as a moment of rupture in the otherwise seamless suture between the mother and the malignant parental legacy.

The fantasized mother and father finally appear in Isak's final dream as a vision of familial bliss and reconciliation. Bergman underscores the importance of this reconciliation when he says, "I appealed to my parents in *Wild Strawberries*: see me, understand me, and — if possible — forgive me" (*Images* 20). Both parents wave to Isak, acknowledging and thereby validating him. *Wild Strawberries*, then, continues the pattern established by *The Seventh Seal* whereby the male protagonist's imagination confronts issues of gender in terms of family structure and rigidly proscribed gender roles. Women function within these acts of imagining as mothers and as Beatrice-like guides to reconciliation with the absent, omnipotent father.

The binarism inherent in patriarchal ideology, the opposition between objective and subjective that complements that between masculine and feminine, is thus subverted only to a very limited extent. Isak's first nightmare depicts him as dead though alive, as do a number of later scenes, including the examination sequence that shows him diagnosing Berit as dead even though she awakens a moment later. Although death and life are presented as a single matrix and thus might serve to disrupt binarism, the oppositions between interior and exterior, male and female, upon which dominant culture bases its privilege are rigidly adhered to. Thus, while in many respects the examination dream would seem to be a combination of the two preceding dreams, a kind of mergence of the grotesque nightmare reality of the dream of the empty city and the idealized summer landscape of the family dream, the film's impulse toward the deconstruction of binarism is disrupted by the idealization of the father and the ideological system he represents.

The impulse towards mergence and a deconstruction of binarism is also apparent in the many dissolves that figure in the film. While they certainly function visually to privilege spectator identification with the fluid consciousness of the protagonist, they also serve Bergman's goal of reintegration, the reintegration of both Isak and the spectator within patriarchal structures. Even the technique with which he introduces these mental event sequences is drawn from dominant cinema: they are all introduced in conventional fashion with a fade into or out of, and onto or from, Isak's sleeping face, thereby reinforcing the opposition between objective and subjective realities. The film also merges temporal categories; one time frame butts up against another. Isak's ultimate awareness of the guilt he bears not only toward those whom he has injured in the past, but also toward those of a future generation, affects the rest of the film and stands in ironic juxtaposition to the song the three young people sing, "Yes, may he live; yes, may he live; yes, may he live for a hundred years." Significantly, the song is led by Sara as she and Marianne represent the forces of futurity in the film.

If the father is the past, the innocent desexualized female lover (for Sara is both virgin and tomboy) and the mother are the future. Since the film is an exploration of Isak's mental and emotional landscape, Marianne's flashback indicates a movement within his psyche toward the futurity represented by woman and suggests his willingness to allow his subjectivity to be influenced and affected by that of the other. He has moved from the static isolation of the initial nightmare sequence, through the non-participatory idealized reality of the first summerhouse sequence and the participatory reality of the second, to the point where another person's subjectivity can impinge on his, his mergence paralleled by that of the spectator and the diegesis. Marianne's narrative is thus pivotal to Bergman's depiction of Isak's emotional growth. We note also that this is the first mental sequence in which time is "real" and unfiltered by the mind of the narrator. In his treatment of temporal issues, then, Bergman depicts Isak's reintegration into a specifically patriarchal sense of both time and history.

Significantly, too, the representation of consciousness merging in this film is different for men and women. The two Saras merge as a single character energy embodying the maternal, and, because this mergence is essentialist, the film aligns itself with the dominant ideological notion of the feminine as formless and incoherent and of women as intuitive and incomprehensible blessers of the masculine order. The mergence of consciousness centered on the male protagonist, however, suggests expansion rather than limitation, growth rather than confinement. Furthermore, Isak's authority as a narrator combines with the film's privileging of an identification between the specta-tor and the male protagonist to define imaginative mergence as a male activ-ity. The film ultimately attempts to affirm the patriarchy, at least as it is redeemed by the imagination and what Bergman sees as the emotive, pro-creative force of the feminine. Positive though the ending may be, Bergman is still struggling to meld the dominant order with the ostensibly vitalizing female force. Woman is sign, man the signifier.

But, in the early sixties, Bergman becomes less ambivalent about the pa-triarchy. He says of this period, "My top-heavy religious superstructure col-lapsed" (Björkman *et al.* 112). Thus, the subjects of his filmic imaginings also change; they less overtly represent the male's quest for reabsorption into the idealized family in which father-god is all-powerful and mother all-loving and nurturing. Thus, the first film in the trilogy, *Through a Glass Darkly*, pre-sents an imagining of God as a combination spider and machine who tries to rape the female imaginer. Bergman has said of this film, "The legacy of my childhood was liquidated. There I assert that every concept of God that is created by people must be a monster" (*Images* 238). The god behind the wallpapered door (suggestive of Charlotte Perkins Gilman) is "a powerful, two-sexed being who direct[s] what happen[s] in the magic room" (*Images* 68). But this god is evil:

> Sometimes he gives her incomprehensible commands, drink saltwater, kill animals, and so on. But he . . . gives her intense experiences, even sexual ones. He climbs down and disguises himself as Minus, her younger brother. At the same time the god forces her to forswear her marriage. She is the bride who awaits her bridegroom and she may not defile herself. She draws Minus into her world. And he follows her willingly and with enthusi-asm since he finds himself in the border country of puberty. (*Images* 249)

The fact that this destructive divinity is "two-sexed" suggests that, while the transgression of gender boundaries may be energizing and enriching, as it largely is in his treatment of cross-dressing, it is also threatening, a marker of this god's perversity. But the designation of him as a rapist god, as distorting male/female relations, as demanding both purity and sexual fidelity of his female victim and appropriating her body for his own desire, indicates how corrupt and malevolent his influence on female reality is. He is also a cor-rupter of male youth, a force that despoils youthful male innocence, an allu-sion to Bergman's sense of God as a destructive force in his own develop-ment. Karin's victimization by a cruel divine patriarch is also Bergman's vic-timization.

Not surprisingly then, when Karin sees this god, David (her malevolently neglectful father, who has been watching her), makes no attempt to inter-vene in her anguished hallucination and is seen walking away from her, leaving her alone with this terrifying vision. The mother, with all that she represents for Bergman of love, nurturing, and wholeness, is absent from this family; the father's power is malevolently absolute and absolutely malevolent. Furthermore, the corruption of the actual family through incest renders impossible the ideal of the divine family. Indeed, Bergman was dissatisfied with the patched-on "God is Love" ending: "I realized just how dishonest the whole film was. That was why I couldn't give form to my insight and rescued myself by regressing in the final episode" (Björkman et al. 167). His film, then, is "a falsification" (Images 248), a work in which he "missed the point" (Magic Lantern 220). In Through a Glass Darkly God is most certainly not Love; on the contrary, he is Violence and Appropriation.

Thus, as Bergman increasingly acknowledges the malevolence of God, he rejects the patriarchy and its system of hierarchy. The divine and human family structure collapses, and women replace male protagonists with a new sense of both agency and authority. But these women and the acts of imagination Bergman enscreens on their behalf are by no means free of patriarchal authority. On the contrary, it continues to pervade every aspect, public and private, of their lives. While here as earlier, Bergman valorizes subjective over objective reality, he does not question the validity of that dichotomy until Persona. Furthermore, while the collapse of Bergman's religious ideology also precipitates a collapse of the male ideological system with which it is complicit, he seems to find it difficult completely to jettison male values, for the female protagonist in Through a Glass Darkly, however accurate her imaginative vision may be, achieves this vision through mental illness. One is reminded of R. D. Laing, who was especially prominent in the debate of the period and who argued that, because society itself is so sick, mental illness is paradoxically a sign of mental health. But the fact that Karin is mentally ill, schizophrenic, is a thoroughly traditional male stereotype of women's mental activities, closely aligned with the image of women as hysterics. Her authority is further undermined by the fact that she does not see the helicopter descending outside her window; only her husband and the spectator witness this image and can thus know that the spider God is also an automaton God. While Bergman probably does use female protagonists in his later films because women have historically experienced the social, cultural, and ideological marginalization that he himself feels on the collapse of his God- and male-centered ideology, he nonetheless presents them within certain androcentric parameters, undermining here and in Cries and Whispers their authority in various ways.

If imaginings in the earlier films enact narratives of male-male and male-mother relations, female-female relations become increasingly prominent. It is significant that only when Bergman has repudiated the patriarchal order and its hierarchy of meaning and subjecthood does he compose films that disperse authority across multiple points of view. While the imaginings in *Wild Strawberries* (with the exception of Marianne's flashback) derive from a single mind, those of *Persona* arise out of multiple subjectivities. While the mental events in the pre-1960 films are experienced as a trajectory toward self-realization or self-fulfillment with a concomitant concentration on the (male) individual, acts of imagining are now less concerned with the individual self than with mutability and boundlessness of the self, with a mergence of consciousness that also extends to the spectator's relationship with the film, at the same time that Bergman problematizes that mergence as appropriation. The last third of *Persona*, imaginings from some unspecified consciousness, addresses issues of specifically female subjectivity, rejecting the concepts of fixed identity and gender that characterize much of male discourse and yet also rejecting dominant cinema's false mergence of spectator and spectacle.

As I argued earlier, the imaginative sequences of *Persona*, precisely because they are not ascribed to either Alma or Elisabet, subvert the equation between the female voice and the female body. The extensive use of screening surfaces, as images of that body, denaturalizes this equation. While penetration through surfaces like the wallpapered door in *Through a Glass Darkly* leads to an acknowledgment of the horror and destructiveness of God (the interior of the closet is "darkness"), only with *Persona* does Bergman explore the particular genderedness of such transgressions. In the film's extensive use of self-conscious strategies, it points to itself as an artificial construct of male discourse that speculizes the female body and appropriates female subjectivity.

The film's acts of imagination further deconstruct both male culture's binarism and the false mergence of spectator and spectacle by asserting that such mergence is appropriation and violence. It is, significantly then, in *Persona* that Bergman for the first time hints that mothering may also be a social construct as well as a biological and therefore immutable fact. To be sure, the burden of the work still defines the mother as rooted in biology; the male child who strokes the screen at the beginning and end of the film is at least in part a Bergman stand-in seeking connection with the mother. At the same time, the allusions to the coercive effect of social definitions of the maternal at least partially undermine a biological definition of the mother. This work, then, both reifies and problematizes the concept of the feminine aspect of the imagination.

I do not mean to suggest, however, that *Persona* represents a complete reversal in Bergman's perception of the imagination and dominant ideology. After *Persona*, his ambivalence returns. For example, in *Hour of the Wolf* he reverts to a male protagonist and an imaginative subject matter that focuses again on a nuclear family. In describing the hour of the wolf, Johan associates his demons with a memory from childhood when he, like Bergman himself, had to kiss his father's hand and beg forgiveness for some minor childhood offense; the nuclear family, a patriarchal structure, institutionalizes humiliation. The von Merkens family, on which Johan's visions center is deeply and thoroughly malevolent, constituting a force that ultimately provokes the death/disappearance of the male. This chain of events implies that the nuclear family, with its roots in divine patriarchal ideology, is overwhelmingly threatening to the male.

Tellingly, too, in this film, as in *Persona*, spectatorial identification and point of view are dispersed. No longer do we identify with a single male-gendered consciousness; rather, Johan and his wife Alma share a consciousness, and the viewer is manipulated into identifying with this merged subjectivity, even as that identification is subverted by the uninterpretability of events. The whole notion of authority here, as in *Persona*, is undermined as the spectator is challenged to question what is real and what is fantasy, itself very much a feminist enterprise, since, as many critics have pointed out, specificity of meaning, of identity, and of spectator identification is in and of itself a reinforcement of traditional systems of discourse.

But *Hour of the Wolf* also entails a retreat from the extreme insights of *Persona*. The homosexual overtones of Johan's fantasies are menacing; witness the effeminate make-up and "feminizing" (*Images* 35) silk robe he wears to his tryst with Veronica Vogler. Bergman describes him as "transformed into a strange androgynous being" (*Images* 42). But most telling is Johan's encounter with and murder of a young boy. Both Wood and Gado point to some of the phallic symbolism in the scene (the fishing pole and the three fishes themselves), but Bergman's description of the scene in *Images* is quite sufficient: "The only mistake was that the demon should have been naked. And if one takes it one step further: Johan also should have been naked . . . . When the [boy]-demon clings to Johan's back and bites him, he is crushed against the cliff with an orgasmic power" (35). There is significantly no dialogue in this sequence; sexual ambiguity and the mutability of the self are again associated with a subversion of linguistic systems, and the soundtrack is filled with crashes and bangs like those during the breaking and burning segment of *Persona*. While both films posit the transgression of sexual boundaries as frightening and threatening, such transgression leads not to a higher level of awareness, as in *Persona*, but instead to madness and death. Both the feminizing of Johan and the threat of homosexuality posed by the boy, as well as the sequence's extremely harsh, grainy, high-contrast lighting (reminiscent of the Frost and Alma sequence in *Sawdust and Tinsel* which also centers on the sexual humiliation of the male) indicate a return on the director's part to the gender binarism of his pre-1960 production, to the androcentric view that gender is identity and gender is absolute.

But, if homosexuality is threatening, so too is the female body. Veronica, whose last name is Vogler, one that throughout Bergman is assigned to strange, threatening people, is described as "passive and indecisive" and yet is also the embodiment of insatiable female sexuality, and as such constitutes a threat to Johan's male autonomy. In *Images* Bergman associates her with "the demons" (42) (insofar as we know, Johan draws or paints only women and demons!). The director furthermore photographs Ingrid Thulin's naked body as though it were a corpse, her eyes closed and her body stiff, laid out on what looks like a bier, an image that suggests a desire to destroy and erase the female body. Johan describes their painful past sexual history as a personification of the Bible's injunction that man and woman "shall become one flesh," indicating that such a union is threatening to male autonomy, and it is significantly his sexual encounter with her that precipitates his death/disappearance.

The character of Alma is also troubling. Bergman describes her very simply; she is "twenty-eight years old and childless" (*Images* 33). But now she is pregnant, and the film defines her in terms of fecundity on numerous occasions. As Wood points out, we first see her, large with child, next to a pile of apples (an image she shares with Anna in *Cries and Whispers*, who is also an embodiment of maternal plenitude); she later handles a growing plant and is seen by a flowering apple tree (161). She is visualized opening windows and letting in light, airing the bed clothes, and pumping water. As Wood argues, "Alma, as wife and mother . . . embodies the possibility of wholeness and health in life: Johan has praised her as having 'whole thoughts and feelings' — God 'made her in one piece'" (161). In *Images* Bergman says that Alma represents "that which is alive." One might also point out that the name Alma, which recurs throughout Bergman, derives from one of the female servants in his childhood home and is clearly a name that he associates with maternal, self-sacrificing nurturing. Later in the film, Johan refers to "a mother-animal" and "creep[ing] into the mother-animal's belly," an image similar to Frost's recounted dream in *Sawdust and Tinsel* about crawling into Alma's(!) womb and getting smaller and smaller until he completely disappears. Both fantasies indicate the threat of motherhood to male subjectivity at the same time that motherhood is a place of retreat, nurturing, and comfort, a state defined in terms of its function for male, not female, experience. Too, Alma tells us that Johan liked the fact that she was so "tystlåten" ("quiet" or "silent"); she has no identity except as mother and support for the male. Alma is further idealized by Bergman's equation between her and Pamina in *The Magic Flute*; twice we see Alma's face while a voice cries Pamina's name. Her authority as a subject is further undercut by the fact that she is depicted as a silent recipient of and repository for her husband's wishes, needs, and desires. Her authority as narrator is borrowed from her husband, who experiences the events she merely recounts.

The mother, however, is also implicated in the destructive sexuality of these visions; von Merkens' mother coquettishly flirts with Johan, asking him to help remove her stockings, to admire her toes and nails, and then to kiss her foot. Only after he obeys does she tell him where to find Veronica. Too, one of Johan's recurring fantasies is of a very old woman, who, in taking off her hat, also takes off her face, another image of the horror of female exposure. These scenes both suggest that the sexual female body must be contained and repressed in order for the male to achieve reconciliation with the "good" mother.

The film does, however, avail itself of some disjunctive strategies that contribute to a feminist reading, strategies that are presumably grounded in Bergman's sense that it deals with "a hidden and carefully guarded ambivalence that is in evidence in both my earlier and later production: Aman in *The Magician*, Ester in *The Silence*, Tomas in *Face to Face*, Elisabet in *Persona*, Ishmael in *Fanny and Alexander*" (*Images* 29). It begins, for instance, with a male voice-over calling attention to itself as the site of narrative authority. The credit sequence soundtrack emits sounds of set construction and stagehands' voices, and the second half of the film is introduced by an interposed title, both of which privilege the kind of passionate detachment so integral to *Persona*. That issues of breakdown and uninterpretability are central to the film is apparent in Bergman's claim that "everything should be intimated, not pointed out or solved. The elements restrained as in the theater. No realism. Everything should be blindingly pure, softly easy, eighteenth century, unreal, the colors never realistic . . . . *The Hour of the Wolf* is played out in a land of twilight" (*Images* 26, 41). This quality of the elusive and allusive is apparent in the many dissolves, a number of them to black screens. But these dissolves and black screens are not problematized in terms of gender; on the contrary, they seem instead to posit the absolute permeability of Alma's consciousness. She is a text to be read and a vacuum to be filled with the contents of her husband's mental life, for she seems to have no life independent of him. Alma's exclusive function in the film is as a guide to Johan's imaginative world. If *Persona* figures a deconstruction of the fantasy of mergence between spectator and spectacle, *Hour of the Wolf* reverts to a much more conventional treatment of this issue. Alma's consciousness merges with Johan's, but she never has full access to his subjectivity, while the film implies that the spectator can and does know fully and completely the subjectivity of the female narrator, who is never problematized as either subjectivity or spectacle. These issues culminate in Johan's final utterance in the film, an utterance so important that Bergman repeats it verbatim in *From the Lives of the Marionettes*. "The boundary has finally been crossed. The mirror shattered, but what do the splinters reflect? Can you tell me that?" (81). Unin-terpretability is gendered as male while female subjectivity is absolutely per-meable.

The recurring use of male voice-over to introduce the fantasy sequences and the complete absence of female voice-over, even though Alma is the os-tensible narrator of this tale, all the more reinforce the male bias of the film. At its conclusion, Alma seems willing to blame herself for Johan's fate, as she wonders whether or not she could have "protected" him better, or perhaps if she did not love him enough. The end of the film does manifest a certain re-sistance to closure: we do not know what has happened to Johan, and Bergman refuses to append the customary "The End;" instead, the final im-age is an irised close-up of Alma that serves to idealize her at the expense of any feminist potential of the film. Alma's presence at the end, as at the be-ginning of the film, as an ostensible narrative authority further undermines the film's resistance to closure, just as her blaming herself for his fate recoups the film for male cultural ideology.

The family and its pivotal role in the development of the child is also central to the imaginings of *Cries and Whispers*. Like *Persona*, this film fo-cuses on female subjectivity and drastically marginalizes the male, and the priest describes the plight of humanity as "left here on the dark, dirty earth under an empty and cruel heaven" (75), thereby intimating that God is re-sponsible for human misery. But, as I argue earlier, while the film acknowl-edges the bankruptcy of the patriarchy and its values, it also, like *Wild Strawberries*, projects the failings of the male onto the female by designating suffering and pain as a product of the destructive maternal legacy. The female body, represented as ugly, corrupt, and diseased, is consistently erased or re-pressed so that the invisible male narrator might achieve reconciliation with the "good" mother who is both non-body and all-body. The potentially disjunctive devices that in *Persona* privilege a feminist experience of the text here are repeatedly subverted and recouped in a view of women as rooted in biology. Screening surfaces posit female subjectivity as absolutely permeable and appropriable by the spectator's gaze. The red dissolves, while more am-biguous than the mental event introductions from *Wild Strawberries*, are far less ambiguous than the seamless gliding between reality and mental event in *Persona*. While the film intradiegetically valorizes mergence as an enriching alternative to the notion of fixed subjecthood, unlike *Persona* it does not question the false appropriating mergence of spectator and spectacle. In *Cries and Whispers*, as in *Hour of the Wolf*, the imagination is aligned with women only in part because of the possibility of an alternative subjectivity they pose; the film's representation of the imagination centers on the female body as a sign in the male signifying process.

Not surprisingly, the last acts of imagination that Bergman enscreens in his career also center on the family. In *Fanny and Alexander* Bergman returns to a fantasy of the failings of the father, of his desertion of the male child, and of the destructiveness that is his legacy. Much of the film takes place in the grandmother's apartment, a replica of Bergman's own grandmother's residence in Uppsala, a place he associates with "security and magic" (*Magic Lantern* 18). The magic lantern, the iron stove in the hallway, the lame servant Maj, uncle Carl, and the Esmarelda story are all part of Bergman's personal history (*Magic Lantern* 15, 19, 20, 26, 11) and indicate the extent to which this film is an attempt to come to terms with childhood and the family. Like Jof, Alexander is, Bergman says, a visionary, and "Jof and Alexander are in turn related to the child Bergman" (*Images* 238). Accordingly, the film has frequently been read as nostalgia on Bergman's part, but nostalgia, as Hollis Frampton observes in discussing his own film by that name, is a complex experience: "The word 'nostalgia' . . . seems to be equated with the German word *Sehnsucht*, which means 'longing.' It is nothing of the sort. In Greek, the word means 'the wounds of returning.' 'Nostalgia' is not an emotion that is entertained; it is sustained'" (ctd. in Creekmur 45). Bergman's self-avowedly "last" film enacts precisely these "wounds of returning."

The film's first imaginative act occurs after Alexander, his hand on a window like Johan and the boy in *Persona*, has witnessed a distressing scene from the reality outside his insular family. He stares at a statue of a girl and sees the statue's arm move, again a detail from Bergman's childhood (*Magic Lantern* 21). Thus, the boy's "vision" is a response to an otherwise frightening reality and gives him some control over that reality. But it is also important that the spectator shares the imaginative image, that we see it as he does. We share the first-person created mental events of the character and thus come to identify with his experience of the mergence of fantasy and reality: a mergence between spectator and spectacle ensues, privileged by a subjective camera that employs frequent panning and point-of-view shots. Bergman seems by and large to have abandoned the multiple viewpoints of *Persona* and *Cries and Whispers*. Even though the film is named for both the boy and his sister, it is his viewpoint that is privileged while Fanny is relegated to a supporting role. Thus imagination and the film's narrating authority are largely gendered as male at the same time that the film seems to subvert androcentrism through an intra- and extradiegetic consciousness mergence that posits male experience as susceptible to penetration by the spectator's gaze. But this appropriable consciousness is, significantly, not that of an adult male; rather, it is located in a prepubescent boy. Like Johan in *The Silence* and the boy who strokes the screen in *Persona*, this child is clearly a directorial surrogate. Thus, Bergman invites spectator mergence with his own experience at the same time that he disguises his own adult sexuality and gender agenda. Only the presexual male body is a text to be read; the adult male body remains hidden from view.

But there are several other mental event sequences in which Alexander sees his dead father, including three times in the apartment and once in Isak's shop. In the first instance, Fanny and Alexander are playing with the magic lantern when Fanny hears something in the apartment and calls to Alexander. While she is looking into the room from which the music is coming, we see only her face; when Alexander joins her and looks into the room, the camera cuts to a point-of-view shot of the ghost of his father Oscar at the harpsichord. This distinction establishes Alexander's authority of vision and excludes Fanny from that imaginative power. This vision also comes to Alexander while he is engaged in projecting images; the visualization of his father as a ghost is directly linked to Alexander's incipient artistry, both because he creates through the projection of images and because it implies a sensitivity in the boy to extranatural realities.

Alexander's last vision of his father occurs in Isak's shop, a kind of junkroom of culture and history strewn with artifacts that figure Alexander's adventure as symbolic of a larger culture movement. After urinating in a potted plant (a very male act of rebellion), Alexander espies his father across a mistily lit, dusty room. This phantom brings two important messages: there is no God (or if there is, not even the dead have seen him) and the boy-artist "must be gentle with people." Alexander upbraids Oscar for leaving them, a sentiment that is linked with his subsequent claim that if there is a God, he is "a shit and piss God," and with his equation between God and the illusory power of the huge puppets. As in *Cries and Whispers*, the ultimate source of patriarchal power is paradoxically both malignantly present and absent.

Interestingly, the advice Oscar gives is precisely the opposite of that imparted by the ghost of Hamlet's father earlier in the film, a significant contrast since it is while playing this theatrical role that Oscar becomes ill. Instead of commanding Alexander to exact vengeance on his brutal and malevolent stepfather, Oscar counsels tolerance and forgiveness. Oscar is but one instance of what one might call the feminized father in Bergman's work, a patriarch who, like Jof in *The Seventh Seal*, is aligned with feminine values. In both cases, the father is gentle and loving, devoted to his children but also totally ineffectual, powerless, having relinquished his control of the family to the mother. Bergman in his depiction of these men seems to allow only two possibilities in fatherhood: love and impotence or cruelty and potency. Binarism endures.

Tellingly, in this film God manifests himself most potently in the children's brutally patriarchal stepfather, who as a minister is a literal representative of God and is also consistently depicted as oppressing women. In opposition to Edvard, Isak has magical powers and is a source of male authority located outside and in opposition to the Lutheran patriarchal tradition. Aron's description indicates that his uncle is part of the cabalistic Jewish tradition, far removed, in Bergman's view, from the repressive patriarchy of Christian ideology. (Bergman ignores here the patriarchal aspects of the Jewish tradition) But Isak is also feminized; he is closely associated with Helena, who, as her maiden name indicates, may also be Jewish, and one suspects that Bergman in his portrait of him is reinscribing the offensive stereotype of the "feminine" Jewish male. Thus, it is appropriate in Bergman's scheme of things that it should be Isak, the female-identified male and the adversary of the Lutheran patriarchy, who should "save" the children. It may be precisely because he stands outside the Christian patriarchal framework that Bergman imbues him with so much more power than the female-centered males (and especially fathers) in the rest of his production.

Although most of the imaginings derive from Alexander's male consciousness, there are important exceptions: Helena's vision of Oscar's ghost, the scene in which the children are stolen, and Alexander's mergence with Ishmael all problematize the film's coherent male point of view. When, for instance, Helena sees Oscar's ghost, she engages him in easy, everyday conversation, her casual acceptance of his appearance disrupting the film's mergence of spectator and spectacle. The fact that she shares Alexander's ability to project an image of Oscar strengthens the association between them (foreshadowing Alexander's mergence with her at the end of the film), even as her ability to project an image of her dead son is of a slightly lower artistic order, for it is less the product of waking artistic consciousness than of her sleepy stupor.

The scene in which Isak rescues the children from the bishop also presents a consciousness of diegetic events that is not linked to Alexander. Here Bergman confuses the spectator: are the children in the chest Isak takes away, or are they on the nursery floor? "Isak's magic foils Vergerus's self-righteousness and faith in the absolute power of a Christian God, replacing it with a reality manipulable by desire and imagination — divinity's human form" (Bundtzen 91). Isak's magical power, to which Alexander has access through Helena and the female, is stronger than the bishop's; the matriarchy's allusive, imaginative supernatural is more powerful than the patriarchy's destructive religious hierarchy. The mergence of fantasy and reality and the interjection of fantasy events that do not derive from the consciousness of the male protagonist join with the uninterpretability of this scene to disrupt binarism and monolithic male authority and to problematize the narrative and the mergence of spectator and spectacle. The film posits the mergence of spectator and spectacle as both a positive, enriching connection and, in the Ishmael sequence, a threatening, invasive act of appropriation.

Uninterpretability and identity mergence, both as positive values that are associated with the female and undercut patriarchal authority and as acts of invasive appropriation, are also manifest in the scene with Ishmael when Alexander is empowered by his mergence with this strange androgyne to kill his tormentor. Like his biblical namesake, Ishmael has been exiled and is illegitimate, and as such constitutes a threat to the patriarchy. A shot of Aron with Alexander knocking at a door cuts to the bishop's house, where Emilie is telling her husband she has put sleeping powders in his bouillon and will be gone by the time he awakens. The continuation of a high piano key striking intermittently and the fact that this scene of rebellion against the patriarchy and the preceding one both take place at night suggest that they are occurring simultaneously, an impression strengthened by the fact that a reverse cut shows Alexander and Aron at the same door, Aron repeating the same dialogue and the same action as before. This repetition functions like the repeated monologue in *Persona* to imply mergence. Linear time is displaced by synchronous time. Like the other imaginings in the film, this scene undermines the hierarchy of time and space, of subjectivity, and of narrative authority, all aspects of patriarchal ideology.

Because s/he is androgynous, Ishmael is an embodiment of the transgression of sexual boundaries, and Alexander's mergence with him/her not only liberates him from the repressive patriarchy but also, because this mergence is represented as an act of the imaginative projection of images, suggests that sexual ambiguity empowers the artistic enterprise. There is a sense in which the voice-over of this sexually ambiguous being *creates* the images that lie latent in Alexander's mind; androgyny is the site of imaginative and artistic authority. The intradiegetic consciousness mergence between Ishmael and Alexander also privileges an extradiegetic mergence between spectator and spectacle, according to which we share the characters' mental images at the same time that the blatant fantasy of the sequence disrupts the cohesion between the two.

The scene ends, then, with another duplication — a repeated shot of Elsa aflame, tearing out of her bedroom door. The Ishmael scene concludes, as it began, with a visual expression of the doubling process (the duplication and mergence of identity) we have just witnessed. Bundtzen points to the importance of this repeated image: "The image hesitates as apparently Alexander's will does, but also, significantly, as a film-image stutters in a projector" (109). This hesitation, like the self-conscious strategies of *Persona*, privilege a critical distance to the film.

But Alexander is also linked to Ishmael through their illegitimacy. The screenplay describes Alexander's mother as having been unfaithful to Oscar and intimates that Alexander is not Oscar's son at all. While this information is deleted from the film, it nonetheless suggests that the sexual immorality of the mother is less unambiguous than in *Cries and Whispers*. While Emilie, by marrying the bishop, is responsible for the children's suffering, she also provides them with a model of rebellion against the patriarchy. Both Emilie and Helena are represented as unfaithful wives whose sexual expressiveness enrich them and the world. This maternal force is furthermore associated with the vitalizing power of consciousness merging. Emilie tells the bishop:

> My God is different, Edvard. He is like myself, fluid and boundless and intangible, both in his cruelty and his tenderness. My God wears a thousand masks. He has never shown me his real face, just as I am incapable of showing you or God my real face. Through you I shall learn to know God's being. (101)

In contrast, Edvard, aligned with patriarchal authority, claims, "You said you change masks constantly so that finally you didn't know who you were. I have only one mask. It's burned fast into my flesh" (188). Although Emilie's and Alexander's experiences of the fluidity of the self are tortured and difficult, they are also somehow much "truer," more authentic than the bishop's rigid patriarchal concept of human identity. Their depth and richness of experience, the mutability of their subjectivities, is juxtaposed with the bishop's spiritual, emotional, and psychological atrophy.

Perhaps not surprisingly, the conclusion of the film charts the emergence of a kind of matriarchy: Oscar and the bishop are dead, the philandering Gustaf has been taken in hand, and Emilie and Helena are now in charge of the theater and of Alexander's life. The boy's final act of imagination, in which the ghost of the bishop knocks him to the floor and promises he will forever pursue him, is overshadowed by the final shot of Alexander with his head in his grandmother's lap, listening to her read the prologue of Strindberg's *A Dreamplay*. The maternal has displaced the father, and Alexander, as clear-cut a directorial alter ego as one can find in the cinema, is finally unified with the good mother (Helena has previously said that of all the roles she ever played she liked the one of mother best), the mother whose emotive powers nourish his imagination, for this powerful matriarchy is linked to the realm of imagination and fantasy. At the same time, Strindberg's authoritative aural presence — a presence that reflects the immense shadow Strindberg, as the "father" of modern drama and of Swedish literature, casts over Bergman's entire artistic enterprise — suggests that Alexander, like Jof, must be realigned with the paternal, with the masculine symbolic order. The imagination is, then, for Bergman, an enactment of reconciliation with issues of family and childhood that both challenges and reifies the position of the subject within patriarchal structures.

Bergman suggests the complicity of culture in both the construction of subjectivity and the representation of gender, even as women for Bergman ultimately remain signs in the male signifying process. To a certain extent,

Bergman joins in that complicity by presenting his women as victims with whom, to be sure, he identifies (thereby to a limited extent subverting the equation between female victimization and male dominance) and nurturing maternal figures aligned with the imagination. One is reminded of that self-described "last romantic" Yeats, who later laughed at himself for asking in his youth, "How could life be a ritual if woman had not her symbolic place?" Indeed, in some respects Bergman's conception of the imagination and of gender are not dissimilar to that of such late Romantics as Yeats, or of the Strindberg of *A Dreamplay.* For Bergman, positive women are usually nurturers, the embodiment of both the maternal and the imaginative force that inspires the artist at the same time that they, as is not the case for Yeats and Strindberg, represent an experience of alienation within a repressive androcentric reality that Bergman feels himself to share.

But Bergman has moved beyond his earlier films: all the acts of imagining he enscreens treat the impingement of external reality on internal reality, the ways in which the patriarchy invades and corrupts life. But, while *The Seventh Seal* may present a dualistic vision with female values redeeming the harshness of a patriarchal world, in his later films Bergman, in a much more nuanced and multivalent way than has previously been assumed, problematizes subjectivity, representation, and spectator/text relations as gender-related issues central to his filmic enterprise. And it is this practice, although it is not necessarily a proto-feminist one, that nonetheless privileges a feminist spectator experience of his texts. But his insistence on the maternal and on women as symbols for an imaginative order finally prevents him from completely succeeding in his effort to give women a voice, and from realizing how pervasively patriarchal culture encroaches upon their identities and appropriates their bodies. He sees "film as . . . well-suited to destructive acts, acts of violence. It is one of the cinema's perfectly legitimate functions: to ritualize violence" (Björkman *et al.* 227). Although his films frequently expose that violence, they also at least in part perpetuate it. If, as Susan Sontag remarks, a work of art "is an experience of the qualities or forms of human consciousness" (*Against Interpretation,* 27), Bergman's works represent women's subjectivity as a rich and compelling alterity to masculine experience that is both ideologically and discursively compromised. While his films systematically disrupt and subvert male notions of subjectivity and discourse, the image of a young boy stroking a screen remains emblematic of Bergman's production: by the time Bergman makes his last film, the screen has become a simple window (Koskinen 151); unproblematized as screening surface, it reflects the director's retreat from the extreme insights of the mid-1960s. At the same time, a sexually ambiguous, male and yet-not-male subjectivity seeks both connection with and appropriation of the female other. Like Bergman himself, this provocatively gendered figure struggles with the dominant culture in which he finds himself in a constant attempt to assert, to assess, and to assimilate a subjectivity beyond gender.

# Works Cited

Abel, Elizabeth, ed. *Writing and Sexual Difference* (Chicago: U of Chicago P, 1981).

Alexander, William. "Devils in the Cathedral: Bergman's Trilogy." *Cinema Journal* 13:2 (Spring 1974). 23–33.

Allen, Carolyn. "Dressing the Unknowable in the Garments of the Known: The Style of Djuna Barnes's *Nightwood*," in *Women's Language and Style*, ed. Douglas Butturff. 106–18.

Alpert, Hollis. "Style is the Director," *Saturday Review* 23 December 1961. 39–41.

Altman, Janet Gurkin. "Graffigny's Epistemology and the Emergence of Third-World Ideology," in *Writing the Female Voice*, ed. Elizabeth C. Goldsmith. 172–202.

Arbuthnot, Lucie. "Main Trends in Feminist Criticism in Film, Literature, and Art History" (dissertation: New York University, 1982).

Arnheim, Rudolf. *Film as Art* (Berkeley: U of California P, 1957).

Auerbach, Nina. *Communities of Women: An Idea in Fiction* (Cambridge: Harvard UP, 1978).

———. "Why Communities of Women Aren't Enough," *Tulsa Studies in Women's Literature* 3 (1984). 153–57.

Ayfre, Amedée. "The Religious Scope of the Seventh Seal," trans. Kristine Hughie in *Focus on The Seventh Seal*, ed. Birgitta Steene, 112–116.

Barthes, Roland. *Camera Lucida: Reflections on Photography*, trans. Richard Howard (NY: Hill & Wang, 1981).

———. *Mythologies* (London: Paladin, 1973).

———. *Roland Barthes*, trans. Richard Howard (NY: Hill & Wang, 1977).

Baudry, Jean-Louis. "The Apparatus," in *Apparatus*, ed. Theresa Hak Kyung Cha, (NY: Tanam, 1980), trans. Jean Andrews and Bertrand Augst. 41–62.

———. "Ideological Effects of the Basic Cinematographic Apparatus," *Film Quarterly* 28:2 (Winter 1974–75). 39–47.

———. "Masque, surface, et profondeur," *Les lettres françaises* 19 July 1967.

Baym, Nina. "The Madwoman and Her Languages: Why I Don't Do Feminist Literary Theory," *Tulsa Studies in Women's Literature* 3 (1984). 45–60.

Benjamin, Jessica. *The Bonds of Love* (NY: Pantheon, 1988).

Benstock, Shari. "From the Editor's Perspective," *Tulsa Studies in Women's Literature* 3: 1 & 2 (1984). 5–28.

Berger, John. *Ways of Seeing* (NY: Viking, 1973).

Bergman, Ingmar. "Den fria, skamlösa, oansvariga konsten," *Expressen* 1 August 1965.

———. *Fanny and Alexander*, trans. Alan Blair (NY: Pantheon, 1982).

———. *Filmberättelser: I-III* (Stockholm: Norstedts, 1973).

———. *Four Screenplays*. trans. Lars Malmström & David Kushner (NY: Simon & Schuster, 1960).

———. *Four Stories*, trans. Alan Blair (NY: Anchor, 1977).

———. *Images*, trans. Marianne Ruuth. (NY: Arcade, 1990).

———. Interview in *Filmnytt* No. 6 (1950).

———. *The Magic Lantern*, trans. Joan Tate. (NY: Viking, 1987).

———. *Persona and Shame* , trans. Keith Bradfield (NY: Grossman, 1972).

———. *Three Films by Ingmar Bergman*, trans. Paul Britten Austin (NY: Grove, 1963).

Bergom-Larsson, Maria. *Ingmar Bergman och den borgerliga ideologin* (Stockholm: Pan/Norstedts, 1973).

Bergson, Henri. "Laughter," in *Comedy*, ed. Wylie Sypher (NY: Doubleday, 1956).

Billquist, Frithiof. *Ingmar Bergman: Teatermannen och filmskaparen* (Stockholm: Natur och kultur, 1960).

Björkman, Stig, Torsten Manns & Jonas Sima. *Bergman on Bergman*, trans. Paul Britten Austin (NY: Simon & Schuster, 1973).

Blackwell, Marilyn. *Persona: The Transcendent Image* (Chicago: U of Illinois P, 1984).

Bovenschen, Silvie. "Is There a Feminist Aesthetic?," trans. Beth Weckmueller in *New German Critique* No. 10 (1977). 111–38.

Boyd, David. "*Persona* and the Cinema of Interpretation," *Film Quarterly* 37:2 (1983–84). 10–19.

Brightman, Carol. "*The Silence*: Problems of Evaluation. The Word, The Image, and The Silence," in *Ingmar Bergman: Essays in Criticism*, ed. Stuart Kaminsky (London: Oxford U, 1975). 239–53.

Brown, Anita. "Undermining the Gaze: Voyeurism in Ingmar Bergman's *Smiles of a Summer Night*" (unpublished graduate student paper, Ohio State University, Spring 1992).

Bundtzen, Lynda. "Bergman's *Fanny and Alexander*: Family Romance or Artistic Allegory?," *Criticism* 29:1 (1987). 89–117.

Butler, Judith. *Gender Trouble: Feminism and the Subversion of Identity* (London: Routledge, 1990).

Butturff, Douglas & Epstein, Edmund L. *Women's Language and Style* (Akron OH: U of Akron P, 1978).

Byars, Jackie. "Gazes/Voices/Power: Expanding Psychoanalysis for Feminist Film and Television Theory," in *Female Spectators*, ed. Diedre Pribram. 110–131.

Caplan, Jay. *Framed Narratives: Diderot's Geneology of the Beholder* (Minneapolis: U of Minnesota P, 1985).

Carson, James. "Narrative Cross-Dressing and the Critique of Authorship in the Novels of Richardson," in *Writing the Female Voice*, ed. Elizabeth C. Goldsmith. 95–113.

Chodorow, Nancy. *The Reproduction of Mothering* (Berkeley: U of California P, 1978).

Cook, Pam & Claire Johnston. "The Place of Woman in the Cinema of Raoul Walsh," in *Raoul Walsh*, ed. Phil Hardy (Colchester, England: Vineyard, 1974). 93–100.

Cowie, Peter. *Sweden 2* (London: Zwemmer, 1970).

Creekmur, Corey. "The Cinematic Photograph and the Possibility of Mourning," *Wide Angle* 9:1. 41–49.

Davidson, Ann Morrisett. "A Great Man Who Humiliates Women," *Village Voice*, 29 March 1973, pp. 70–80.

De Beauvoir, Simone. *The Second Sex*, trans. H. M. Parshley (NY: Random House, 1974).

De Lauretis, Teresa. *Alice Doesn't: Feminism, Semiotics, Cinema* (Bloomington: Indiana UP, 1984).

——. "Now and Nowhere: Nicholas Roeg's *Bad Timing*," in *Re-Vision*, ed. Mary Ann Doane. 150–69.

——. *Technologies of Gender* (Bloomington: Indiana UP, 1987).

Doane, Mary Ann. *The Desire to Desire* (Bloomington: Indiana UP, 1987).

——. "The Dialogical Text: Filmic Irony and the Spectator" (dissertation: U of Iowa, 1979).

——, et al. *Re-Vision: Essays in Feminist Film Criticism* (Frederick MD: University Publications of America, 1984).

——. "The 'Woman's' Film," in *Re-Vision*, ed. Mary Ann Doane. 67–82.

Donner, Jörn. *The Films of Ingmar Bergman*, trans. Holger Lundbergh (NY: Dover, 1972).

Donovan, Josephine. "Afterword: Critical Re-Vision," in *Feminist Literary Criticism*, ed. Josephine Donovan. 74–82.

——, ed. *Feminist Literary Criticism* (Lexington: U of Kentucky, 1975).

——. "Towards a Women's Poetics," *Tulsa Studies in Women's Literature* 3 (1984). 99–110.

Dyer, Richard. "Don't Look Now: Instabilities of the Male Pin-Up," *Screen* 23:3–4 (1982). 61–76.

Ellmann, Mary. *Thinking About Women* (NY: Harcourt Brace, 1968).

Epstein, Julia. "Fanny's Fanny: Epistolarity, Eroticism, and the Transsexual Text," in *Writing the Female Voice*, ed. Elizabeth C. Goldsmith. 135–53.

Erens, Patricia, ed. *Sexual Stratagems: The World of Women in Film* (NY: Horizon, 1979).

Fischer, Lucy. *Shot/Countershot: Film Tradition and Women's Cinema* (Princeton NJ: Princeton UP, 1989).

Flitterman, Sandra. "Women, Representation, and Cinematic Discourse: The Example of French Cinema" (dissertation: U of California-Berkeley, 1982).

Foucault, Michel. *The Archeology of Knowledge and the Discourse on Language*, trans. A. M. Sheridan-Smith (London: Tavistock, 1972).

——. *Discipline and Punish: The Birth of the Prison*, trans. Alan Sheridan (NY: Vintage, 1979).

Fried, Michael. *Painting and Beholder in the Age of Diderot* (Chicago: U of Chicago P, 1980).

Friedman, Susan Stanford. *Psyche Reborn: The Emergence of H.D.* (Bloomington: Indiana UP, 1981).

Fussell, Paul. *The Great War and Modern Memory* (NY: Oxford University Press, 1975).

Gado, Frank. *The Passion of Ingmar Bergman* (Durham NC: Duke UP, 1986).

Gallop, Jane. *Thinking Through the Body* (NY: Columbia UP, 1988).

Gentile, Mary. *Film Feminisms: Theory and Practice* (Westport CT: Greenwood, 1985).

Gilbert, Sandra M. "Costumes of the Mind: Transvestism as Metaphor in Modern Literature." *Critical Inquiry* 7 (1980). 391–417.

Gillman, Linda. "The Looking-Glass Through Alice," in *Gender and Literary Voice*, ed. Janet Todd. 10–22.

Gledhill, Christine. "Developments in Feminist Film Criticism," in *Re-Vision*, ed. Mary Ann Doane. 18–48.

Goldsmith, Elizabeth C., ed. *Writing the Female Voice: Essays on Epistolary Literature* (Boston: Northeastern U, 1989).

Gordon, Linda. "What's New in Women's History?," in *Feminist Studies/Critical Studies*, ed. Teresa de Lauretis (Bloomington: Indiana UP, 1986).

Haskell, Molly. *From Reverence to Rape: The Treatment of Women in the Movies* (NY: Holt Rinehart, 1973).

——. "*Madame de*: A Musical Passage," in *Sexual Stratagems*, ed. Patricia Erens. 62–71.

Haverty, Linda. "Failing at Autobiography: The Examples of Mark Twain, August Strindberg, and Rainer Maria Rilke," (dissertation: Harvard University, 1989).

Hayes, Julie C. "Writing to the Divine Marquis: Epistolary Strategies of Madame de Sade and Milli Rousset," in *Writing the Female Voice: Essays on Epistolary Literature*, ed. Elizabeth C. Goldsmith. 203–220.

Heilbrun, Caroline & Stimpson, Catherine. "Theories of Feminist Criticism: A Dialogue," in *Feminist Literary Criticism*, ed. Josephine Donovan. 61–73.

Holland, Norman N. "*The Seventh Seal*: The Film as Iconography," *Hudson Review* 12:2 (1959). 266–70.

Holly, Marcia. "Consciousness and Authenticity: Toward a Feminist Aesthetic," in *Feminist Literary Criticism*, ed. Josephine Donovan. 38–47.

Holman, C. Hugh. *A Handbook to Literature* (NY: Odyssey, 1972).

Houston, Beverle. "The Manifestation of the Self in *The Silence*," in *Film and Dreams*, ed. Vlada Petric. 139–45.

Höök, Marianne. *Ingmar Bergman* (Stockholm: Wahlström & Widstrand), 1962.

Irigaray, Luce. *This Sex Which Is Not One*, trans. Catherine Porter (Ithaca NY: Cornell, 1985).

Jensen, Katherine A. "Male Models of Feminine Epistolarity; or How to Write Like a Woman in Seventeenth-Century France," in *Writing the Female Voice*, ed. Elizabeth C. Goldsmith. 25–45.

Johnston, Claire. "Dorothy Arzner: Critical Strategies," *The Work of Dorothy Arzner: Towards a Feminist Cinema*, ed. Johnston (London: British Film Institute, 1975).

——. "Towards a Feminist Film Practice: Some Theses." *Edinburgh 76 Magazine* (n.p.). 55–56.

——. "Women's Cinema as Counter-Cinema," in *Sexual Stratagems*, ed. Patricia Erens. 133–43.

Kakutani, Michiko. "Ingmar Bergman: Summing Up a Life in Film." *New York Times Magazine*, 26 June 1983, 32.

Kaplan, E. Ann. "Is the Gaze Male?," in *Powers of Desire: The Politics of Sexuality*, ed. Ann Snitow, Christine Stansell & Sharon Thompson (NY: Monthly Review P, 1983), 309–327.

——. *Women and Film: Both Sides of the Camera* (NY: Methuen, 1983).

Kawin, Bruce. *Mindscreen: Bergman, Godard, and First-Person Film* (Princeton NJ: Princeton UP, 1978).

Koskinen, Maaret. *Spel och speglingar: En studie i Ingmar Bergmans filmiska estetik* (Stockholm: Norstedts, 1993).

Kozloff, Sarah. *Invisible Storytellers: Voice-Over Narration in American Fiction Film* (Berkeley: U of California P, 1988).

Kristeva, Julia. "Interview — 1974: Julia Kristeva and *Psychoanalyse et Politique*," trans. Claire Pajaczkowska, *m/f* (1981). 162–72.

Kuhn, Annette. *The Power of the Image: Essays on Representation and Sexuality* (London: Routledge, 1985).

——. *Women's Pictures* (London: Routledge & Kegan Paul, 1982).

Kustow, Michael. "*The Silence.*" *Sight and Sound.* (Summer 1964). 142–43.

Laing, R. D. *The Divided Self* (London: Penguin, 1967).

Lakoff, Robin Tolmach. "Women's Language," in *Women's Language and Style*, ed. Douglas Butturff. 139–158.

Lederer, Wolfgang. *The Fear of Women* (NY: Harcourt Brace, 1968).

Leed, Eric J. *No Man's Land: Combat and Identity in World War I* (Cambridge: Cambridge UP, 1979).

Lenne, Gérard. "Monster and Victim: Women in the Horror Film," in *Sexual Strategems*, ed. Patricia Erens. 31–40.

Livingston, Paisley. *Ingmar Bergman and the Rituals of Art* (NY: Cornell UP, 1982).

Mambrino, Jean. "The Seventh Seal," trans. Marie Georgette Steisel, in *Focus on the Seventh Seal*, ed. Birgitta Steene. 50–54.

Mayne, Judith. *The Woman at the Keyhole: Feminism and Women's Cinema* (Bloomington: Indiana UP: 1990).

——. "The Woman at the Keyhole: Women's Cinema and Feminist Criticism," in *Re-Vision*, ed. Mary Ann Doane. 49–66.

Melchiori, Paola. "Women's Cinema: A Look at Female Identity," in *Off-Screen: Women and Film in Italy*, ed. Guiliana Bruno & Maria Nadotti (London: Routledge, 1988).

Mellen, Joan. "*Cries and Whispers*: Bergman and Women," in *Ingmar Bergman: Essays in Criticism*, ed. Stuart Kaminsky (London: Oxford U, 1975). 297–312.

Metz, Christian. "The Imaginary Signifier," trans. Ben Brewster, *Screen* 16:2 (Summer 1975). 14–76.

——. "Photography and Fetish," *October* 3:4 (1985). 81–90.

Miller, Nancy K. "'I's' in Drag: The Sex of Recollection," *The Eighteenth Century* 22:1 (1981). 47–57.

Mosley, Philip. *Ingmar Bergman: The Cinema as Mistress* (London: Marion Boyers, 1981).

Mulvey, Laura. "Visual Pleasure and Narrative Cinema," *Screen* 16:3 (1975). 6–18.

Nystedt, Hans. *Ingmar Bergman och kristen tro* (Stockholm: Verbum, 1989).

Oates, Joyce Carol. "Is There A Female Voice?," in *Gender and Literary Voice*, ed. Janet Todd. 10–11.

Oldin, Gunnar. "Interview with Ingmar Bergman" for Swedish Radio-TV, broadcast 26 October 1966.

Penley, Constance. "Cries and Whispers," in *Movies and Methods*, ed. Bill Nichols (Berkeley: U of California P, 1976); pp. 204–08.

Penlington, Norman. "Symbolism and Meaning in *The Silence*." *University College Quarterly* 11:4 (May 1966). 30–33.

Persson, Göran. "Bergmans trilogi." *Chaplin* 40 (October 1963). 224–38.

Petric, Vlada. *Film and Dreams* (South Salem NY: Redgrave, 1981).

Pribram, Diedre, ed. *Female Spectators*. (London: Verso, 1988).

Register, Cheri. "American Feminist Literary Criticism: A Bibliographical Introduction," in *Feminist Literary Criticism*, ed. Josephine Donovan. 1–28.

Rich, Adrienne. *On Lies, Secrets, and Silence* (NY: Norton, 1979).

Rich, B. Ruby. "From Repressive Tolerance to Erotic Liberation: *Mädchen in Uniform*," in *Re-Vision*, ed. Mary Ann Doane. 100–130.

Rohmer, Eric. "With *The Seventh Seal* Ingmar Bergman Offers us his Faust," trans. Kristine Hughie, in *Focus on the Seventh Seal*, ed. Birgitta Steene. 134–35.

Roller, Judi Miller. *The Feminist Novel: The Politics and Ideology of Style* (dissertation: U of Michigan P, 1981).

Rose, Jacqueline. "The Cinematic Apparatus: Problems in Current Theory," in *The Cinematic Apparatus*, ed. Teresa de Lauretis (NY: St. Martin's, 1980).

———. *Sexuality in the Field of Vision* (NY: Verso, 1986).

Rosen, Marjorie. "Popcorn Venus or How the Movies Have Made Women Smaller Than Life," in *Sexual Strategems*, ed. Patricia Erens. 19–30.

Rosenberg, Jan. *Women's Reflections: The Feminist Film Movement* (Ann Arbor: U of Michigan P, 1983).

Sadoul, Georges, "Un vaste drame et une tragedie locale," *Les lettres françaises*, 12 July 1967.

Samuels, Charles. *Encountering Directors* (NY: Putnam, 1972).

Sandberg, Mark. "Rewriting God's Plot: Ingmar Bergman and Feminine Narrative," *Scandinavian Studies* 63:1 (1991). 1–29.

———. *Missing Persons: Spectacle and Narrative in Late Nineteenth-Century Scandinavia*. (dissertation: U of California-Berkeley, 1991).

———. "Motherhood and Modernism in Early Swedish Cinema: Victor Sjöström's *Ingeborg Holm*," lecture delivered at Ohio State U, 26 February 1992.

Sarris, Andrew. "*The Seventh Seal,*" in *Focus on the Seventh Seal,* ed. Birgitta Steene. 81–91.

Showalter, Elaine. "Women's Time, Women's Space: Writing the History of Feminist Criticism," *Tulsa Studies in Women's Literature* 3 (1984). 29–44.

Silverman, Kaja. *The Acoustic Mirror: The Female Voice in Psychoanalysis and Cinema* (Bloomington: Indiana UP, 1988).

——. "Dis-Embodying the Female Voice," in *Re-Vision,* ed. Mary Ann Doane. 131–149.

Simon, John. *Ingmar Bergman Directs* (NY: Harcourt Brace Jovanovich, 1972).

Siska, William Charles. *Modernism in the Narrative Cinema: The Art Film as a Genre* (NY: Arno, 1980).

Sjöman, Vilgot. *L 136: A Diary with Ingmar Bergman,* trans. Alan Blair (Ann Arbor MI: Karoma, 1978).

Sontag, Susan. *Against Interpretation* (NY: Delta, 1966).

——. "Bergman's *Persona,*" *Styles of Radical Will* (NY: Farrar, Straus, Giroux, 1968).

——. *On Photography* (NY: Farrar, Straus, Giroux, 1977).

Spacks, Patricia Meyer. "Female Resources: Epistles, Plot, and Power," in *Writing the Female Voice,* ed. Elizabeth C. Goldsmith. 63–76.

Spelman, Elizabeth V. "Woman as Body: Ancient and Contemporary Views," *Feminist Studies* 8:1 (1982). 109–32.

Steene, Birgitta. "Bergman's Portrait of Women: Sexism or Subjective Metaphor?," in *Sexual Strategems,* ed. Patricia Erens. 91–107.

——, ed. *Focus on The Seventh Seal* (Englewood Cliffs NJ: Prentice Hall, 1972).

——. *Ingmar Bergman* (Boston: Twayne, 1968).

——. "The Milk and Strawberry Sequence in *The Seventh Seal.*" *Film Heritage* 8:4 (1973). 10–18.

Strindberg, August. *Samlade Skrifter,* vol. 36, ed. John Landquist, (Stockholm: Bonnier, 1916).

Taylor, Anne Robinson. *Male Novelists and Their Female Voices: Literary Masquerades* (Troy, NY: Whitson, 1981).

Taylor, John Russel. "*The Seventh Seal,*" in *Focus on The Seventh Seal,* ed. Birgitta Steene. 135–36.

Teghrarian, Salwa. "The Cracked Lens: The Crisis of the Artist in Bergman's Films of the Sixties" (dissertation: SUNY-Buffalo, 1976).

Todd, Janet, ed. *Gender and Literary Voice* (NY: Holmes & Meier, 1980).

——. *Women's Friendship in Literature* (NY: Columbia U, 1980).

Törnqvist, Egil. *Filmdiktaren Ingmar Bergman* (Stockholm: Arena, 1993).

Treichler, Paula A. "Escaping the Sentence: Diagnosis and Discourse in 'The Yellow Wallpaper,'" *Tulsa Studies in Women's Literature* 3 (1984). 61–78.

Williams, Carolyn. "'Trying to Do Without God': The Revision of Epistolary Address in *The Color Purple*," in *Writing the Female Voice*, ed. Elizabeth C. Goldsmith. 273–86.

Williams, Linda. "When the Woman Looks," in *Re-Vision*, ed. Mary Ann Doane. 83–99.

Winnett, Susan. "Coming Unstrung: Women, Men, Narrative, and the Principles of Pleasure." *PMLA* 105:3 (1990). 505–518.

Wittig, Monique. "Paradigm," in *Homosexualities and French Literature: Cultural Contexts/ Critical Texts*, eds. George Stambolian & Elaine Marks (Ithaca NY: Cornell UP, 1979). 114–121.

——. "A Point of View: Universal or Particular?," *Feminist Issues*, 3:2 (1983). 63–70.

"Women and Film: A Discussion of Feminist Aesthetics." *New German Critique* 13 (1978). 83–107.

Wood, Robin. *Ingmar Bergman* (London: Studio Vista, 1969).

Woodward, Kathleen. "May Sarton and the Fictions of Old Age," in *Gender and Literary Voice*, ed. Janet Todd. 108–118.

Woolf, Virginia. *A Room of One's Own* (NY: Harcourt Brace & World, 1957).

Zern, Leif. *Se Bergman* (Stockholm: Norstedts, 1993).

# Index

CPSIA information can be obtained at www.ICGtesting.com
Printed in the USA
LVOW13*1434121213

365042LV00005B/86/A

9 781571 130945